This humble effort is dedicated

To my Wife Nutan (the wind beneath my wings),

my two sons -Aneesh and Rohan (the Hull of my ship)

and Finally my daughter Aishwerya (the sails).

"To all those who guided me, taught me orinfluenced me:

THE EVO-DEVO* is a FACT waiting to Happen"

(Ashish "Ash" Paul)

*Evolutionary Developmental biology (evolution of development or informally, evo-devo) is a field of biology that compares the developmental processes of different organisms to determine the ancestral relationship between them, and to discover how developmental processes evolved. This evo-devo theme has been further evolved in this book and other writings by the Author, to demonstrate the effect of culture (memetics or meme) and hereditary traits (genetics or gene) that work together to form an Individual. The meme of high technology without the compassion gene and Technical Civilization combined with low Digital IQ will have a devastating effect on the human species unless the evo-devo of leadership occurs. (The Wiki)

The Evo-Devo of Leadership

INDEX

CHAPTER 1

Author's Spear- THE QUEST

The IDIOCY and the BRILLIANCE of the Human Species is an awesome spectacle. The limits of both these naturally occurring phenomenon is finite yet infinite. The paradox of living in a box vs. living outside the box is only solved by the evo-devo that sees "No Box". As humans we play not only with space and time but thought and motion as well. The fact that we are not rigid bodies in space but flexible, independent thinking yet interdependent beings occupying a multi-dimensional metagenome is sometimes ignored. The fact that we operate under a set of Natural Laws that are interconnected yet ambiguous, when observed for large bodies and Quantum particles simultaneously, is sometimes forgotten. Herein lays the spear of Success and the start of the Quest for the evo-devo of Leadership.

The evo-devo of Leadership is mandated; whether we achieve it on our own in a controlled "implosion" or are forced to acquire the desired traits in an uncontrolled implosion" is your choice: your "free will". This quest is not about one person, one enterprise, one nation, or utopia. The words "I", "Me", "Mine" are used rarely and only to indicate that the current integral weaknesses are solely owned by the self. The words "You", "Our", "We" or "Us" abound to indicate the collectively derived strengths that innovate synergy.

The examples and processes utilized are mostly natural or organic as these have stood the test of time. Success has been measured in "quantas" of sustainability, stability, and synergy alone; unfortunately most economic and cultural innovations have not even survived the 100 year mark. The natural organic processes that have stood the test of time and distance have been repeated across the 'quest' intentionally in order to "connect the dots" throughout the leadership canvas. The fact that Leadership is a domain expertise that is horizontal across all the verticals of human activity is the basic tenet of the quest. The GIFT of the quest is in its **guarantee of unmatched value and success for your communities and hence your evo-devo.**

The practice of the evo-devo principles is not the exclusive domain of some but the path to great Leadership is open to all. The quest also defines that the evo-devo of leadership is a sorely needed competitive advantage for the masses to battle the challenges that face all the communities today. The success of this quest is mired in the uncertainty and the ambiguity of evo-devo. Religion and Science both fail to explain the ambiguous, the inconsistent and the different. Religion calls them miracles and science ignores them as inconsistencies. The evo-devo of leadership and its faith in the virtues of the consistencies within the inconsistencies is the only solution for long-term sustainable growth of the entire leadership metagenome. The tools of evo-devo are in the Trust, Patience, Honesty, Wisdom and Empathy of the practice of the principles truthfully. Falsification is best left to the diplomats and politicians not the evo-devo leaders.

Implode your weaknesses and use the released "free energy" to explode your existing, acquired and learned strengths for a higher than normal "peak performance" for the benefit of your "sphere of influence." Accept the quest and go with FAITH!!

ASHISH "ASH" PAUL

Chapter 2

OPEN LETTER TO ALL LEADERS FOR THE EVO-DEVO OF LEADERSHIP

"DO LEADERS MAKE HISTORY OR DOES HISTORY MAKE LEADERS?", "Is Contingency the cause and effect of leadership or is it adversity?", "Is Leadership charismatic or humble?", "Is Leadership a belief or a value?", "Is a leader a manager or can a manager be a leader?", "Is leadership interactive or is it powerful?", "is leadership inclusive or exclusive?", "Is Leadership goal based or path based?"_____???- YOU are the Leaders of this Quest and the benefit of this quest. The answers to these questions for you and an unmatched value of sustainable SUCCESS for all those around you.

From a systematic and theoretical point of view, you can imagine this quest, for the processes and knowledge of leadership and its evolution, to be a continuous cycle of induction. This would entail theories that are mired in the study of a large number of observations which are individual in nature yet extrapolated across the populace to predict communal behavior. Unfortunately, Great Leadership is not a function of pure observation or theory or empirical laws. The actual process includes the important parts played by intuition, ideation, faith, and synchronicity. The BIG "G" i.e. the creator, trust, deduction and an uncanny ability to "Connect the Dots" and visualize a new choice that was not envisioned. YOU, then have to execute this "preferred wise choice" flawlessly and deliver the benefits to the community.

It is said that the nature of the Leader is well known by the community and to understand the nature of the community you need to be a leader. Human existence is not just an occupation of a 3-dimensional space. It is multifaceted and profound. Its leadership is complex but the fundamentals are simple. The choices are varied but the benefits are constant. The evo-devo wise choice is the key to unlock the unmatched value hidden in the PAIN of needs and wants of the community. You will see the empirical evidence, the facts, the observations, the ambiguous yet consistent deductions and the guarantee of results as this quest progresses. The frame of reference is yours, the journey is yours, the honest effort is yours, the weaknesses or strengths are yours, and the opportunity is yours and the WOW!! Of Esteem is yours but the unmatched value is ours. DROP the shackles, RAISE the bar, PRACTICE and JUMP. We will celebrate your success.

The planet and its communities are becoming smarter every day. On a smart planet, the wise leader is akin to the central nervous system. The "particles of evolution, development and integration" start and stop here. The competitive advantage of an elegant and evolved central nervous system is apparent and abundant and will continue to remain so in the future. The paradigm of the wise leadership culture that sets no limit to benefits other than continuity requires great leaders that do not feel obliged to excuse their failures but have a process to assimilate facts and investigate their own value systems for transformation. **These evolutionary and developmental innovations, from a gathering of incremental predispositions, are then shuffled into advantageous configurations for competitive advantage as acquired traits. The leadership of acquired traits through this evolution (Evo) genetically and the development of the beneficial traits through culture (Devo) mimetically and their transmission across the leaders "sphere of influence" is the deduction you have to see.**

This vision is not an exclusive domain of the <u>few</u> but needs the evo-devo of the masses to meet the challenges that we have created for ourselves. The entropy of the system from the perspective of "how leadership ought to be" versus" how leadership is" provides you with a tremendous source of "free energy" to create the needed transformations. The processes are defined and the tools made available as a part of this quest so that you can unlock the value. Leading the "Implosion Effect" of chaos to create explosive and stable growth is your goal. The randomness and uncertainty of adversity is the constant that will fuel the growth once the "free energy" is released by the variable of Great "STAR" Leadership.

The current practice of leadership to view itself as an isolated organism looking after its own survival, within a global interdependent population, is the cause of the unmanaged "implosion effect" we are observing in the world. The practice of the existing leaders in their politics whether it be democracy, capitalism, communism, faith, monarchy and dictatorship, are all tending to promote exclusion in order to protect their selfish interests. These interests are the ones that are the cause of the chaos and adversity in the first place. The evo-devo paradigm that will be inclusive in its nature and sharing in its culture will create great leaders. A farmer, A Teacher, A Soldier, A Guru Nanak, A Moses, A Mohammed, A Washington, A Churchill, An Einstein, A Ramunajam, A Mother Teresa, An Ambani, A Gates, A Jobs, A Buffet, A Mittal, A Tata, A Manmohan Singh, A Putin, An Obama, A Buddha, A Li Kai Shin, An empathetic Doctor, A Patient Scientist, A Servant Politician, A competent Manager, A wise Parent, A honest Friend and An Intelligent Enemy, are all part of this evo-devo paradigm. The constant amongst all such wise leaders is that they all operate within the Quantifiable metrics of results and the Continuity of Qualitative benefits for their communities. They do not preach Leadership but practice a "way of life" that is self-explanatory.

In a recent study conducted across a vast majority of leaders, managers and employees, it was found that less than 37% of the audience was fully aware of what was going on in the enterprise. Less than 28% had an interest in transforming the way things were to the way things should be. Less than 14% desired to implement change. Less than 8% took action to implement the desired change. Less than 1% was willing to admit failure or share their knowledge with others to transmit the beneficial processes of success and failure through evaluation and feedback. This is our current attitude and will remain so as the environment evolves to become smarter than our leaders.

This apathy of Trust and Faith is the primary reason for the current crop of problems that face all manners of leadership today. As we shed our values to conform in order to solve these self-inflicted issues, we expend huge amounts of energy, Natural Capital and economic value through the inefficient and ineffective process of "crisis management". This onetime situational response strategy is neither evolutionary nor developmental. The evo-devo processes and knowledge you will gain as part of the journey will not only provide a rational, logical and planned decision cycle that will allow you to overcome the problem but as part of the solution it will illuminate new avenues of growth and synergy. The evo-devo process does not recommend that you throw the "baby out with the bath water", rather it promotes the concept of mining your existing business logic and diversity that has billions of dollars' worth of economic value locked up in its entropy. The available business logic is an integral part of the evo-devo process which will allow you to learn to fail successfully each time while developing the tools to innovate multiple alternatives to each predicted failure point. The process to create a Knowledge Library of Business Logic Objects that can be modernized and evolved will become apparent as a key to enhance the leadership decision choices through innovation and shared access. The evo-devo of Leadership will also guide you to make the Right Choice the "preferred choice" consistently and in the process achieve the Leadership of symbiotic relationships that will be highly beneficial to you.

The Leadership of Relationships and their competitive advantage is a tremendous source of Natural capital; combined with ethical consumption and communication it will allow you to create low Cost, low risk, and a high value client retention strategy that will be a net generator of "free energy" rather than the existing high Cost and unstable customer acquisition tactics that constantly uses energy. The paradigm shift that will assist you in migrating from the constant distraction of a "scarcity" of money consciousness i.e. CASH to the sustainable abundance of community potential, relationships, knowledge, skills and "virtualization" i.e. KASH is one of the important rewards of this fruitful quest.

The Leadership Parabola that identifies the leadership traits from an evo-devo questioning methodology of Who, When, Where, What, Why and How will provide the answers that will evolve GOOD Leaders to become GREAT "STAR" leaders who can transform the nature and culture of leadership itself. The "STAR" Leaders are the ones that are crucial to the evo-devo of sustainable growth as these great leaders will be responsible to understand the needs and wants of their communities; the "STARS" will combine this knowledge with the individual potential and the predisposition of the masses to create processes for SUCCESS which will release energy for further growth. **The "STARS" as you will observe are bright with esteem not ego**. Every and each one of you has his or her own "STAR" within you that needs to be nurtured with all your strengths while the weaknesses that lower your "STAR" value need to he transformed through the evo-devo process. This cycle of transformation is the basis of the evo-devo of leadership. The constant questioning of an evolved culture vis-à-vis its value system is another important tool of the evo-devo of Leadership. The evo-devo of transformation through Questioning is illustrated below:

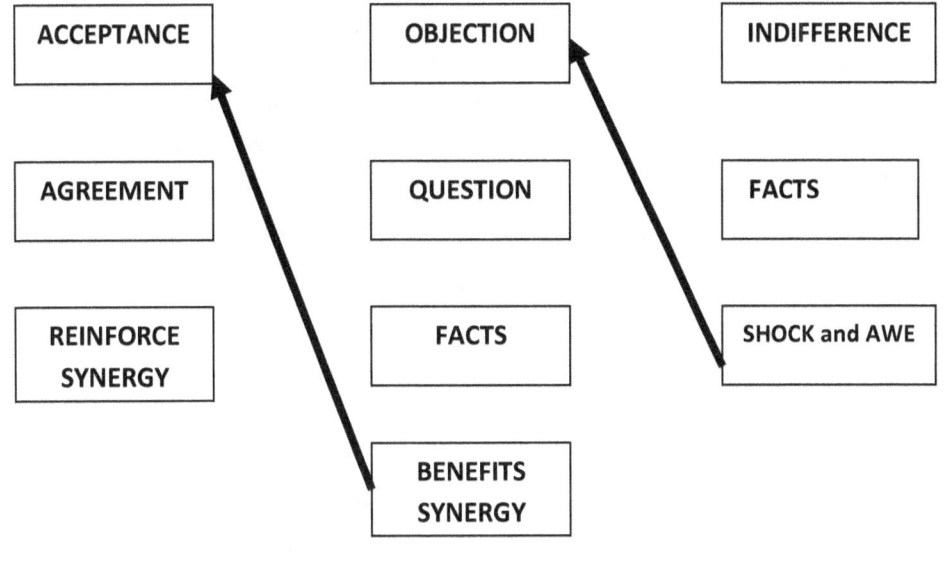

EVO-DEVO QUESTIONING

The evo-devo questioning process that you will gain as part of this quest, for "STAR" esteem, is an attribute that will transform objections and indifference to the "Right Solutions" into acceptance and synergy. It will permit you, the evo-devo leaders, to innovate and become Transformation Drivers rather than change managers. It will also give you the Knowledge and Process to lead the quagmire of chaos and adversity of the "Implosion effect" to create the purity of the explosion of Shared SUCCESS for the innovator and the community. The Leadership of this Energy will transform the Good Communities into GREAT "STAR" communities through the foci of long term sustainable growth based on Facts.

The debate of nature vs. nurture becomes moot when you will recognize the Leadership habits that are consistently based on a set of Global laws that are wise and just as well as locally sympathetic to the needs and wants of ethical consumption. The process that ensures that leadership follows ethical global practices with local execution to develop the potential of their communities is an important element of the evo-devo of Faith. This will not only reduce the conflict since the process promotes shared goals but also assist in equitable distribution of rewards. In case conflict rationally becomes the "preferred choice" as a means to fight oppression and discrimination then the

The Evo-Devo of Leadership

Leadership of Conflict and Aggression will guide you on the tools for victory as well as using the conflict and its adversity to build new relationships. The question that you will learn to handle: **What happens when you meet a valid objection that conflicts with your value system? Do you falsify facts to push consumption or do you follow the path of evo-devo and adapt your belief system to the new paradigm??** The process of the 5A's will assist you in the collection and understanding of the Facts that will ensure a logical decision that will transcend individual bias to create the Leadership of Energy with Thought.

Empirical studies have repeatedly shown that the single most powerful prediction of Great STAR" leadership is the sheer number of influential and beneficial decisions a leader has made for the community to increase its competitive and comparative advantage. At the same time you will find that leadership has to avoid the temptation of always trying to be "Right" by resorting to a "Falsification" strategy that molds the "Truth" to suit Leadership decisions. The methodology to set up processes to create traits and habits to ensure the "Right Cube" paradigm of the Right Solution will be revealed to you as we travel on this exciting journey. The reason current leadership cannot avoid the pitfalls of the temptation of falsifying results to gain a false sense of greatness is that the "I", "Me" and "Mine" of the existing value system never allows us to let go of this temptation completely within our enterprise. The illusion of GLASS (Greed, Lust, Anger, Self Aggrandization, Self-Ego) based on the principle of unworked for gain, especially in times of the "Implosion Effect", is the key reason for the wide spread virus of "Falsification". The Leadership of Governance will show us that even though this temptation will always exist within the system we can use certain strategies to innovate a culture that will forgo the "cheating" option in favor of the "Right Solution". You as the "STAR", will comprehend the economic value of "cheating" and the Leadership of Economics that creates unmatched value by lowering the number of "cheaters".

The evo-devo of Leadership will demand the price of Commitment, Accountability and Responsibility from the leader as a guardian of the "Natural Capital" that belongs to the community and to play the role of the "servant" of the constituents within the metagenome. The Leadership of Natural Capital that goes "beyond resource" through the aegis of ethical consumption will provide the basic foundation that will enhance the Leadership Energy Value (LEV) while increasing the "communal wealth" for sustainable growth. The leadership traits of Competence with humility, Character with wisdom and Contentment with patience will result in lowering the "internal back-flux" of adversity, chaos and resistance to evo-devo that currently depletes the Total Leadership Energy Value. This ends up destroying the Leadership Core Values which in turn lowers the competitive advantage of the community.

The cyclic nature of the Faith, Beliefs, Values, Ethics and Thought is a function of both the nature of our environment as well as the culture of the Leadership you create. You will also observe, as we travel through the various dimensions of leadership and its "brand Value' of esteem, that Facts are the building blocks of the evo-devo leadership culture. The key Facts defined, as the DNA of the Leadership of SUCCESS, are from reliable sources, have adequate proofs and are verifiable. The various formulae for SUCCESS and verifiability will be given to you to unlock the multiple alternatives available to you from which you can then select the ones that are most likely to succeed. The paradigm that indicates evo-devo SUCCESS is based on the simple concept of "Leadership is as Leadership does". This way of life that will ensure the long term growth of the community, including "acquiring what is needed to be acquired" will also lead to the Leadership of Global Interdependence both from an individual "domain expert" criteria and the communal "centers of excellence" based on best practices. Unfortunately, you will also learn that the reverse is true as well If leadership follows the policies of unfair practices then their communities will not be sustainable and will be acquired in order to create a "new" community that is stable. The image of the "new" community will be in the image of the new evo-devo leaders and in turn the constituents of the community will learn to have faith in their new leaders.

The crucial lessons that will be learnt as a part of this evo-devo quest will need to be assimilated into the value system of the leaders, in order to release the "free energy" of entropy, by learning to be "GOOD" and "BAD' as and when needed to meet the needs of the community. This as you will see means that as an integral part of the evo-devo process an environment of managed chaos through "implosion" will be utilized to collapse the non-beneficial areas of the acquired, owned or inherited communities to create synergy. The methodology that is essential to retain both justice and symmetry within this process will be another milestone of this journey. This new value system of "communalism" that sees what is in the BOX before jumping out of the Box and in turn creating a "no Box" syndrome will mandate a sharing and inclusive mentality that is far removed from the current "ism" driven ideologies. The difference will become apparent to you and the path of "communal benefits" that are in line with global benefits will be lit.

The "Have It" gene and meme of evolution and developmental culture in the evo-devo of Leadership, in your quest, will leave its interfaces that are "open sourced" so that future generations and other "Have It" leaders can emulate and adapt on an ongoing basis sustainably. The "Have Not" leaders will also be a constant source of learning to avoid their failures and evolve accordingly. A Leader is one who "Goes, Travels, Guides, Conducts and Influences". An evo-devo leader lives the "way of life" that transforms others in his journey and continues to create positive change through his "sphere of influence" even when he is not present in the world physically.

Let us begin our quest to understand, assimilate, componentized and evaluate the multi-dimensional Image of the "STAR" Leader to create a culture of the "EVO-DEVO of LEADERSHIP".

"The Greek word a-po-ka'ly-psis basically means-unveiling or uncovering-or as evo-devo says-A REVELATION"

CHAPTER 3

THE LEADERSHIP PARABOLA

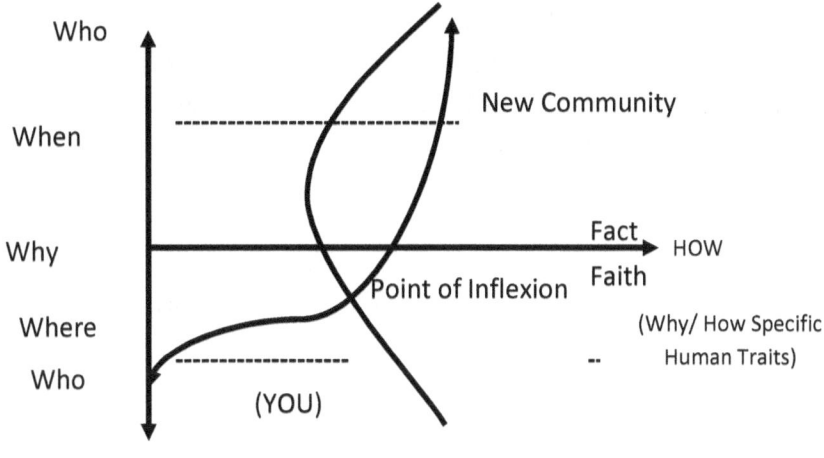

(Fig. 1) LEADERSHIP PARABOLA

Leader status whether acquired through inheritance, acquisition or founded anew is always capable of being redefined both voluntarily and involuntarily for the community in the Image of the Leader. The paradigm of the Evo-Devo of Leadership will require us to answer the Who, Why, What, Where, When and How questions as part of the Leadership Parabola in line with the needs and wants of the community. We will also need to understand the correlation between the Community and the leader in terms of the Image of the leadership. This also puts the onus on leadership to harness the unused energy of Chaos or Entropy in the system and innovate the predisposed qualities within the community to create SUCCESS. In order to gather all the empirical evidence around this Leadership Parabola let's take each of these questions and answer them one by one to understand the "cause and effect" of these attributes as individual traits as well as the "summation" of these traits for the "SIGMA Effect" on the evo-devo of Leadership.

THE "WHO" of the EVO-DEVO of LEADERSHIP:

The Leader has to clearly define his image as a person of the people, an embodiment of the community, who is accountable and responsible for the good of the constituents. This is applicable whether the community is acquired, inherited or founded by the leader. This nature of accountable and responsible leadership will give him or her right to create his or her own brand of leadership. The Leadership Core Values he or she defines will become essential for managing both the adversity of the "implosion" as well as the success of the explosion of growth in the leader's image. This "Who" also frees the Leadership from any obligations to find excuses for past failures or debts to any other person or entity other than the community. The intermingling of the Leadership Core Values of the "WHO" of Leadership with the Community Values will create a "Sigma Effect" of Summation that will become the image of the entire community. The "Sigma Effect" is crucial since the synergy of the Leader and the community to reach "Summation" results in the fact that the WHOLE-Community-actually becomes larger than the SUM of its parts, This Sigma Effect is due to the fact that at the point of Summation where the WHO of the Evo-devo Leadership and the WHO of the Community merge the synergy and release of "FREE ENERGY" create an additive effect in the overall "Brand Value" or perception of the community.

In order to achieve the Sigma Effect and the Competitive Advantage of Summation for the leader and the community it is essential to create the foundation of the "WHO" of the evo -devo of Leadership on Facts and Faith not Fortune or "Gut instinct". The "Who" of Leadership that can survive under chaos as well as transformation to produce the Right Solution at the Right Time and for the Right Reason needs the **RIGHT People at the Right Place** on the Leadership team? The Individual traits of the "Right People" have to be in line with the desired Sigma Effect of Leadership. In order to be synergistic and well defined the leader has to set the selection criteria and communicate the vision succinctly. The focus on the selection of the Right Traits for the "WHO" of the Right People is the responsibility of the leader and in turn provides him with an excellent opportunity to define his leadership Brand and core Values.

This initial opportunity under Chaos and change for the overall benefit of the community (through summation) will give the leader the impetus to implement the "WHO" as defined by him using the energy stored within the community. This will give both the leadership and the communities the energy survive "The Implosion Effect" of adverse circumstances as well as enhance its chances of success since the summation will have a holistic effect across the enterprise or community. What then are the desired traits in the "WHO" of evo-devo?

The evo-devo of leadership desires a **strong Diagnostic trait,** in the "WHO" of the leader. This diagnostic nature of leadership will have the ability to assimilate the Facts into the belief System as well as the value system of the leader and the community. The Leader also has to be ruthless in his focus to implement the transformation in order to get the community focused on success and growth. This will mean that the "WHO" of leadership in its initial phase of transformation may need to be viewed **as taking less from the community but not giving away too much in the early stages.** It is not in the nature of evo-devo leadership to be good at all times. The focus has to be on the overall competitive advantage of the community. This essentially requires the "WHO" of leadership to be in its nature a synergistic whole that is focused on the "Communal Wealth" and the needs of the community. At the same time the need of leadership to get the Right people in the Right place demands "bad" in order to implement the transformation of an entire community through the local change drivers.

The need to Do it Right the first time based on Facts and faith is another "Who" of the evo-devo of Leadership. This means that the Leadership core value will need an illative sense. A sense that can take the ratiocination of thinking and reasoning and be able to connect the dots for ideation and illation for a "First Call Resolution" i.e. one that can deliver the Right Solution in the first instance. This will greatly enhance the "WHO" of leadership in terms of the faith of the community in the Leadership. This implies a rational, logical and unbiased thought process with a strong sense of commitment for the community by the Leader.

The combination of the Diagnostic Ability with an **Illative sense** will also mean that the Leader should have the virtue of handling both the **Fear of punishment and the Love of Reward equitably.** Fear and Love are both strong tools for leading in the adversity of the "Implosion effect" in order to generate energy for sustainable enhancing growth. The sense to use these tools effectively for the process of enhancing "Communal Wealth" will imply that the end does justify the means in order to create advantageous configurations for the community.

The "WHEN" of the Evo -Devo of Leadership:

The timing of the Evo-Devo of Leadership, within the aegis of the new value system as defined by the "WHO" of the Leader, is crucial for the success of the evo-devo process. Leadership with its fixed nature and habits is currently resistant to change. The alternative is that the "WHEN" of Leadership will either move them or change the value system around them by redefining the communal belief system. The "When" question, in the context of the evo-devo, is thus clearly addressed that the time to implement the positive transformation is governed by the environmental stimuli. These stimuli indicate the changes required for competitive advantage of the community to have a balanced and sustainable growth process.

This requires leadership to prepare for the "Implosion Effect" i.e. adversity during the growth phase. At the same time processes need to put in place that can utilize the energy released from the adversity of the implosion to fund and transform itself as well as the community for explosive growth. The flexibility of the leader to act in a timely manner with the necessary facts and faith in his leadership will answer the "WHEN" question of the evo-devo of leadership. The concept of leadership and leaders that are consistently in the 'Right Place at the Right Time" is not a matter of luck but more of foresight and planning. This is achieved by creating an organization or community that is ready to accept positive change during growth rather than trying to respond to adversity by changing when forced to change in a crisis.

This is the key to the survival of great communities in the current era of changing Value Systems and collapse of the so called established paradigmatic "Towers" of success that are falling apart under the stress of a decaying values. The problems are common be it New York or London and Mumbai and Beijing or Tokyo and Seoul or Dubai and Riyadh. The solution lies within **the ideation of innovation that predicts future problems based on present facts and past experience** to ensure that the timing of the solution is in line with both the Implosion and planned explosion. **This will also mean that the solution is in place before the event occurs** or the problem becomes incurable leading to the ultimate collapse of the community. A modern day example of this paradigm is the "Health Care" system: A system that is effectively about "Disease Care". This is due to the fact the system only responds when the person is sick. It is difficult to diagnose a health issue at the inception or before but much easier to cure it. On the other hand it is much easier to diagnose the disease once it is full blown but it will be nearly impossible to cure. Therefore, the "When" of the evo-devo of leadership in terms of the right timing for implementing transformation, factored on the correct diagnosis, is crucial to the success and health of the community.

The above is only possible within a **New Value system** that is constantly monitoring the health of the system, both internally and externally, with facts to use evo-devo leadership skills that will design innovative solutions which in turn will provide the means for a beneficial end. **This brings us to the next question of "WHERE" or the points of inflexion for implementing the evo-devo of leadership.**

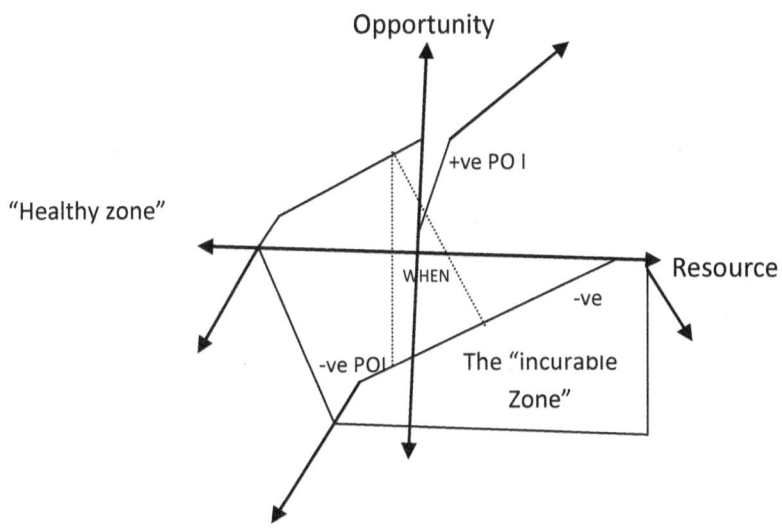

THE "WHEN" and "WHERE" POINT OF INFLEXION (Fig. 2. (i))

THE "WHERE" of the EVO-DEVO of Leadership.

The point of inflexion (POI) between the implosion and the explosion is the place of the "WHERE" of evo-devo leadership. In the above figure you observe that the "incurable zone" is one where there is negative opportunity but huge resources are being expended. A waste. On the other hand, the "healthy zone" is one where the minimum amounts of resources are required for the maximization of gain from the existing opportunity. APOI. As leadership creates avenues of balanced and sustainable growth, using the right solution and the right resources to induce positive transformation at the POI, it is also leaving the dentations of innovation as the building blocks for the "WHERE" of future communal growth. The wisdom to discover these points of inflexions is the "WHERE" to commence the evo-devo.

The areas needing the evolutionary leadership for the induction of the New Value System is governed by the nature of the community and its need of competitive advantage to ensure sustainable success. The instability at the point of inflexion in the "Where" of leadership arises when transformation is implemented for the sake of transformation rather than based on the needs and wants of the advantageous configuration for the community. In cases where leadership uses change to control the community the change will itself become the catalyst for the uncontrolled implosion and adversity leading to chaos by triggering the "Implosion Effect". On the other hand planned transformation at the desired POI, that utilizes the entropy or waste within the community and the leader, will release a tremendous amount of "free energy" for innovation resulting in sustainable growth in incremental advantageous configurations for competitive advantage for the community. Simply put, the POI is the location at which evo-devo leadership can transform the community positively using the potential of the community itself.

The POI can be identified using both observation and experience. The pace of innovation and success may be slower in places "where" the evo-devo of leadership is following in the path of other leaders as it has to be tweaked to meet the local conditions for execution but it will be sustainable and in the image of the leader. Alternatively, the leaders own experience can be a good source for discovering the POI and transforming the community into a "New Order" that is beneficial.

The paradox is that the setting of "New Order" within an existing community or even a new community is one of the most thankless "Where' or place to be for any leader. The POI that establishes the "New Order" will be supported by weak defenders and opposed by strong adversaries. It is therefore essential that at the POI or the "WHERE" of the evo-devo, the Leader has acquired both the facts and the faith of the community. The

leader has to be ruthless in the implementation of the required chaos before the "New Order is implemented. This can be accomplished by eliminating the adversaries who benefited from the existing order and resist change; at the same time communicating the benefits of the New Order to the community to gain their support and commitment to change.

The POI in the Leadership Parabola is therefore most beneficial where minimum effort and energy of the leader will result in the maximum sustainable gain for the community. The key to discovery of this exact point of inflexion hinges on the understanding by the leadership of the predispositions, in terms of strength and weaknesses, of the existing or acquired community. This requires that the Leader physically live inside the community and not delegate this essential task. This physical presence of the leader will result in creating faith within the community and the facts will become known to the Leader first hand. This will not only help manage any implosion or failure by eliminating or lowering any waste in the process, it will also identify the areas of excellence within the community to generate explosive growth based on the "Free Energy" i.e. energy that exists unutilized within the system.

At the same time the presence of the "WHERE" in the evo-devo of Leadership will shore up the confidence of the weak defenders and scare the adversaries into accepting change. This will also assist the community to imitate the leader to project the community in the image of the leader. It is crucial to take cognizance of the fact that in this New Value System the Leaders presence at the POI is mandated to take advantage of any opportunity that exists or will present itself in the future.

This opportunity has then to be transformed from its state of potential i.e. "matter" by adding the "mass" of the Leader's vision and the effort of the community to create a sustainable entity. The "Where" of the evo-devo of Leadership is the place that offers the best opportunity for the leaders to maximize the benefits for the community by utilizing its potential most effectively. This is the evo-devo "PRESTROIKA".

The "Where" or the POI can also be defined as the point at which the "PRESTROIKA" occurs. "Prestroika" is the point at which we can create transformation by changing the operating parameters. The evo-devo leaders who can use the "Where" of the Prestroika to add new processes and knowledge can generate the "symmetry" of chaos for the positive evolution of the enterprise. The innovative process changes implemented at the Prestroika and their symmetry will result in the beauty of an evolved, stable and sustainable community which will bear the image of the evo-devo leader. The POI at which the Prestroika has to be introduced needs to be pre-determined. This point should be such that it does not compromise the STRUCTURAL STABILITY of the enterprise during the creation of the Symmetry of Chaos and Adversity. **Structural Stability is a sophisticated mathematical concept with an intuitively simple interpretation. The flawless execution of the "Where" of the POI and the Perestroika allows you to attain global competitive advantage without losing the intrinsic value of the local beneficial traits of the community, Any added traits need to complement and fill the gaps within the enterprise to achieve efficiency and enhanced "Life Cycles".** The peaceful coexistence of the enterprise during the Prestroika and the evolution of the beauty of symmetry is the key to the "Where" of Leadership.

This simply means, roughly but accurately, that quantitatively small changes have quantitatively small consequences. At the same time quantitatively small but effective processes applied at the POI will have Large Qualitative consequences i.e. Prestroika. The desired qualitative transformation is:

SYMMETRY + CHAOS = BEAUTY of "Communal Benefit".

Thus it becomes essential to understand the "Where" of evo-devo to apply the Prestroikas effectively. The mathematical representation of the Prestroika:

PRESTROIKA = $\dfrac{\text{OPPORTUNITY OF CHAOS x RESOURCE of COMMUNITY}}{\text{SYSTEM INEFFICIENCY (No. Of SMALL PERTUBRATIONS)}}$

(PERTUBRATIONS = Ineffective small changes)

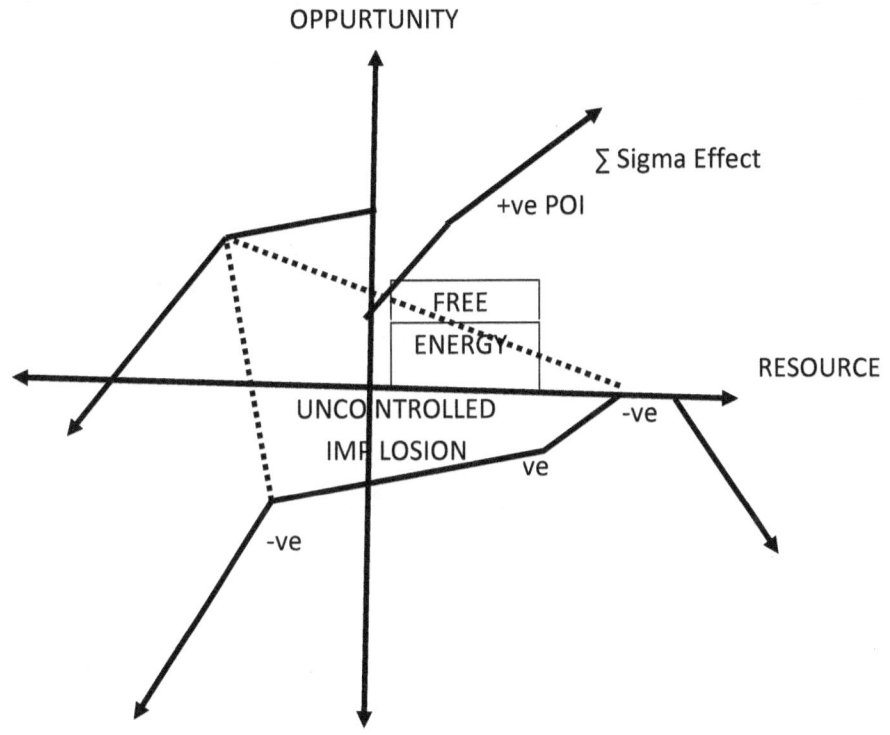

THE "WHERE" POISIGMA-PRESTROIKA FIG 2(ii)

It might be beneficial to look at a simple example in order to understand the advantage of the play between the POI, Prestroika, structural stability, transformation, qualitative results and the "WHERE" in the evo-devo of Leadership. In the diagram above you see the 1st quadrant, where the Opportunity and Resource are in synchronicity, the community sees explosive growth. In the 2nd quadrant where there is Opportunity and potential but a lack of resources there is complete failure. The 3rd Quadrant is one where there is neither Opportunity nor Resource therefore the system fails. The worst case of all is in the 4th Quadrant where there is no Opportunity but the leadership continues to allocate resources in an attempt to extend the life cycle through falsification and for their own aggradations, this is the cause of chronic failure and triggers the "implosion effect".

If we diagnose the chronic disease of the U.S.A. fiscal deficit we will learn that the federal taxation at 18% of GNP only accounts for spending in 5 areas i.e. retirement and disability, medical care, Veterans Programs, Defense/Homeland Security and lastly payment of interest on Public debt. All the other needs of the community such as Education, Science, Technology, Diplomacy, Wars, Public Assistance, Energy, Broadband etc which are at around 5% of GNP are funded out of debt. The solution that the US government has devised inappropriately is the concept of "infinite debt" and unethical consumption. This is a negative spiral wherein new energy in the form of printing money, creating debt and passing the debt on to consumers both domestic and foreign is a constant requirement. This vicious cycle of debt which only funds short term unsustainable growth needs more resource each timewe need to expand. This phenomenon has compromised the structural stability of the entire global economic system. This strategy lies in the 4th quadrant wherein we are burning up resource just to maintain an unsustainable growth pattern. The solution of the "WHERE" lies in understanding where to apply the PRESTROIKA in order to generate sustainable growth using "FREE ENERGY" as in the 1st quadrant where the minimum utilization of resource results in the highest, opportunity for success. This opportunity of Chaos in the system is a tremendous opportunity for the evo-devo of leadership to find a long term sustainable solution to the chronic problem of public debt.

We will discuss this solution later as we define the structure to the "WHAT" of the evo-devo of Leadership to answer the question to the best solution for existing or future issues.

THE "WHAT" of the EVO-DEVO of LEADERSHIP:

The "WHAT" in the leadership parabola for the evo-devo of leadership is essential to define the Leader, the community, the Opportunity, the Resources, and the Facts in the right order to preserve the sustainable growth concept? The goal of Leadership is to Inspire others to understand their potential at the same instant create an environment that allows them to utilize and hone their unique talents. The word "Inspire" comes from the Latin word "Inspirer" which literally means to breathe life into another. This is the level of relationship and trust between the leader and the community. The relationship and trust interplay that coexists in the community and the leader is translated in the "What" of the evo-devo of leadership as Faith. The faith in the leader by his community to find the Right solution through a clear understanding of the strengths and weaknesses of the existing value system as well as inducting a new Value System that will give the Leader and the Community the required impetus to gain competitive advantage.

   The **"What" of the evo-devo of Leadership operates best in Four Dimensions: <u>Vision, Process, Knowledge and Wisdom</u>**? : The Vision is the Leader, who thinks Big, Thinks New and Thinks ahead. The Process is to remain in touch with Reality, have Courage and Ethics to achieve the Vision through flawless execution. The Knowledge is the Empathy, Passion and Illative sense to make the right Choice consistently. The Wisdom is to keep in touch with the communities Human Consciousness and Creative potential to share benefits in order to deliver the required results. The intelligence to perceive and communicate to get the results as well the strength and energy to control the success for the long Term sustainability of the community is the "What" of the Leadership Parabola. The harmonious balance of the four dimensions is crucial for the "What" of Leadership that can inspire Faith. The "What" trophy of evo-devo and its unmatched value of Faith are shown in the next illustration:

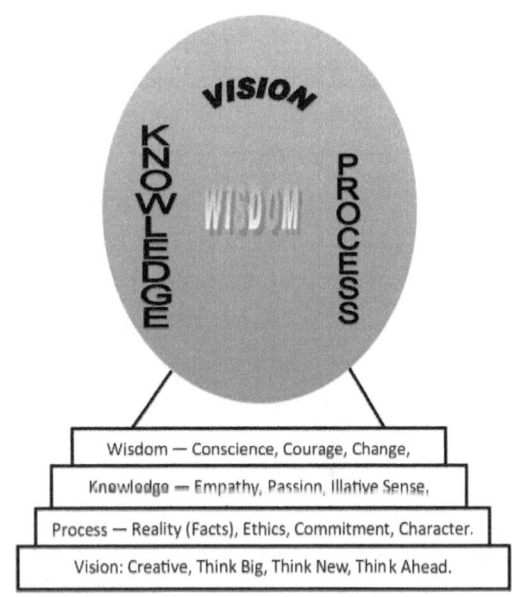

THE "WHAT" TROPHY OF EVO – DEVO (Fig. 3)

The "WHAT" of Leadership Faith may seem like an ethereal concept, but this eschatological faith in a bright future has motivated leaders and their communities to achieve their potential. Leadership needs faith at the core of its character in order to achieve the desired results. Leadership needs to use the faith to induce the community with a passion that "wants" the future. To achieve this passion the "What" of Leadership evo-devo will need to streamline the diverse and ambiguous policies into a single focus of the "STAR" paradigm. This "EYE of the BIRD" focus on the "STAR" is the Key to the "What" of Leadership. (Note: In the 3000 years old Indian mythological tale -" MAHABHARATA"- when Arjuna, a famous warrior, was asked by his teacher as to what he saw when he was, shooting his arrow at the bird in a tree. He replied "Only the eye of the Bird, O Guru." The other students, when asked the same question, answered that they saw the sky, the tree, the branches, the fruit and the bird. Arjuna's focus is the evo-devo that is required in a leader). This faith that focuses solely on the desired result and shared rewards, simultaneously, creates a value system that ensures flawless execution. This is the "What" of evo-devo leadership. **The current global economic crisis is a crisis of confidence in leadership and has a single cause i.e. a Lack of Faith.**

The "What" of Leadership that can get the needed results of <u>winning BIG in small increments to create competitive advantage is the foundation of leadership faith and the evolution of "STAR" leaders.</u> The "STAR" concept is the focus that will deliver the maximum benefit for the community while minimizing the use of the Natural Capital. This "STAR" is the "What" of evo-devo and requires the innovation of an evolved leader that finds the "STAR" within itself which is based on the predisposed strengths of the community. The "STAR" should also result in achieving the advantageous configurations desired by the community and the Leader. This entails that at no time can the "STAR" be defined in character as being biased towards a few. The fair and just nature of the evo-devo "STAR" is essential to the "WHO" of leadership.

In the software world there is a constant struggle between up gradation and status quo in-the legacy application world. The evo-devo of leadership is similarly required to "Modernize° the "Who" of leadership at the same time retain the "What" i.e. the existing business logic that is built over time and has proved to be effective for the sustainable growth of the community. Evo-Devo Leadership requires that the a "STAR" develop his or her own "Leadership Modernization Tools" that can be used as a resource for the community on an ongoing basis to retain the image of the Leader and to preserve the logic over a long period of time. **This independence of having your own resources without being dependent on others for your success and the success of the community will serve the "Star" in multiple ways to differentiate the core leadership values while conforming to shared communal success.** The Leadership Tools and the personal professionalism of the leader as a practitioner of this art is the definition of the "What" of leadership. The leader that can seize the opportunity of failure to attain success through skill and innovation at the same time drive the transformation within the community to self- sufficiency is another element of the "STAR". This also entails that both the adverse and the beneficial be used effectively for growth through preparedness and planning that are founded on facts and faith.

The "STAR" is the harbinger of a leadership domain that is not deceived by the vagaries of the environment. The "STAR" leader who understands that one cannot have all the strengths required by the community will cover the risks by preparing and acquiring the relationships that cover the gaps. At the same time it also mandates that the "STAR" leader investigate all the weaknesses that are solely his and be prudent to avoid them and their negative impact on the community.

In defining the "What" and "STAR" of leadership it is of paramount importance that the enterprise does not depend on external help alone to achieve its goals. A leadership with a strong and well-defended community that owns its tools for success in economics and war as well as faith in the leader is essential to retain the "STAR". The "STAR" has to maintain its focus under the adverse conditions of the "Implosion effect" and be able to lead the success in a stable manner to acquire the "What" of evo-devo. The assimilation of the "What" traits have to be in line with the global trends and natural laws to create an interdependent Global "STAR" for the community. This synergy of the "STAR" traits alongside the character of the Leadership is represented below:

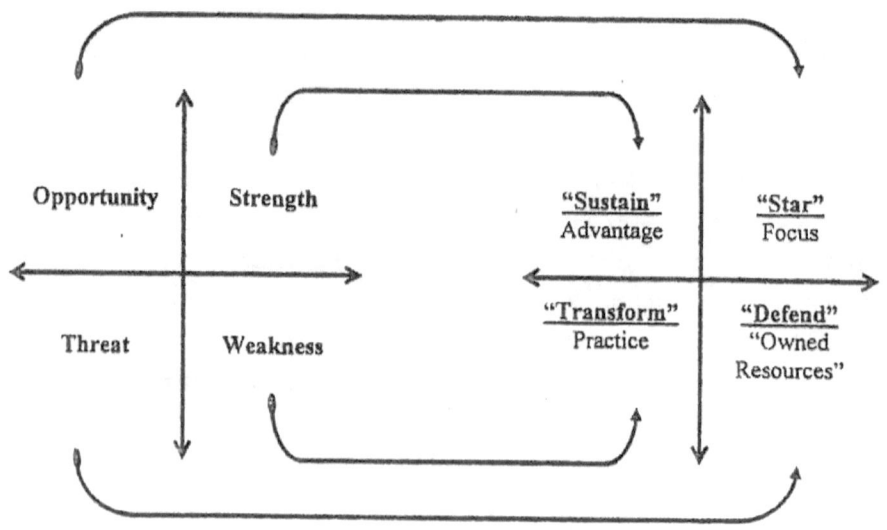

| Opportunity | Strength | "Sustain" Advantage | "Star" Focus |
| Threat | Weakness | "Transform" Practice | "Defend" "Owned Resources" |

The "STAR" and the "SWOT" (Fig. 4)

The "What" of Leadership that can acquire and grow in a sustainable and balanced manner in incremental steps, based-on-the local predispositions, and operate with a ruthless and dedicated focus for the good of the community will result in the evolution of GREAT COMMUNITIES. The great communities will show "above normal" recovery from the adversity of the "Implosion effect". In summary: A Leader who has the art and tools of leadership but lacks the resource will always prevail over leaders who have resources but Lack the art of Leadership."

The "What" of evo-devo and its "STAR" will open the door to the crucial "HOW" and "WHY" of Leadership. The "HOW" and "WHY" the two traits that are exclusive to humans and are not are shared with the rest of the animal kingdom. The "How" and "Why" need to be aligned with the rest of the Leadership parabola in order to achieve the "No Box" syndrome for success. It is the natural tendency for leadership to box themselves into adverse situations and using biases to extract them from this untenable situation.

This process is the ultimate recipe for disaster. The "NO BOX" paradigm of the Leadership Parabola is to acquire the business logic available in the box, find the "HOW" and "WHY" of the situation and create a "Third" alternative that has not been envisioned to achieve the goals. The "third" alternative may include multiple solutions that are synergistic and lead to sustainable growth.

THE "WHY" of the Evo-Devo of Leadership:

The primary responsibility of a Leader is to lead and create advantageous configurations for the community. This competitive advantage ensures a high win ratio for sustainable growth. At the same instant the Leader has to protect the community from adverse circumstances that could or will affect the long term strategy of survival or even immortality. This then is the "WHY" of the evo-devo of Leadership.

The importance of planning and preparedness of the evo-devo leader in the art of managing the "Implosion" and creating the explosion for growth, both by innovation and acquisition is the key to success in the new paradigm of evo-devo. Simultaneously, leadership needs to arm the community with appropriate tools and resources to defend and enhance its competitive advantage. The passion to create the Competitive and Comparative Advantage for both the Leader and the Community is in essence the "WHY" of the Leadership Parabola. In no way should we delude ourselves that survival and sustainable Growth under adversity are not akin to War. The Leader and hence the community need the discipline and order within the New Value System to keep the entity in a state of alert to any external or internal stimuli that threatens it survival, both genetically and mimetically, to be able to respond professionally with facts and a wise choice.

Imagine a huge pile of bricks. It has resource, mass and matter linked with it but it takes a leader who is aware of its potential to mould this "Natural Capital" into a wall with the appropriate tools including vision, knowledge and process as well as the wisdom of planning. This will then ensure that the wall is built on a foundation that will stand the test of time. At the same time if the evo-devo leader can be alert to future needs the wall can be built with interfaces or dentations that permits many walls to connect and grow into a house .If the house is also built with the dentations and flexibility for expansion in incremental predispositions we can create a community that will grow on a sustainable basis.

There is no match between a leader who is prepared for transformation than one who is unwilling to accept change. The unprepared Leader will not be able to impose on the prepared leadership and the inevitable will happen. The "WHY" of the Leadership Parabola will get triggered and the prepared Leader will use his competitive advantage to acquire what is needed from the unprepared Leader. The prepared leadership will then transform the acquired community in its Image. In this process of forced transformation the leadership has to be focused which reinforces the paradigm that the evo-devo leader be able **to not be good to all at all times**. This is necessary in the "WHY" of the evo-devo of leadership as selection advantage for the entire community lies in the fact that the leader has to survive in the real world not a world of his imagination. This entails the leadership to accept both blame and praise for the actions of the community. The leadership is required, to be liberal in the utilization of natural capital to maximize the opportunities for the community rather than giving away resources to be called Liberal. If there is a need to "appear" liberal the leadership should find ways **to give away resources that belong to others in order to lower their competitive advantage at the same time enhance its own Leadership reputation and brand value.**

A leader who tries to buy support in the existing or acquired community will find that none of these will stand behind him in times of adversity. The support that is given at a price rather than, need, want, or inspiration of a common goal are bought but not owned by the leader or the community. It is paramount for the evo-devo leader to have at his command resources, facts and the faith of the community to follow leadership vision and the strategy in both times of growth and adversity of the "Implosion Effect".

GROWTH

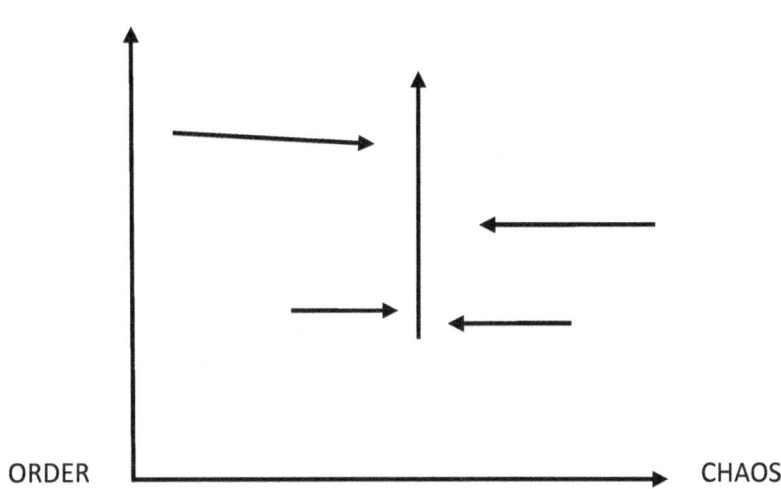

CHAOS

ORDER

CHAOSAND ORDER (Fig. 5)

The leader in the evo-devo paradigm has to exist in the understanding of the harmony of Chaos and Order to create a Value System that will be strong yet flexible to handle ambiguity. The system has to be able to continuously auto correct itself between Order and Chaos under the guidance of the leader in order to gain competitive advantage for the community. The "WHY" of the evo-devo of leadership requires the Leader to live every moment learning and perfecting skills to react to the Chaos chaotic events will appear in an Imperfect State in the day to day execution of the long term strategy? Oh the other hand leadership should resist the temptation of looking for the Utopian State or the "Should Be" state since the order and resource to achieve that will create more chaos. The "Why" of evo-devo which utilizes maximum free energy and creates sustainable growth lies in the state of entropy between Order and Chaos wherein both exist in the Harmony?

THE "HOW" OF THE EVO DEVO OF LEADERSHIP:

The last but not the least servant of evo-devo leadership is the "HOW". HOW and WHY are the only two questions that differentiate us from the rest of the animal kingdom and therefore provide the key to leadership innovation for evolution and creativity?

The concept of "HOW" is attached to the ideation of incentives is clearly the view that will be used in the Leadership Parabola to define the Evo-Devo leader. These "Incentives" that play between the swings of "Chaos and Order", "Fear and Faith", 'Doubt and Facts", "Punishment and Reward" or "Implosion and Explosion" will be employed in the "HOW" of the evo-devo of leadership as we push the community towards sustainable success. It is extremely important to keep this "incentive" driver simple so that it is clearly understood and in turn serves the leader to achieve the goals for the benefit of the community.

This Incentive driver is designed in the "HOW" of the evo-devo of leadership to inculcate desired behaviors. These behaviors are those that will create transformation. This transformation aligned with communal objectives will result in the Evolutionary Development of the community. This evo-devo is the key to Competitive Advantage.

The incentive drivers designed by the leader, in line with the vision, should result in evolving the community towards a harmonious state with the knowledge and flexibility to work in the Imperfect state of chaos and temptation. This essentially brings us to the basics of the "Who" of, the Evo-Devo leader: One who can eliminate his bad traits (that are depleting the overall communal value) by replacing them with traits that are conducive to enhancement of "Communal Wealth". This again has to happen in incremental steps based on the pre- disposition of the leader and the community. The truth is that this kind of incremental transformation using incentive drivers has to motivate and evolve the 3 C's i.e. the clients, the custodians and the community to perform "above peak". This can only happen through mass proliferation of these performance drivers within the community which will then evolve in the image of the leader and his or her value system. The system cannot support a duality of incentives or value systems that are different for the Leader and the Community. The incentive drivers inherently need to similar working towards a common goal.

The other factor to evolve the incentive drivers is to ensure that the desired behaviors have to confer advantage to the entity both at the individual and community level in order for it to be propagated reliably and sustainably across the community. It is also true that as the entity evolves to accept beneficial transformation and makes it a part of the New Value system it will become easier to introduce further changes. Initially though there will be a resistance to change and it will take time with the right incentives for the transformations to reach a replicable frequency or "fixation". The "HOW" of the evo-devo of Leadership establishes the relationship curve to ensure that the desired behaviors is spread at a steeper growth rate as it the moves down from the leader to the community for the goal of achieving "Fixation". Fixation in turn will assist in transforming "desired behavior" into an "Accepted Behavior".

At the same time to maintain harmony between the systems during transformation the "HOW" of the evo-devo of leadership requires the insertion of an important process within the system in the shape of the "FEEDBACK LOOP". This feedback loop should ensure that the desired traits are actually providing the advantage required for the community before these traits become accepted behavior. This feedback loop being cyclic in nature will move between the relationship curve going from the leader to the community and vice-versa. The feedback loop should measure the effect of the transformations against the value chain and provide input to the leader for personal evolution. This constant feedback loop is "HOW" the leader can motivate the system and to ensure that only the right desired behavior becomes accepted behavior for the leader and the community.

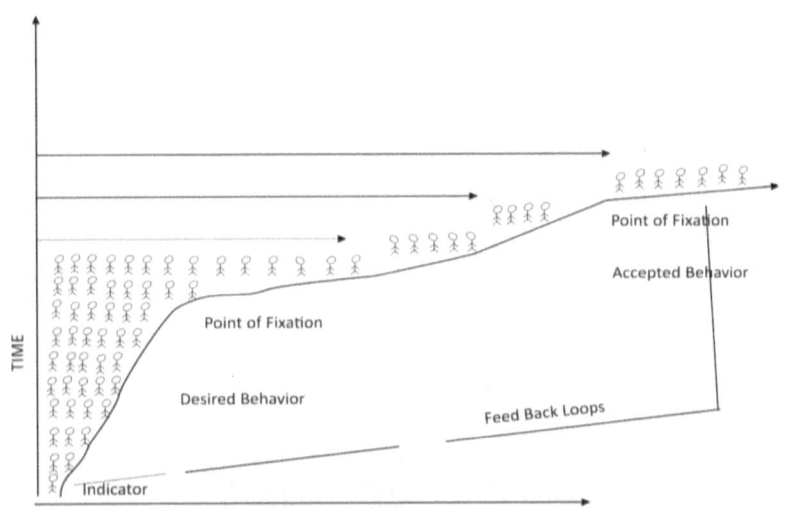

RELATIONSHIP CURVE (Fig. 6)

The Evo-Devo of Leadership

The "HOW" of the evo-devo of Leadership necessarily involves having a strong belief system alongside the New Value System. The heart and the mind both play together. The leader needs to have the confabulation of both the emotion and the I logic of faith and fact between the community and self. The leader who just stays within the "comfort zone" based on the past successes or limited knowledge will not be able to meet the adverse effects of chaos and adversity during the "IMPLOSION EFFECT". In order to capture the entropy of the Implosion to fuel the explosion using free energy to gain competitive advantage leadership will need to move away from its "comfort zone." If leadership continues to base its strategies on past successes and "luck" of previously successful strategies to achieve sustainable success he or she will fail. The environment needs innovation therefore the community will also fail. Thus in effect the "HOW" within the Leadership Parabola becomes the culture that is created by the leader for sustainable success that will become the most powerful tool for its growth or alternatively the wrong leadership culture will result in its demise by becoming, its own potential nemesis.

The figure below shows the relationship between violence, change and evolution. The periods of mass violence were also periods of the lowest levels of cultural evolution and evo-devo Leadership.

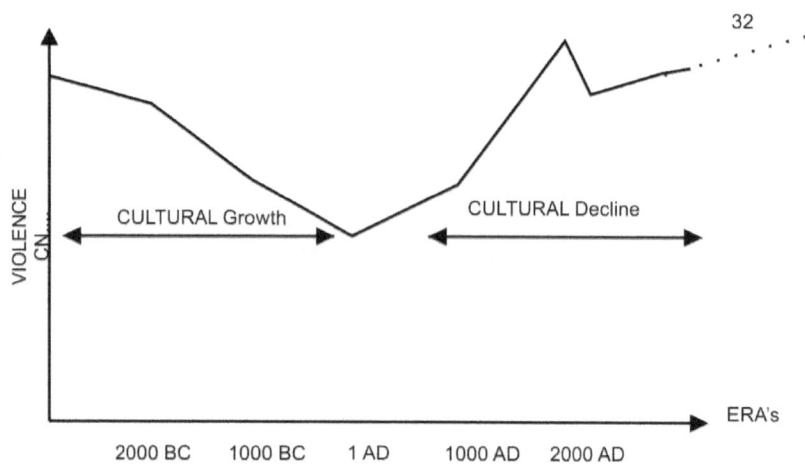

CULTURAL EVOLUTION (Fig. 7)

"SUCCESS IS NECESSARY BECAUSE THE OTHER OPTION IS FAILURE. CHAOS IS NEEDED IN ORDER TO ACHIEVE ORDER. EVO-DEVO IS MANDATORY BECAUSE CHANGE WILL HAPPEN."

"A LONG VIEW OF EVOLUTION REVEALS THE EDGY COEXISTENCE BETWEEN LEADERS AND PLACE TO SHAPE THE ORGANIZATION"

An EVO-DEVO Statement

CHAPTER 4

THE ENTROPY OF LEADERSHIP

The huge expanse of the universe gives one the impression of a non-chaotic and perfect state. This is the ultimate illusion. An urban myth. As an evo-devo leader you have to observe the universe in smaller increments to understand the chaos that lies within this "perfect" state. As you delve deeper into your community and yourself you will discover the flawed nature of the system due to your weaknesses. A famous saying by an evo-devo Leader is " It's Fun to do the impossible.". The Indian Army has gone one step further. They state "The Impossible is not a problem; Miracles will take a little more time". The value system that defines the impossible as achievable and understands that the flaws within the system are a source of energy realizes the Entropy of Leadership and its inherent competitive advantage. Entropy is a measure of chaos and isolated systems will always tend towards the highest state of chaos. The energy stored in the entropy is higher than the energy expended. Thus the evo-devo concept of the "free energy" from chaos for prevention and recovery from failure to sustainable growth.

The interplay of facts and faith intermingled with the right choice is the key to opening the store of leadership entropy. Unfortunately, the facts are not easily available. In most cases the facts are buried, hidden, unused, falsified or ignored. The only time these facts are uncovered is in adversity or chaos. The paradox though is that Chaos and Order can peacefully coexist within a perfect system. The intricate dance to balance the two is the evo-devo of leadership that is needed. The unavailable energy or the free energy is present in the randomness and uncertainty of chaos. This free energy will fuel the incremental transformations required in the community and the leaders to achieve the goal of sustainable success. The identification of the entropy in any system and its processes, whether owned or acquired, is a task that requires complete focus. It also needs a transformed value system that includes vision and innovation to utilize the potential of the community for the extraction of facts and using the facts to generate "free energy" from the Entropy of Leadership.

The advantage of free energy is manifold since this sustainable source of energy is the cheapest and best form of fuel available to the leader to pull the community towards the "STAR" of Greatness. The metrics of this entropy of chaos and the "STAR" lie amongst the pre-dispositions of the community aided by the art of skillful planning and preparedness. The tools of extraction of this "free energy" are also available within the Leadership sphere of influence.

As the leadership parabola oscillates between the diverse parameters of chaos and order to attain its point of equilibrium, the Leadership capabilities are stretched to the limits of continuity. This mandates that both the leadership and the community become RESILIENT. **The evo-devo of Leadership that commands the entropy of the system to withstand the extreme environmental flux during the "implosion effect" without collapsing into a qualitatively different forced state is known as the RESILIENCE QUOTIENT (RQ).** In terms of the RQ and its relationship with the entropy of leadership it is known that the more variegated or divers a system the more resilient it becomes in adversity. In actuality the higher RQ allows the system to enhance its normal Life Cycle by utilizing the entropy of the constituents and the Leadership.

The "Ecological Economics" of Resilience and the Entropy of Leadership in the 21st century and beyond will redefine the growth curve of any enterprise based on its wisdom and fortuity. In an attempt to understand this crucial area of evo-devo it might be prudent to look at some logic:

a) The Entropy, The RQ and the diversity of the enterprise are all benefits that are both tangible and intangible quantities. In order to understand these quantities and measure their power we need to observe their absence to realize their presence in any system.

b) For example Silence cannot be measured except for the absence of Sound.

c) Similarly cold, even as low as Absolute Zero is only a measure of the absence of Heat. Darkness is only a measure of the lack of Light. The universe contains Dark Matter as its major constituent and its presence is measured by the absence of matter. In the same tone, the measure of the RQ is linked directly to its absence within the leaders and the community. The measure of the RQ is a direct result of the **Liquidity of the Entity (L) and its Diversity Value (D)**. The RQ is also inversely proportional to the Rate of Change (@C) and the Frequency of Change (face). The RQ is a defining factor in gauging the competitive advantage of the community and its "STAR" value.

The mathematical representation of the RESILIENCE QUOTIENT (RQ), which is therefore the measure of an entities ability to withstand catastrophic and apocalyptic chaos, is as under:

$$\text{RESILIENCE QUOTIENT} = \frac{\text{No. of Days of Liquidity X Diversity VALUE}^2 (\%)}{\text{RATE of Change (\%) x Frequency of Change}}$$

OR

$$RQ = \frac{LD^2}{@C \times fC}$$

In this formula, in order to quantify the resilience of system, you can enter various values for the rate and frequency of Change to verify the ability of the system <u>to withstand adversity and implosion without compromising its structural stability.</u>

The Key to an enhanced RESILIENCE QUOTIENT is therefore a consequence of the Entropy hidden in its Diversity and Liquidity of resources as well as a planned rate and frequency of Qualitative Change. As an example, a Democratic Nation stricken by Ecological, Economic and Ecclesiastical chaos having a lack of Diversity will collapse if multiple changes are applied frequently at a fast pace. Simply put: Frequent changes (quantative) applied rapidly to any system will lower its resilience and increase waste. This waste is a source of free energy that will fund recovery when the system collapses if you follow the evo-devo principles stored within the ENTROPY OF LEADERSHIP.

The entropy is a function of the fact that as the leadership shapes the Nature and Culture of the Community simultaneously the Community is transforming the Image of the Leadership as well. There are numerous examples of the Entropy of Leadership and the Diversity of resources that exist today. The current Diversity and its attached impact on the Resilience Quotient need to be redefined in an attempt to gain competitive advantage via the qualification and quantification of advantageous configurations that exist within the enterprise. This redefinition is the "watershed" that will divide the good from the Great "STAR" communities and their leaders based on the innovation and knowledge of the diverse constituents to identify and use the entropy within the system.

One of the premier processes that is currently trying to identify the entropy within the universe is the Large Hadron Collider (LHC). The LHC is focusing on establishing the interdependence that exists at the Quantum Level known as the STRING THEORY as well as identifying the "Higgs Bosun" or God's Particle that theoretically adds mass to matter (July 2012 the "Higgs Bosun was observed). Both these theories have a common goal to further our understanding of the unseen dark energy around us that helps in creating the observable gravitational force across the universe. This $8 Billion tool is set to redefine the nature of resources available to leadership for creating "perpetual" growth and is an indication of the sophistication of technology available to evo-devo leaders for gaining a competitive advantage. The 21st century is the century of evo-devo where you will see a rapid rate of change but you, as leaders, will need the wisdom and enduring patience to use the free energy realized in a technically civilized manner. Technical Civilization will be the key to high Digital iQ that will be used to measure, map and enhance the capability of "STAR" leaders to extract the store of free energy.

A similar example is the $5 Billion being spent on the biological processes known as the Genome Mapping Project. This project and its ramifications are expected to transform the entire Human Evolution paradigm. These examples and other such discoveries are indicative of the technological liquidity and diversity of resources available to leaders today. Unfortunately, the lack of technical civilization and low Digital iQ has resulted in the misuse of these powerful "game changers" to create scarcity and fear.

The real "game changer" though lies in the transformation of our belief system to move away from the dogma of "scarcity" of resource to the evo-devo of "abundance" of Natural Capital. The Natural Capital stored in the

Entropy around us and its associated "free energy" is both sources of abundance that is present in all our existing processes. The Higgs Bosun of Leadership and its evo-devo is the latent energy that lies within the quality of leadership and the quantity of the potential of the diversity of talent in the community. The harnessing of this latent energy will automatically provide the desired transformation in tune with Leadership vision through innovation.

This latent energy and the concept of "abundance" of Natural Capital that exists within our own bodies can be observed from the three examples we will analyze as below:

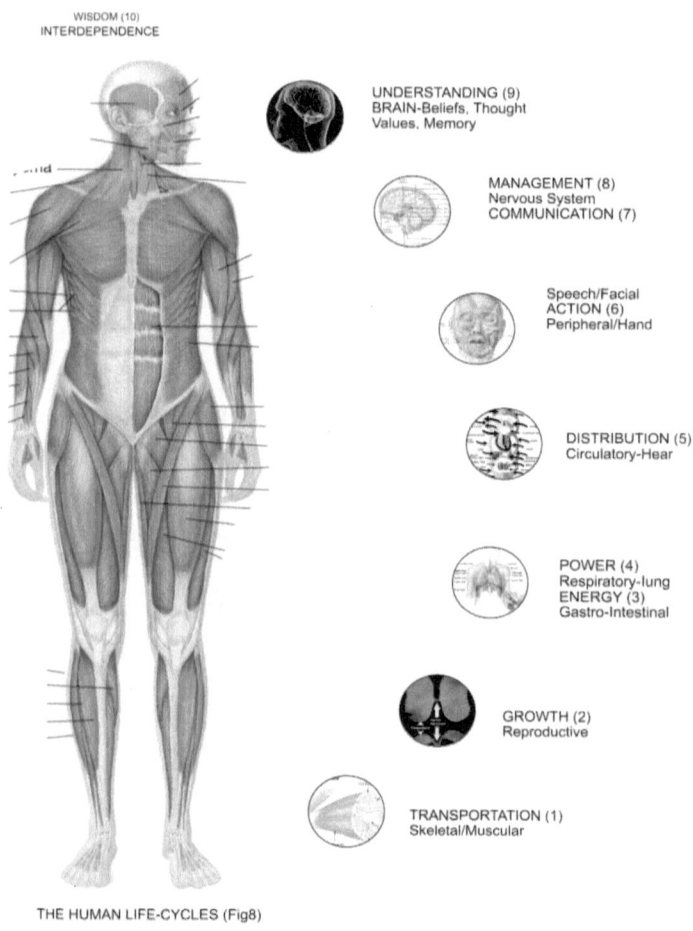

WISDOM (10)
INTERDEPENDENCE

UNDERSTANDING (9)
BRAIN-Beliefs, Thought
Values, Memory

MANAGEMENT (8)
Nervous System
COMMUNICATION (7)

Speech/Facial
ACTION (6)
Peripheral/Hand

DISTRIBUTION (5)
Circulatory-Hear

POWER (4)
Respiratory-lung
ENERGY (3)
Gastro-Intestinal

GROWTH (2)
Reproductive

TRANSPORTATION (1)
Skeletal/Muscular

THE HUMAN LIFE-CYCLES (Fig8)

THE 10 Cycles of the Human Body Fig. 8

The Evo-Devo of Leadership

a) The HUMAN LIFE CYCLES

b) The HUMAN BRAIN- Size and Usage

c) The HUMAN DNA- Usage

(a) Your body has been "fast-forwarded through time and is currently in a catch-up mode as it tries to adjust its prehistoric nature to the modern culture. The Sumerian's and the Hindu Veda's divide the Human body into Life-Cycles. The 9th and the 10th life cycles are the ones that pertain to Understanding and Wisdom. The 8th cycle is the one that manages the other cycles that in turn are the physical layers for survival. The 5 senses are sight, sound, touch and smell. These senses are subordinate to the 10 Life-Cycles. The harmony is in the co-existence of both peacefully and efficiently.

As you will gather from the next two illustrations, which compare the unutilized brain usage and brain sizes amongst various species. The size of the brain is not a clear indication of the intelligence of the species. The entropy of the unutilized portion of the brain though has a direct correlation to the competitive advantage of the species in the future. The "survival of the fittest "paradigm is closely linked to the Entropy of leadership and its diversity and is a signature of the species' selection advantage over other systems. On the other hand, The Human Life Cycles loses efficiency once the 5 senses start controlling the other layers by promoting unethical consumption. The process also starts affecting our understanding and wisdom. This imbalance is the source of entropy and free energy through evolutionary change that is available.

Your body is in a never-ending fight for survival. As you rest or work or consume, the battle continues. In this chaos lies the answer for growth. As Benjamin Franklin said" Balance is the basis of all good health. Everything in moderation.", similarly the secret of growth is in the entropy of chaos as it can take the moderate consumption and create abundant energy for success. In recent studies it has been proven that this "Bonus" of extracting the unutilized energy is the extra flexibility needed for the "STAR" leadership of greatness. Similarly, it is now a fact that nearly 97% of our DNA is classified as "junk" as the function of the DNA is not yet established. The energy stored in this 97% is the "Bonus" that can be selected for the entropy of Leadership The hidden potential as we see in the illustrations relating to the unutilized DNA or the Brain or the Human Life-cycles is a powerful source of energy for growth and can be found in all the processes around us and within our "sphere of influence".

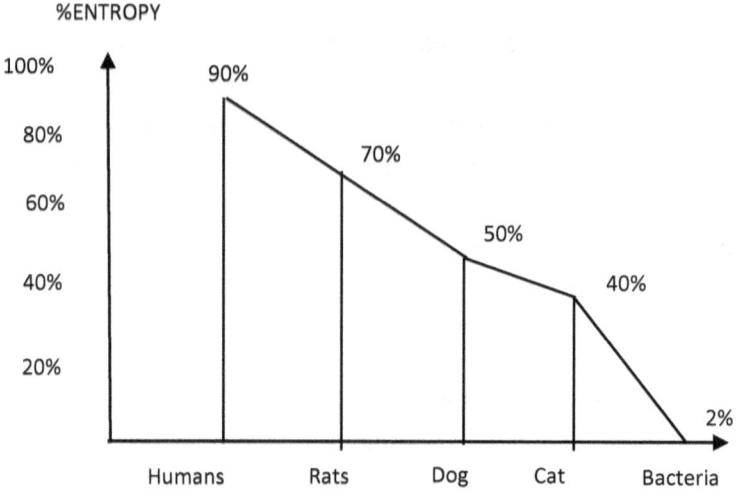

DNA USAGE (Fig 9)

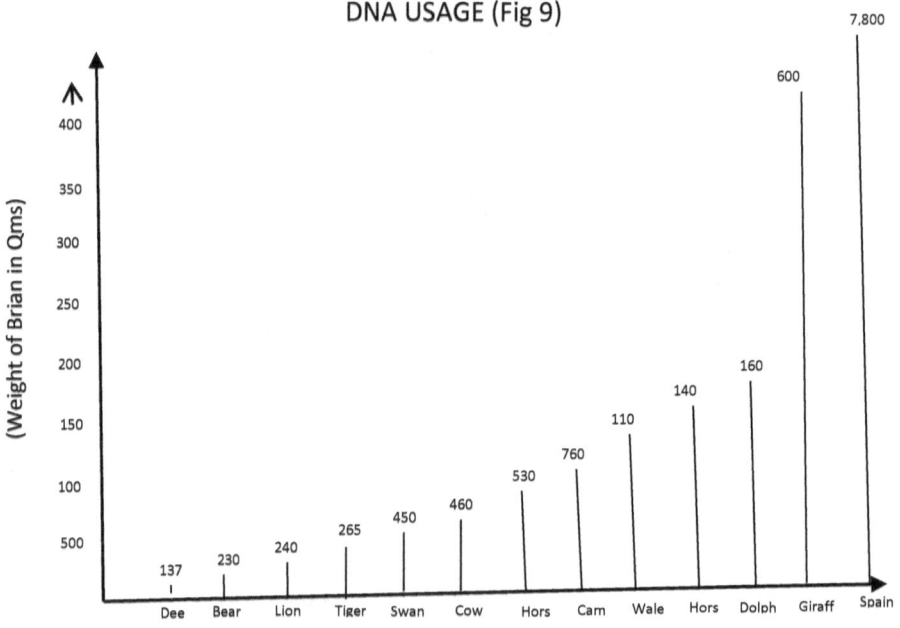

UTILIZED BRAIN USAGE (Fig 10)

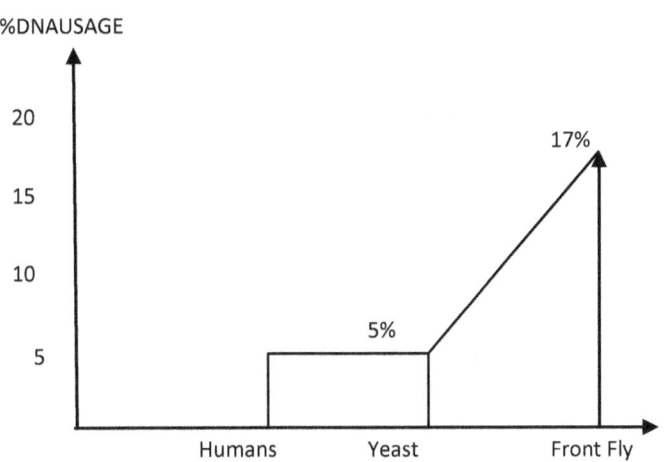

COMPARITIVE BRAIN SIZES [Fig 10 (i)]

BRAIN SIZES OF MAMMALS Fig. 10(i)

The current chaos in the financial and banking sectors may be a good example of the entropy of Leadership in adversity in modern times. The "Greater Depression of 2009", was a result of the combined effect of the economic and financial collapse hitting simultaneously in a classic case of the unmanaged "Implosion Effect". The "Implosion Effect" was triggered since the policies of "infinite debt" as a source for consumption were unsustainable. The global systems had to return to some order as the chaos was stretching the structural stability of the financial and economic processes. In comparison to the similar phenomenon in the 1930's i.e. The "Great Depression" and its underlying chaos and the subsequent order that was established is an excellent source of facts that could help us today.

In the 1930's for 3 years there was no growth as the system corrected itself within the extremes of chaos and order. In the 4th year the markets rose nearly 60%. The industries contributing to this growth were Tobacco, Oil, sugar, leather and other such commodities which can loosely be termed as "community products". The entropy of the demand and the unutilized energy of the consumers were transformed from a need based strategy to a want based pattern of guilty pleasure even as the consumers faced economic hardships. The "BUCK" was passed on. You may observe that there is a direct comparison between the two economic disasters of the 1930's and the 21st century. The economic recovery index i.e. the stock exchange took 3.5 years to come back to its 2007 high. The industries that fueled this growth are similar to the consumption based industries of the 30's, only the consumption pattern has changed. There are various similarities including the process of "passing the buck" to unwary consumer.

The current crisis is in no small way the aftermath of the "Dot.com" bust of 1999. The stock market crisis that was fueled by the un-sustainable valuations was passed on from a few investors to the mom's and pop's through liberalized credit lines for consumption. The "credit card" economy was linked to the subconscious pleasure of the "American dream" i.e. the Housing sector. The insane valuations of the "Dot.com" era were now transformed into the crazy real-estate values that were used to fund the consumers: an epidemic of debt. The 1999 virus was now an epidemic that was passed on to the American public. The unethical consumption resulted in spreading the virus globally as well. The economies of the emerging markets set out to satisfy the unfulfilled demand for goods and services in the developed markets. The collapse of the housing sector resulted in a global recession that was unparalleled. The solution: consume more. The economists in the developed world have decided to solve the crisis by providing subsidies and grants through stimulus packages in an attempt to prop up the financial and economic sectors. This has created a new commodity i.e. "Debt", which is being sold to countries like China, India, Japan, Germany and the Middle East. The virus is now a pandemic as the underlying causes of the disease are unchecked. The "Buck" continues to be passed.

The question - **What would be the evo-devo solution**? The evo-devo Leadership would create an "implosion effect" by de-debiting and de-leveraging the market in "debt locked" nations. The fiscal deficits and the trade deficits would be corrected to release the intrinsic value of the market. The individual "core competencies" would then be focused on the "STAR" to deliver the maximum gain for the constituents on a global basis through the aegis of sustainable growth. The type of entities that would play a major role in this transformation would fall into three distinct categories as under:

a) **INFRASTRUCTURE MODERNIZATION**: The idea of "unemployment reduction" versus the push for "employment creation" is an excellent strategy to unlock the hidden potential within the community. The use of infrastructure projects as a source of "unemployment reduction" will provide a double benefit for the constituents. Firstly, it will become an investment for the future that will assist the next generations in building wealth. These projects, as a store of wealth and entropy, will also be able to offset the cost of the investments made today Secondly, the planned nature of these projects as a tool for existing and future growth will ensure ethical consumption of the resources and the honest effort of the current unemployed populace by increasing their knowledge. The infrastructure projects would include the traditional i.e. roads bridges, communication, power, alongside data centers, intelligent buildings, technology incubators, green energy and "thin-wired" business logic libraries.

b) **NEED to HAVE vs. NICE TO HAVE ENTERPRISES**: Trustworthy branded corporations with manageable debt that are focused on satisfying the needs of their existing, consumer base would be another strong contributor to the resurgence of economic growth. The qualitative nature of these enterprises that would be innovating to meet the current and future needs of their clients in terms of process improvement would be using the "STAR" processes of customer retention not a constant push for customer acquisition. The focus of such companies on quality not quantity would also promote the "need to have" paradigm rather than the "nice to have" focus that is promulgated by the leadership of today. The "need to have" nature of the enterprise would be to provide unmatched value of both lower risk and cost. **The smart communities will reduce the time and distance between the client and the provider.** The current examples of such enterprises would include: Amazon, Wal-Mart, Commodities, Craig list, Xerox, Google, Fed-Ex, Toyota, etc.

c) **"INFLATION-PROOF" CONSUMPTION**: Economies and Organizations that have reached the zenith of consistent and guaranteed results linked to sustained growth are another candidate for the desired economic transformation. These enterprises have utilized technology and knowledge to "inflation proof" their offerings. The "inflation proof" methodology is not only in relation to their incomes but also encompasses the fact that they do not need to constantly upgrade or reinvest for growth. These enterprises can also create mass employment due to the monopolistic nature of their goods and services. In order to retain their competitive advantage and create an "entry barrier" for any competition these enterprises will have to maintain a strategy of Rapid Return on Investment through constant innovation and technical civilization. The same can be achieved through the harnessing of intellectual capital hidden in the potential of the "individual" experts across the globe. Enterprises such as Microsoft, Apple, Time Warner, Pharmaceutical and Bio-Tech industries, Space Exploration, Art and Music etc. would fall into this category.

All the three solutions and enterprises mentioned are also prime examples of the evo-devo Leadership of Entropy through their use of the natural laws of the equilibrium of chaos and order to fund sustained growth. At no point do these enterprises and their leaders think about "Passing the BUCK" as a strategy for growth.

The question -**"Is existing Leadership willing to gain the wisdom to harness the potential to achieve this transformation that moves them from the goal of self-preservation to the advantage of Communal benefits?"** If the answer is YES, then there are methodologies that are tried and tested in terms of short, medium and long term fiscal frameworks that can convert the existing chaos into the order of growth. If the answer to the above question is NO then you need to understand that the BIG "G" and the natural laws will force us to learn the evo-devo processes, to unlock the energy of entropy that exists in our leadership, through the chaos of an implosion.

Let us try to answer these Key questions of our survival as we move to the next port of good leadership vs. the great "STAR" .The evo-devo of the "STAR" in the ideation of communalism and the part played by faith or the BIG "G" to create the small "g's" that exist today is an important component of our quest.

"EDUCATION IS NOT ABOUT MAKING KIDS GIVE THE"RIGHT"ANSWER,BUT ABOUT GIVING KIDS METHODS BY WHICH TO DECIDE WHETHER AN ANSWER IS "RIGHT"

Bill Gates in "The Road Ahead"

CHAPTER 5

<u>**THE LEADERSHIP OF "STAR" GREATNESS- The BIG "G" vs. The small "g"**</u>

"A rising tide lifts all boats." The epitome of the Great "STAR" Leadership in its nature and culture will energize the entire community to a higher state of achievement and success. The higher state of achievement that is beneficial and shared is also the evo-devo paradigm of communalism. The objective of this quest is to define this nature and culture of Great "STAR" leadership in relation to both good and bad leadership styles. The point of Inflexion between the higher state of communalism and the existing states of non-performance will also need to be defined. **The "BONUS" of the BIG "G" or the creator in tune with the small "g" or the Great "STAR" leader is the harmony that is desired as a function of the evo-devo of Leadership.**

The harmony that is created when the natural laws of the BIG "G" are in line with the local laws of the small "g" the foundation of transforming adversity into sustainable growth is laid. This also allows the small "g" to harness the "free energy" of the implosion to innovate explosive growth that is the hallmark of the Great "STAR" leaders. These traits are therefore the ones that need to be acquired by the good leaders to achieve the "STAR" status. The good leaders react to the stimulus of "situational change" while "STAR" leaders create evolutionary positive transformation. The good leaders are focused on meeting the challenges of their environment while the Great Leaders are focused on creating an environment that provides the community and the Leaders to achieve their potential in incremental steps. The onus of the "STAR" leaders is also to ensure that the transference of the states is stable yet expanding.

The uncanny ability of Great Leaders to be able to consistently pick the "preferred choice" is sometimes attributed to luck or fortune. The fact is that the Great Leaders build a value system around an illative sense and a dichotomy of thought that allows them to "SEE" the "preferred choice" as the "RIGHT" choice. The golden rule of achieving this dichotomy of thought is to believe that there "are no rules" while having the knowledge that certain "rules do exist". This ambiguity is a "way of life" for the "STAR" leaders as they possess the wisdom to understand that as the protectors of the "communal wealth" the "preferred choice" is always the one that benefits the community more than the leadership. This then becomes the basis of their actions in the paradigm of "communalism." Communalism in its evo-devo avatar is in no way to be confused with the current definitions that border on religion or with communism that is a failed governance methodology.

An "ism" by definition is a distinctive doctrine, cause or theory. The word communal is further clarified as - "relating to one or more communes or communities." The combination of the "ism" with "communal" though turns out to be "a social organization on a communal basis". This division is not our goal. Our goal is synergy. The communalism of evo-devo is triggered by the value system that believes in the truth that at the quantum level energy and matter become symbiotic and transferable. The energy also has a advantage that it is not constrained either by time or space. This energy that can be transferred across space and time to create communities that prosper in synergy is the evo-devo of the Leadership of Greatness and the foundation of "STAR" leaders and communes.

The two pillars of the "STAR" of Communalism are "Communal Wealth" and "**Communal** Benefit". The end goal of the communalistic paradigm is Sustainable Growth. The three fundamental laws of communalism are based on:

a) An honest effort to achieve one's potential or "do not sell yourself short",

(b) Just rewards for your effort and in line with your individual and communal contributions or "Get our Fair Dues" , and

(c) Sharing the rewards to create an environment that ensures that the individual and communal potential is achieved and the energy of communalism is abundant for ongoing growth.

The re-emergence of communalism as an evo-devo mechanism to evolve into "STAR" communities with the Leadership of Greatness will automatically result in competitive advantage in the areas of Natural and Artificial selection.

The current typical or even good leaders have created an unethical whirlpool that is overburdening the physical, economic and cultural resources of the global community and testing the resilience of the entire human species. The negative effects of this downward push is being felt all around the world in various forms with the loss of stable and sustainable communes that can self-replicate and self-sustain their expertise. The result of the disappearance of these capabilities will automatically mandate the extinction and elimination of communities and organizations through the natural laws of selection. The Key to understanding the vagaries of this process and the advent of Communalism linked to the Leadership of Greatness is the only method to lead the constituents out of the current adversities. The fact that communalism is time and space independent also means that our current focus on "clocks and watches" that only help in crisis management has to be replaced by the concept of time that is aligned with the evo-devo processes of sustainability. Let's examine the two pillars of Communalism to understand the evolutionary processes:

a) **COMMUNAL WEALTH**: The search for meaning is a quest and our journey now brings us to the port of Leadership of "STAR" Greatness. This quest is complex since the communal wealth is hidden in the ambiguity of natural and man-made laws that differ according to the local conditions. The fact that the secret of the communal wealth is a combination of the individual potential available locally with the global unused energy of entropy, hidden in the inefficiencies of the process and knowledge, is the ultimate tool of "STAR" leaders. Communal Wealth thrives in adversity and sustains during the "Implosion Effect." **The "Implosion Effect" is a crucial milestone in the interplay of the forces of Chaos and Order which test the resilience of the entity. The "STAR" of Leadership Greatness is directly proportional to its ability to "fund" the store of communal wealth using the energy of the implosion itself. This self-generating process of sustainable growth is the measure of the "communal wealth" in communalism.**

The entire concept of "communal wealth" that encompasses individual wealth and community potential, in a social structure that promotes the free transference of knowledge and processes is the crux of the strategy of communalism. It is a well-known phenomenon that if we throw a stone in a body of water it will create ripples. Typical and good Leaders are watching the ripples while "STAR" leaders focus on the fact that can reuse the stone to keep on generating ripples. Similarly in the commercial environment today the hidden energy and wealth in the existing relationships within the global communities is ignored in a race to keep acquiring new relationships.

As a thumb rule 20% of our constituents account for 80% of the benefits and only 40% of our cost in an ongoing relationship. The other 80% only account for 20% of our benefits but consume nearly 60% of our resources. As an example it costs nearly $1000 to acquire a new insurance client or $550 a new banking client with their initial revenue covering only 30% of their costs when you include customer turnover. A new telecom customer will only be able to cover a small portion of their cost initially but if we can retain the customer relationships over large periods of time we can make a huge contribution to the store of communal wealth. This retention strategy for key constituents in our communal success is mandated as a source of communal wealth.

b) **COMMUNAL BENEFIT**: Sun Tzu, the great Chinese strategist and tactician said "The Greatest Generals are ones that can win without fighting a war." The above quote is equally matched by the saying that "the definition of insanity is to keep performing the same actions over and over but still expect a different result". The key thought process behind both these is the elimination of Waste. The waste we are discussing is not your average garbage or trash but the "BONUS" hidden in the processes of the Leadership, the commune, and the individual. Communal Benefit is directly linked to the elimination of waste. The Leadership of Greatness and its "STAR" of communalism is a value system that identifies and innovates consistently to transform waste to communal benefit. The problems we face today whether in the governance of capitalism, monarchy, dictatorships, socialism, communism, democracy and globalization is that without the "STAR" leadership that can eliminate wasteful processes the political and social structures are doomed to failure. **In some of the examples ahead you will observe the fact that communal benefits are inversely proportional to the amount of waste in any enterprise.** Technology is a major tool that can be successfully employed to identify waste but it will finally be the human ingenuity and determination that will innovate the processes itself to transform the waste into communal benefit. This one key factor of communalism can clear the cobwebs that separate the good leaders from "STAR" leadership.

The three laws of communalism are the foundation that supports the two pillars of "communal wealth" and "communal benefit". The laws also define the nature and culture of "STAR" leadership that can unleash the energy required for sustainable growth of the enterprise. **The first law states that the "STAR" leaders have to practice the <u>art of honest effort</u> constantly to achieve their potential.** Simultaneously, they need to create an environment that allows the community to hone their domain expertise. The Honest Effort desired is mired in the fact that evo-devo "STAR" leaders should not focus on what they cannot control and plan adequately to cover these points of failure. At the same time they need to focus on what they can control and eliminate any loss of energy in that process without worrying about failure. In this process of honest effort the "STAR" leaders, over time, should attempt to enhance their control incrementally over the points of failure that can affect the communal wealth.

The second law of communalism is in the equitable distribution of reward and risk. The "STAR" leaders would use this law to have an ubiquitous distribution policy rather than one that is based on the kurtosis of benefits. The kurtosis of rewards that only satisfy the leader and has small band of supporters is a certain recipe for disaster. The current fiscal disaster is a prime example of the violation of the second law of communalism. The aftermath of the catastrophe has added a tremendous amount of waste to the entire global economy in the form of unemployment, over capacity, rising prices, rising inflation, currency deflation and war. The reasons seem simple now in hindsight and were avoidable if the evo-devo laws were followed. The financial markets were over burdened by the billions of dollars in derivatives without any sustainable benefit to the economy. The risk was distributed amongst the unsuspecting community through the sub-prime mortgage innovations of the unethical lenders who ended up reaping the rewards. The result of this inequitable distribution and wasteful strategy was an economic and financial downturn of epic proportions. The second law of communalism that mandates a "fair" share of both risk and rewards is only possible if we investigate our processes, beliefs, values and accept that the blame lies with you. Then we need to find innovative ways to reduce the effect of these processes on the system and utilize the benefits of the economic advantage achieved for the growth of the community. This will promote further reduction of waste and thus the advent of ongoing communal benefits. There will always be some loss of efficiency in the system through waste as a part of "doing business" but even that should be in areas that will assist you during periods of implosion and chaos.

Apart from the afore mentioned laws of communalism the **third law is one of the most crucial elements of its success. This law states that the concept of sharing knowledge, assets and processes is the secret of creating abundance of Natural Capital** for attaining the "STAR" of the Leadership of Greatness. As we share energy across multiple systems the energy of all the systems increases simultaneously. The initial source of energy will also have 'its' energy returned but the entire system will now be escalated to a higher stable state of efficiency. This process can be repeated consistently to achieve growth. The sharing paradigm will allow the Great "STAR" leaders to enhance their sphere of influence and control without resorting to force. The same will also ensure that both technology and knowledge will not be used to deter or impede growth by withholding information as in the past. In fact by sharing the Natural Capital the "STAR" leaders will become the catalyst for releasing the free energy of entropy or waste in the global system. The communal wealth and benefits will thus be translated into a "global gain" that will surpass the sum of individual benefits. For example the knowledge domain that surrounds "Genome Mapping" is again being hampered as the current policies of isolation of information. The patenting of the genes by a few countries or organizations, in the name of research costs, is holding back new innovations. This "olde" value that promotes scarcity through hoarding is "passé". The idea of "Thin Wired" OPEN SOURCE verified local knowledge that is shared across all global individual "domain" experts is the foundation of the evo-devo laws of communalism and the "STAR" leaders. The small "g" who follows these rules in all their processes will start resonating with the creator or the BIG "G".

The Wall Street Journal scheduled-an initiative in Washington named "Finance in Crisis". The theme of this discussion was succinctly advertised under the following headlines "The World's financial system has broken down. Credit remains a constraint, markets and regulatory regimes have failed, and the old rules governing financial flow are moribund." The statements are a desperate cry for an evolved leadership- A "STAR" leader who can replace the existing "zero-risk" mentality with the laws of communalism to create sustainable growth. This can only happen if he or she can focus on the "STAR" of communal and global "gain" rather, than personal gain. This cannot be achieved by having governance policies based on the principles of "DON'T ASK-DON'T TELL". The need is for an abundance of small "g's" who have the "STAR" values and virtues that are required for the Leadership of Greatness. These values and virtues should become a "way of life" through practice and also be transferred to the community to be formed in the leader's' image. As Machiavelli once said "Without doubt Princes become great when they overcome difficulties made for them and opposition made to them" **Thus, the fact is that GREAT CHAOS is also a time of GREAT OPPORTUNITY for GREAT "STAR" leaders. You will agree that there is no better time than NOW.** The "STAR" values can be easily understood if we use the advantage of a comparison table as below;

LEADERSHIP LEVEL:	TYPICAL	GOOD	GREAT "STAR"
PROCESS:	PUSH	PULL	RESILIENCE
	COPY	TRANSACT	TRANSFORM
	CONTROL	COMPROMISE	SYMBIOSIS
	POWER	ALLIANCE	TRUST
	"LONE"GENIUS	SMART	WISDOM
FOCUS :	FEATURE	ADVANTAGE	BENEFIT
	ORDER	ORGANIZE	EMPOWER
	WEALTH	VALUE	UNMATCHED VALUE
	CHARISMA	LOYALITY	INTEGRITY
CHANGE:	IGNORE	ADAPT	SYNERGY
	EGOISTIC	EFFICIENTEFFECTIVE SYESTEM	
STYLE:	TAlK	ACTION FLAWLESS EXECUTION	
CONFLICT:	DEFENSIVE	MOBILE RUTHLESSELY AGGRESSIVE YET MERCIFUL.	
RESPONSE:	MANAGE	CONSENSUS	SERVE

The above mentioned values are in effect the ones that create a UNIQUE SELECTION POINT (USP) for the evo-devo leaders over the typical or good leaders. The USP for the "STAR" leaders in terms of their values generates an ideation strategy that is focused on competitive advantage. The ideas whether exciting innovative, provocative or even mundane are planned in advance and executed with precision. Alfred Hitchcock, one of the most brilliant directors of the 20th century, used to appear half-asleep and bored on his sets. Other directors are worried, anxious, aggressive and hyper-active while shooting a film. The reason Alfred Hitchcock was relaxed to the point of inaction on his sets was that he had planned and prepared for the points of failure down to each meticulous detail. In turn he had also planned for flawless execution of his vision of the film in areas as diverse as set design, costume lighting, sound and emotion. Hence, he was bored and half-asleep while directing the actual movie since in effect he had already directed the movie in his mind and on paper.

The values and KEY VIRTUES of "STAR" Leadership is also their **Center of GRAVITY**. This center of gravity is not only their source of power but the measure of their ability to create a sustainable community. The KEY VIRTUES that sustain the "STAR" values are the energy that surround the center of gravity of great leadership. Let's move forward in our journey to investigate these KEY VIRTUES that define the "STAR". The important factor is to acknowledge the fact that these virtues are common to all communities whether new, acquired, inherited or founded in-spite of their unique challenges. Also these virtues clearly define the **Quality of Leadership (QoL)**.

The primary virtue and the QoL of "STARS" is that they have to stand on their own merit as a private and unprivileged citizen of the community or organization. This implies that each "STAR" leader or small "g" has to have his own center of gravity that is stable, sustainable and synergistic. In effect this really means that the leader has the inherent values that are the intrinsic to him or her that can create the qualities to lead on his own strengths without relying on others. The leader will use this quality to create the vision and opportunity in his or her image in order gain greatness within the community. The community will also be transformed in the image created by the leader. The greatness achieved by the community in the image of the leader will be owned by the leader. The caveat here is that the same people who help him to come to power and achieve greatness are also expecting the most benefit to themselves even if it comes at a price to the community. This is the area that most good leader fail to navigate hence are not able to find greatness. It is therefore a better idea to focus on Communal Benefit and at the same time communicate with "known" enemies who fear greatness and will work with the leader to end any crisis while continuing to support the leader for their own survival. In reality the Great Leader will thus become a small "god" in his sphere of influence. As we are aware the BIG "G" or the One GOD does not want to do everything for us so he has designed the concept of "free will" and helps the Great Leaders or the small "g's" by creating great challenges for them to overcome in order that the glory in the shape of communal faith and Trust can fall on them.

The second QoL of greatness is the virtue to keep the faith on the community as well as on oneself. In this it is important to understand that most of the members of leader's sphere of influence have fixed natures and will not keep faith with the leader at all times. The qualities of greatness in leadership then require the leader to be flexible, cunning and strong at the same time. The nature of leadership greatness demands the cunningness of the fox and the strength of a lion. In order to keep the faith of the community the "STAR" has to be able to consistently deliver the results promised to the community. As in all cases greatness will be judged by the "ends" not the "means". A focus on achieving results that enhance the competitive advantage of the community is the "STAR" of leadership greatness. It-is also crucial to understand that this ruthless focus on results comes with a caveat. The caveat states that in order to achieve greatness that can be sustained and fixated into the community you should not intentionally use unethical strategies that are harmful to the culture of the community in the long run. These unethical strategies would be classified as those that violate the Natural Laws and the evo-devo principles. The sustainable benefits of the "STAR" leaders that are bestowed on the community ensures that the community views the leaders as having the blessings of the BIG "G" and being favored by fortune. This faith of the people adds the advantage of immortality as a virtue of "STAR" leadership.

The Third QoL of greatness is that "STAR" leaders have a "STAR" focus that should be founded on the faith of the masses that are benefited rather than a "few" who are demanding self-Aggrandization. The parameter for this virtue is that any decision that gives more to the masses than to the "few" is correct and ethical. The masses may not necessarily like being led or commanded but are too diverse to focus on the communal goals or the leaders. In fact it is important to lead the masses to achieve synergy without becoming the "common enemy" of the masses. The more diverse the populace the lesser the chance of a "coup" against the "STAR". On the other hand it is easy for the "few" to target you as the "common enemy" and oust you by coordinating their resources against you, the "STAR". The center of gravity that is based on the faith of the community is much more stable than one that is mired in the sycophancy of the "few". At the same time it is critical for the "STAR" not to become a pawn in the fight for power amongst the "few" or the community even though the "few" may have helped the "STAR" in the achievement of greatness. The key is to remember that it is easier and cheaper to replace the "few" rather than trying to change the masses.

The Fourth QoL of great leaders is to be able to be perceived as a master of their own destiny. This in essence is the leader's virtue to own, defend and command his "own" resources and the community's Natural Capital effectively. This ensures that the "STAR" leader can retain the competitive advantage for the community and himself against internal and external forces of adversity and conflict. In an environment of globalization and its interdependent nature it is crucial that even shared resources be under the control of the great leaders especially during chaos. This can be achieved contractually or through interdependent treaties. Also it is an established rule of Natural capital and resources that these automatically gravitate towards and respect the leaders who have the strongest center of gravity. These leaders are also the ones who can faithfully defend the resources in the times of adversity and chaos. The cause and effect of this quality is to transform the community in the image of the leader as a small "g" for the people. Great Leaders such as Moses or Gandhi or Mandela used their own knowledge, process and faith in the BIG "G" to transform the communities for success. All three and other such "STAR" leaders do not try to conform or become "like" others to get respect. They retain their identity and use their position as outsiders to win the community and implement evo-devo transformation. They control the center of gravity of the community from outside while allowing their actions to create the contrast between their successes and the failures of others.

The last but not the least quality that mandates the virtue of "STAR" leaders is founded on the fact that the great leaders have a belief system that is willing to accept and take calculated risk. The difference between them and other leaders is that they understand risk but avoid a gamble. Risk is essential for success but a gamble is unnecessary. The "STAR" leaders know that if a gamble goes wrong you can lose everything but if a calculated risk goes incorrectly you can recover and restart. In risk each ending is a new beginning and has an exit strategy while in a gamble an end is THE END. This virtue of the leadership of greatness may seem fortunate or lucky to others but is in fact the result of a perfect balance between the Yin of Knowledge and the Yang of Process. The magical ability of "a STAR" leader to be consistently in "the right place at the right time" is also a result of this virtue of understanding risk and controlling the failure points. The secret for acquiring this virtue is to practice the art of "connecting the dots" in order to visualize the "BIG PICTURE". The BIG PICTURE has to be seen as a collection, of small increments based on the resources of the leaders and the potential of the community. The practice of "connecting the dots" to find the "STAR" that can mesh the leaders and the community as a whole is also the essence of evo-devo leadership. The illustration below is the "BIG PICTURE" of the Leadership of Greatness where the sum of the values and virtues create the center of gravity that can defy the normal laws of success.

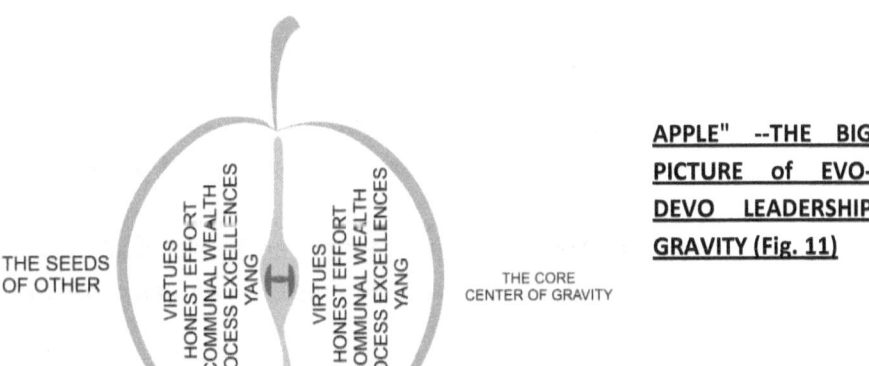

THE SEEDS OF OTHER

VIRTUES HONEST EFFORT COMMUNAL WEALTH PROCESS EXCELLENCES YANG

VIRTUES HONEST EFFORT COMMUNAL WEALTH PROCESS EXCELLENCES YANG

THE CORE CENTER OF GRAVITY

APPLE" --THE BIG PICTURE of EVO-DEVO LEADERSHIP GRAVITY (Fig. 11)

The "Big Picture" capability and the control of luck or fortune through the leadership of facts and truth is the quality that needs to be inculcated into the community in order to create the evo-devo of leadership; and to attain long-term sustainable growth. This control is rather like how a cat, dropped upside down, can twist its body, retrace and extend its legs so that it flips over and lands on its feet. The laws of Newtonian mechanics permit the cat to change its orientation, but not its velocity, without needing to push on anything or be pushed by anything. This "lucky" or "nine" lives phenomenon for cats is also used by Astronauts such as those on board the International Space Station to turn around in non-gravity or weightless environments without having to grab onto a handhold. The fact is that this "great" ability is in reality based on the fundamental principles of the Laws of Conservation of Energy and Momentum. The knowledge and Processes of these laws allows the "great" leaders such as the cats and the astronauts perform these unbelievable feats.

If we were to take the above example further into the realm of the theory of General Relativity we could actually control motion and velocity without the use of any external force by stretching and contracting in an asymmetrical fashion. A space ship equipped with a device that can change the relative speeds by increasing or decreasing the velocity of mechanical extension or contraction could act as a glider even in the absence of air. In this case (as shown by Physicist Mosna) this effect has to do with the temporal rather than spatial qualities of motion. This brings to light one of the key aspects of Einstein's theories which is the connection between space and time.

This distortion of both space and time leads to the effect that is known as frame dragging: a rotating body such as earth exerts a slight force in the direction of its rotation on other nearby objects such as satellites. Speaking loosely the rotating body actually drags space-time itself around. This in general terms implies that the velocity of motion of any mass influences its gravitational field. The above phenomenon is currently used in all the existing Global Positioning Systems. All this from the simple yet uncanny ability of cats being able to turn in mid-air.

Similarly, the evo-devo of leadership is the uncanny ability of "STAR" leaders to innovate a vision, set the goals and execute the process flawlessly for the desired benefits to accrue to the community. This leadership process in turn becomes the inherent competitive advantage for the community and the sphere of influence of the evo-devo leader. The competitive advantage ensures a sustainable and stable growth strategy for all the constituents. The Leadership of "perpetual" Growth that will be the next stop in our journey will further clarify the dynamics of evo-devo through the Leadership of Greatness.

In the next few pages, however, we will take a judicious step back to observe the current financial status around the globe and some of its inhabitants to gain some insights on the needs and wants that exist today.

1) **EMERGING MARKETS**: (China, India, Brazil, Russia, Thailand Mexico, Argentina, Taiwan, Korea and Hungary) - S

The global recession is hitting the world's emerging markets with a speed and ferocity few imagined possible. Emerging Markets as a group contracted from a GDP growth rate of 5% in 2008 to around 1.2% in 2011. Asian economies once again posted the starkest declines with Thailand going down from a growth rate of 3.7% in 2008 to -1% in 2010. In South Korea, the decline in Industrial output over the last 12 months was the largest since the country began keeping records. Taiwan, Philippines and Indonesia are seeing export declines that out paces the 1997-1998 experience. China, the behemoth of the emerging world, will grow 7% in real terms in 2012 compared to the 10-12% of previous years. This is a major de-acceleration for China. India, as you will observe from the chart below has remained relatively stable due to a growing domestic market and stringent Foreign Direct Investment rules which lowered its dependency on the American investors. Still, India has also taken a major hit in terms of its growth rates.

COUNTRY	2008 GDP	2011-2012 GDP
• CHINA	9%	7%
• INDIA	6.2%	5.7%
• BRAZIL	5.8%	1%
• THAILAND	3.7%	-1%

- RUSSIA   6.2%   -1.5%

- ARGENTINA   6%   -1.8%

- MEXICO   2%   -2%

- KOREA   2.3%   -2.3%

- TAIWAN   1%   -2.8%

- HUNGARY   1%   -3%

- EMERGING MARKETS   5%   1.8%

THE EMERGING MARKETS GDP GROWTH RATE TRENDS - 2008 vs. 2011/20102.

The above scenario is bleak but you knew this was going to happen as the signs were clear but leaders across the globe refused to acknowledge the facts and to make matters worse falsified the results for their personal gains. When the Mumbai Stock Exchange and the other regional stock exchanges were rising in tandem with the NYSE everyone was happy. When the NYSE collapsed and the USA stopped its consumption engine the effect naturally was global. Russia lost 5% of its value in terms of its GDP despite having the third largest reserves of foreign exchange in the world. The cause- Russian Ural crude oil blend dropped from $150 to $40 per barrel. Wage arrears, a major cause of Russian unrest in the 1990's, increased to over 50% in 2010. The Emerging Market crisis is a prime example of the global interdependence paradigm.

2) **THE EURO-ZONE**: The Euro-Zone excelled in one area that it surpassed the USA by delivering their worst performance in three decades. The GDP shrank nearly 6% in just one quarter in 2009. Then Greece and Spain went into their individual death spirals and the bottom fell out of the Euro-Zone. Germany is currently spending billions to avoid a total collapse. The German crisis is once again a victim of the unethical practices of the Financial Institutions. The bill for these practices is unfortunately being paid by the both common worker and the middle-class income taxpayer. The decline of both the manufacturing sector and trade alongside the financial crisis will force the Euro-Zone GDP down by 4% in 2013 the solution- "Consume more to get out of the financial

problems". The Euro Zone is in the process of implementing a stimulus package of 500 Billion dollars that is expected to solve all the problems that currently plague the region.

The Eastern European economies that were a beneficiary of the Euro-Zone excesses are now in turmoil as well. The current Eastern European situation is worse than the Asian crisis of the 1990's. The chart below clearly indicates the parallels that exist   :

EASTERN EUROPE		ASIA	
(2010 Debt/2010 GDP)		**(1997 Debt/1997 GDP)**	
CZECH REPUBLIC	24%	INDONESIA	25%
ESTORIA	131%	KOREA	20%
HUNGARY	65%	MALAYSIA	28%
ROMANIA	40%	PHILIPPINES	18%
POLAND	23%	THAILAND	46%

The above situation is a direct result of the short term goals of the Euro Zone to exploit the Eastern European nations to take on additional debt to consume more. The unemployment rate and bankruptcies in the region is a pointer to the growing chaos in the European region. The falsification of facts and results continues as the American model of consumption, that is the current cure for all economic ills, as recommended by the leading global economists is implemented globally. The other alternatives:

a) STATUS QUO: Let the crisis carry through and the manufacturing sector in countries, like Germany, will rebound. (THE KEEP YOUR FINGERS CROSSED STRATEGY)

b) Increase domestic consumption: Increase the local consumption through the increase in credit limits for the consumers. (PASS THE BUCK STRATEGY)

c) Innovate, Diversify and get into new sectors such as "Green Energy", bio-Technology, Robotics and Ecology Repair. (DO THE IMPOSSIBLE STRATEGY)

Remember, somebody had to create a comparative advantage in machinery, chemicals and BMW's in the 1960's for the German economy to grow. Germany, is currently the second last (the last being Belgium), in the number of business start-ups among 18 advanced economies surveyed across the globe. The transformation required to change this scenario is to create a genuine diversification of education, economics, and laws relating to labor and immigration and a wise leadership.

The Third alternative, The Impossible strategy, requires both an honest effort and an evo-devo transformation hence it is most likely to be ignored. The most likely solution will be a mix of the first two: increase domestic spending and pass on the budget deficit to the consumers. AN EXACT REPLICA OF THE 1996-98 disaster of the South-East Asian economies, only this one is going to be much worse. Another prime example of a tired, jaded and confused leadership that is desperately trying to pass the blame while maintaining its own "failure blindness". The current blame targets- Eastern Europe, Greece and Spain.

A small step back into the past may not be a bad idea at this point in the journey. As per the Almanac 2012 - " A worldwide financial panic and economic depression began with the Oct 1929, US stock market crash and the May 1931 Austrian Credit Policy - Anstalt. A credit crunch that caused international bankruptcies and unemployment: 12 million in the USA, 6 Million in Germany, and a million in England. Government Public works programs were obliterated by a deflationary budget balancing strategy." These were the factors that gave rise to one of the major man-made disasters of the 20th century World War II. The current scenario is no different: European unemployment is at an all-time high, the infrastructure programs are at a standstill, public debt is around 30% of GDP and fiscal deficit is a rule rather than an anomaly. Then should we plan for WWIII?

3) TOYOTA: Akio Toyoda, the grandson of Kuchiro Toyoda (The founder of Toyota Motors -The world's largest Auto Maker) in a message to the company on taking over as the President was to abandon "KAKUSHIN" or revolutionary change. The alternatives "go back to basics". Toyota faced its first annual loss in 60 years. He is blaming the fact that Toyota has moved away from its core idea of thrift with high efficiency. A malaise he attributes to the culture of

trying to emulate the American Auto Manufacturers like General Motors who are currently in bankruptcy.

Akio Toyoda has a strong faith in the traditional Toyota practice of "Genchi Genbutsu", a leadership dictum that boils down to "get out of your office and visit the source of the problem." Toyota was the developer of the lean manufacturing philosophy that is a part of the manufacturing bible across the world for effectiveness. The reason for Toyota's reversal over the 2009 and 2011 time frame, including the "quality scare" currently, is the fact that it moved away from its fundamental principles of not to make long term decisions based on short term gains. Toyota added manufacturing plants based on the advantages of currency fluctuations which resulted in overall declines in quality and efficiency. Shoichiro Toyoda, Akio's father, said it succinctly, "We are not God's, and we are not infallible." **A small "g" finally gets it.**

4) XEROX: The Xerox Corporation is trying to go "beyond copiers." For decades Xerox has been playing the product "push" game and making money on expensive consumables. Finally they are seeing the light to get into the **"Serduct" business** (a symbiotic combination of products and services) to provide a higher level of benefit to their current customer base. The OSS (One Stop Shop) methodology of the "Serduct principle" allows Xerox to provide a single multifunctional device those copies, prints and faxes as well as a managed print service that handles all the consumables. Xerox, the leader in the OSS managed services business, has more than 1.6 million devices that the company currently manages. The key transformation is that out of these devices managed by Xerox nearly 50% are from other vendors. The total managed print-services business, per industry estimates, is expected to deliver nearly 40% of the printer business revenue amounting to nearly $50 Billion. Xerox's revenue in the OSS business for 2008 was $3.5 Billion. The message is sustainability and an environmental friendly approach that lowers cost and risk. An evolving company and an evo-devo candidate.

5) Warren Buffet: The Berkshire Hathway group founded by Warren Buffet has consistently provided an annual compounding return of over 28% for the last 40 years. Warren Buffet is the only billionaire in the world who has been in "The Forbes" list of richest men solely on one focus: Investing. His secret: Learn from the follies of others while disciplining your own. His tools: dedication,

practice, honest effort and a willingness to learn. His evo-devo principle: Provable, Predictable and Verifiable facts with a profound sense of business basics that identify the intrinsic and environmental value of any entity. The above combination not only creates a low risk scenario but also allows for a cyclic investment process that has a clear exit strategy linked to unpredictability in any investment. His fundamental principle: Speculation is an invitation to failure. This from a man whose entire focus is stock markets and publicly held companies which are speculative. His evo-devo KEY: Make less mistakes by only making a limited number of Great decisions. Warren Buffet has always acted as a guardian of the "communal wealth" when dealing with investor capital. His strategy: Find the unmatched value of entropy in the pessimism and failures of the competition not in the optimism and successes of the markets. An evo-devo STAR.

6) ALBERT EINSTEIN: In 1905, a young German was working in total obscurity in the Swiss government's patent office in Bern. The young man had been at this job for three years. While working in the patents' office this young man was also trying to reconcile the various and diverse laws of science. Using his intrinsic strengths of mental insights, that were almost alien, and a profound knowledge of math and physics he kept questioning the **consistent inconsistencies** that were prevalent in the scientific community. In   1905, the results of his investigations were published in four separate papers in the prestigious German Journal "Annalen der Physik" or the Annals of Physics. In the first paper he proposed that light be regarded as a stream of particles he named "quanta". This not only contributed to the fundamental theory of the current "Quantum" mechanics but also explained the photo electric effects that would prove to have many practical applications in our modern life. The second paper explained the irregular motion of microscopic particles in liquid or gas - "Brownian Motion"- which actually confirmed the atomic theory of matter. The fourth paper established the correlation between mass and energy with the velocity of light squared acting as a constant. This resulted in the Manhattan Project and the Atomic Bomb as well as a new source of energy i.e. Nuclear Energy. The Third paper that was innocently titled "The Electro Dynamics of Moving Bodies" proposed a theory that affected the entire global community in the aegis of "The Special Theory of Relativity". This theory was the result of his attempts to reconcile the laws of electro-magnetism and

mechanics. This young man and Great "STAR" leader was Albert Einstein who then went on to author the "General Theory of Relativity" in 1916 that finally replaced the Newtonian Law of Gravity. The General Theory also confirmed that gravity was a consequence of the curvature of time and space.

Einstein was born in Ulm, a city in South Western Germany, and in his early childhood and teens rebelled against the conventional and traditional teaching methodologies. He never earned his high school diploma but still went on to study mathematics and physics at the Federal Polytechnic Institute in Zurich. The principles of relativity that linked space, mass and motion with time as a "fourth" dimension are not only profound but to some extent revolutionary in their nature. Einstein went on to publish an article in 1917 that introduced the concept of stimulated emissions that would ultimately lead to the development of Lasers. In 1921, he was awarded the Nobel Prize. His conceptual deductions were always mired in facts that he proved either through calculations or demonstration. His observations of Key phenomenon's such as the "Deflection of Light by a gravitational field", "Motion of the Perihelion of Mercury" and the "Displacement of Spectral lines towards Red" helped in the overall understanding of the then existing inconsistencies. In 1939, Einstein was persuaded to write a letter to President Roosevelt that lead to the Manhattan Project and nuclear fission. Einstein later regretted writing that letter after the Atomic Bomb was used in Japan. His last years were spent trying to create a "Unified Field Theory" before he died in Princeton, New Jersey in 1955. In the evo-devo sense Einstein transformed not only the world of science but continues to impact thinkers, writer, scientists, entrepreneurs, musicians and other leaders to re-examine their worlds. In fact his theories continue to evolve and become milestones in our quest to understand and realize the mysteries of Life. (From John S. Bowman's introduction to the book "Relativity" by Albert Einstein.) . Some say Einstein's brain was wired differently. We say that he achieved the "EVO-DEVO of Leadership Greatness." When Albert Einstein was asked if he believed in the BIG "G", he responded:

"We are in the position of a little child entering a huge library filled with books in many languages. The child knows someone must have written those books. It does not know how or why. That, it seems to me, is the attitude of even the most intelligent human beings towards God. We see the universe marvelously arranged and obeying certain Laws but only dimly understand these laws." A humble, patient and content attitude to an unexplainable paradigm from a man who was a Great "STAR" Leader.

7) ADOLF HITLER: The Wolf's Lair ("Wolf" was one of Hitler's nicknames), an isolated and heavily guarded complex, was the inner sanctum of the German High Command - The Oberkommando der Wehrmacht (OKW). This was the center of power from which Hitler unleashed his devastating vision on an unprepared world in 1939. This vision finally imploded on Hitler itself and destroyed Germany while putting the entire human community in a state of turmoil. A turmoil that still impacts our thinking processes.

In 1936, at the Olympic Games in Berlin, where Jesse Owens made a mockery of the Fuehrer's racial theories by winning four Gold medals, Hitler radiated an almost magical strength. When he appeared in Vienna, during the annexation of Austria in a bloodless coup, wearing a simple gray officer's uniform without any insignia of rank and two medals earned during WW I i.e. The Iron Cross and the Wound Badge, he was not a physically imposing figure. When he raised his arm in the characteristic salute that was his trademark, the notorious blue-eyes alive with diabolical energy, he transformed and seemed to pin all those around him to the wall. Hitler always spoke with passion while slicing his hands through the air in short, compact gestures. The more he spoke the stronger his hold on the audience. He was so persuasive that most people did not even question the success of the enterprise being planned. Hitler had a mystique and charisma but in terms of the evo-devo principles he is the anti-thesis of Great "STAR" Leadership.

On July 25th, 1943 in the Wolf's Lair Hitler said- "**I have already told you, when we discussed this a few days ago, that terror can only be broken by terror. One has to counter attack, everything else is nonsense. Instead of monk eying around let's attack, pick out a target- it does not matter what target. We can't go on this way. Eventually the German people will go nuts Terror can only be broken by terror and in no other war!** Hitler was talking to a senior Air force Officer of the German Luftwaffe. The words may seem like the ranting of a mad man who was deluded, tired and physically sick but the order was carried out to the detriment of the world and the German citizens. The Evo-Devo question- "Did Leadership evolve after this experience? The truthful answer is NO. The current wars in Iraq, Libya, Sudan, Syria and

Afghanistan as well as the continuing tensions across the globe are similar in nature to the above "Insane" strategy. The current economic conditions are no different than the, pre-war scenario. The unemployment rate in the USA is running around 10%. The Euro-Zone is pushing consumption for growth. The Chinese and the Indians are buying toxic western assets. Russia has banned export of commodities like wheat which is pushing up food prices across the globe. The Asian economies are fighting for survival to retain their manufacturing edge against China. The global currencies are playing their own short-term games to combat the falling dollar value. It seems that we are all doomed to repeat our mistakes. We can blame it on the Leadership but at the end of the day-as on April 30, 1945 when Hitler committed suicide- the community has to bear the consequences.

There are 7 notes that create music. The multiple combinations of Sa, Re, Ga, Ma, Pa, Dha and Nee (the Indian classical music notes) has been innovated into millions of songs over centuries and will continue to do so. There are 4 proteins (A, T, C and G) that combine into a string of 7 to create billions of strands of DNA which have resulted in billions of individual entities with specific traits on this planet alone. Therein lays a hidden logic and a rational that exists behind these truths. The Leadership of Greatness and the "STAR" leaders need to understand the business logic stored in the histories or the legacy systems. This leadership trait and its knowledge needs to be "thin wired" and made accessible to leaders on a 24/7 basis. This will not only assist in enhancing the leadership "Life Cycle" of growth but will also allow the leaders to predict the results of their decisions. The "thin wired" capability of this library of legacy knowledge and processes will ensure that mistakes of the past are not repeated. The extended "Life Cycle" of business logic through availability and modernization is a tremendous source of energy to reach the goal of "perpetual" growth.

One of the key leaps of faith in mathematics is found in the world of Fractions. The phenomenon known as the "canceling effect" is an area that children and even some adults struggle to understand. The rule of Fractions that 3/8= 24/64= 240/640...is one example of the "canceling effect". The evo-devo Leadership of Greatness is a demonstration of the cancelling effect as the "STAR" leader is not just a matter of size but at its lowest denominator each individual can attain "STAR" status and prolong the value to the community by extending the "Life Cycle" to forge an era of "perpetual" and sustainable growth. As we cross the stormy ocean of Leadership Greatness to the next port of the "Leadership of Perpetual Growth" we can observe from our 7 examples that the idiocy and brilliance of the human species is an awesome spectacle. It is within these two extremes of our nature wherein the secret of growth and leadership exists.

"To have understood without retaining does not make Knowledge"

DANTE

CHAPTER 6

LEADERSHIP OF SUSTAINABLE "PERPETUAL" GROWTH

Leaders are often the most ordinary of men. The only difference is that they possess the capabilities to perform extraordinary tasks under chaos and adversity. This extraordinary capability is a derivative of a state of higher consciousness that is the hallmark of great leaders. The reason these leaders can achieve this evolved state is based on the fact that they move away from the "I" factor (SELF or "Maan"-a hindu and sikh term that defines Pride or EGO) to the "We" factor (HARMONY-or "Naam"-a hindu and sikh term that defines Truth or Humility). The "I" factor is focused on short-term gain which is part of the MICE system i.e. My Money, My Ideology, My Conscience and My Ego. The "We" factor comprises of the WISE system i.e. Our Wealth, Our Ideation, Our Shared Services and Our Evolutionary Collective Conscience. As soon as the "I" factor is transformed into the "We" factor or MICE evolves to WISE the Leadership of Sustainable "Perpetual" Growth is triggered.

"KUMBAH-YA" is a common motivational epitaph used in parts of Africa which symbolically means "LIFT TOGETHER". The heaviest of weights can be lifted when the philosophy of "KUMBAH-YA" is applied to combine the energy of the leader with the potential energy of the community. The key factor in this process, that you as leaders need to grasp, is that the energy of the leaders is the catalyst that can accelerate the process of transforming the potential energy of the community into usable energy, This "speed-up" effect of great leaders results in a Rapid Return on Energy (RROE) which in turn provides a Rapid Return on Investment creating an Unmatched High Value for all the Stakeholders. This unmatched high value benefits the shareholders, employees and customers of the community which ensures that the engine of growth progresses in a sustainable manner.

The policies of short-term gains, as a measure of leadership, has to be migrated to measure leadership performance on creating self-sustaining communal benefits. The reward system that promotes this mentality includes incentives for both good and "STAR" leaders that are "perpetual" in nature. Alternatively, the reverse will happen and the system will start "rewarding" bad performance linked to greed and self-preservation. The results of this alternative strategy, that encourages bad leadership, are in front of us today. Pythagoras, the great Greek philosopher, once stated that the "most momentous thing in life is the art of winning the soul to good over evil". This momentous thing is also the watershed that identifies the evo-devo of the Leadership of Sustainable "Perpetual" Growth.

The concept of "perpetual" growth is akin to the idea of "perpetual" motion which is alien to our thinking. We have been taught that friction and resistance to motion does not allow perpetuity of momentum. Similarly, the resistance to growth from both internal and external "back flux" is the cause of unsustainable growth. The internal "back flux" is a combination of internal strife within the leadership domain and the communal discords inherent in any system of leadership today. As the enterprise grows the internal "back flux" also increases eventually leading to a slowing down and stoppage of progress and ultimately death unless a new source of energy is established.

As sources of fresh energy become scarce as is the case presently, the survival of the enterprise is now under threat. The current resources i.e. **Natural** (Oil, Coal etc.), **Physical** (Skilled Work-force, Best Practices) and **Financial** (Cash, Credit, Debt) are all under severe constraint. The self-replicating and cyclic resources that are renewable can only be obtained through the transformation of waste and "internal back flux" within the process itself into new energy. This "free energy" that is stored in the entropy of the 2nd Law of Thermodynamics is the only solution that can result in the evo-devo leadership of "perpetual" growth.

The "free Energy" principle will destroy the current demon of the scarcity of resources which is also a major cause of conflict today. In the current scenario, with conflict and back flux, we have created a system that is self-replicating only to generate waste and resistance rather than growth. **As soon as you can learn to transform the scarcity into abundance through innovation and technology linked to a dedicated focus of communal wealth the "perpetual" sustainable growth phenomenon will be unleashed.**

The current macroeconomic scenario of supply and demand under the mantle of scarcity and wealth is progressively defined as under:

Wealth= Physical Resources X Technology^2 or W= PT^2

In the above equation wealth is directly linked to the product of the available resources (Natural, Physical and Financial) and the technology with its multiplier effect. The inherent complexity of this formula for wealth is that it is constantly restricted by the availability of the scarce resources and needs an ongoing investment in technology to find new sources of energy. The technology and resource gaps prevent us from fully utilizing the potential communal wealth and hence we are limited to only individual wealth as a measure of success.

The evo-devo of sustainable growth requires that we unlock the "free energy" available to us in abundance in order to create self-replicating success. The advantages that we will acquire as a part of this quest will benefit us in transforming the above mentioned equation to the one given below:

COMMUNAL WEALTH = Natural Capital X Technology ^{2} X 10 Free Energy

OR

$$C.W. = NT^2 \, 10 \, . \Delta G$$

In the above equation the true measure of SUCCESS i.e. Communal Wealth and it's associated competitive advantage is equal to the product of the Natural Capital of the community that includes all the Physical and Intellectual resources available, the square of the Technology and the "Free Energy" (ΔG) multiplied by a factor of 10. This "free energy" is the one that is locked up in the system due to the entropy or waste in the process. The "Free Energy" is defined as the difference between the existing energy of the system i.e. Enthalpy (ΔH),and the product of the waste in the process i.e. the Entropy (ΔS) and the "internal back flux" or resistance to change i.e. t. Mathematically, this would be represented as under:

$\Delta G = \Delta H - t.\Delta S$ (wherein t is the measure of the back flux and S is the Entropy of the system.

You will observe that as the entropy of the system decreases the "free energy" increases. Also as the internal back flux and resistance decreases the "free energy" rises. This "free energy" is the catalyst for "perpetual" sustainable growth as it will fuel fresh growth without the need for the fresh infusion of energy. If the internal back flux increases and the waste or entropy increases and nears the value of the existing energy of the enterprise the "free energy" is reduced to near zero and the process of growth is halted. Our bodies, The "BIG BANG", Einstein's Theory of Relativity, Quantum Mechanics, Thermo-dynamics and Economics all follow this afore-mentioned law. The 2nd Law of Thermodynamics is infallible.

The difference between Individual Wealth and Communal Wealth as a measure of real success is fundamental to the evo-devo of "perpetual" growth. Let us take a simple example to illustrate the effect of the "free energy" on wealth and communal wealth. Assume that the Physical and Natural Capital that is available to you as the leader is 1 Million Dollars. The Technology and its multiplier are taken at 10. The Enthalpy is 1 and the entropy or waste is 0.7 while the value of the internal back flux is also 1 for the sake of simplicity.

The above data when entered into the formulae for wealth and communal wealth will give us the following values:

$$\text{Wealth (W)} = 1MM \times 10^2 = 100MM$$

$$\text{Communal Wealth (C.W.)} = 1 \times 10^2 \times 10 (1-(1 \times 0.7)) = 300MM$$

The effect of the "free energy" is apparent from the above equation as it triples the value of the invested energy. This effect is further demonstrated in the illustration ahead for multiple values of the different factors that influence both wealth and communal wealth. In all the cases the communal wealth exceeds individual wealth by providing the unmatched value of a rapid return on invested energy. The evo-devo leadership of "perpetual" growth is founded on this principle of sustainable growth that does not require a constant input of investment to survive and lead chaos.

The "STAR" leaders play a major rule in this phenomenon since they will be the ones pulling the community into a cohesive and seamless whole to lower the back flux and find innovative ways to lower the entropy of the enterprise. The leaders will be the catalyst that will set-off this explosive strategy for growth and increase the rapidity of the availability of benefits to the community. At the same time the great leadership will also ensure that the Natural Capital of the community is renewed and utilized judiciously, The competitive advantage of this strategy that identifies and fixes the technology gaps in the process to create efficiency and lower back flux is essential to face any adversity. The evo-devo leaders can actually use the adversity and chaos as a trigger to create an "implosion effect" that will release "free energy" for growth by lowering the waste i.e. entropy and internal resistance to change i.e. internal back flux.

WEALTH vs. COMMUNAL WEALTH - A Comparison of SUCCESS

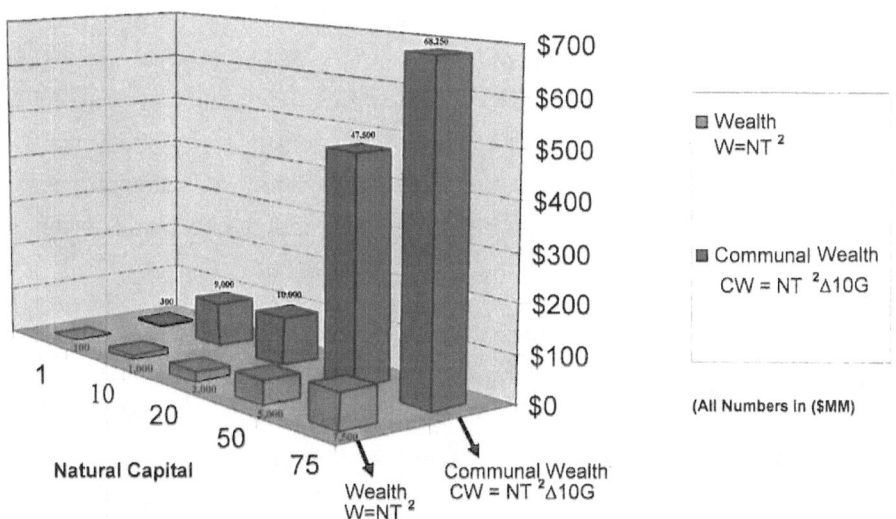

WEALTH vs. COMMUNAL WEALTH - EVO DEVO of "Perpetual" Growth (Fig. 12)

Wealth $W=NT^2$ (MM\$)	Communal Wealth $CW = NT^2 \Delta 10G$ (MM\$)	Capital (MM\$)	Technology^2 $(T)^2 = (10)^2$	Entropy (ΔS)	Backflux (t)	Free Energy $(\Delta G)=10 \times (\Delta G)$
\$100.00	\$300.00	1	100	0.7	1	0.3x10 = 3
\$1,000.00	\$9,000.00	10	100	0.1	1	0.9x10 = 9
\$2,000.00	\$10,000.00	20	100	0.5	1	0.5x10 = 5
\$5,000.00	\$47,500.00	50	100	0.1	0.5	0.95x10 = 9.5
\$7,500.00	\$68,250.00	75	100	0.3	0.3	0.91x10 = 9.1

Another major factor that affects the ability to generate "perpetual" growth is sharing and transparency of knowledge and processes across the systems. The focus of "STAR" leaders to promote the concept of a "TECH SHARE" environment that is based on an "Open Thin-Wired System" will be essential for accelerating growth. The "Open Thin-Wired System" architecture will allow the global Innovation paradigm to come into play to generate a "sigma" effect of benefits. Individual Wealth spread across the world can be combined together with technology to improve the knowledge and process of the entire global community. These individual innovations in a Knowledge share mode will lower the back flux and entropy to enhance the Natural Capital available for growth. The incremental reduction of the duplication of resources by the positive effects of "optimization" will be a tremendous boost to the processes, thus leading to the abundance of Natural Capital. As the "trickle down" effect of this abundance spreads locally and globally the self-sustaining principles will be initiated. This ripple effect of self-replication of benefits is similar to "using the same stone again and again" for a "perpetual" process of motion and success in the lake of Natural Capital.

This syndrome of "perpetual" growth will allow the "STAR" leaders to pull the community forward (with increased rewards to the innovators) from across the entire gamut of users. You may have observed some of the effects of this strategy without a complete understanding of the evo-devo principles around those processes. In the early 90's Mitsubishi followed an "open architecture" with its VHS technology while Sony focused on retaining its Beta cam technology. The effect of licensing the VHS technology by Mitsubishi gave them the competitive advantage over Sony as the video sales far exceeded the sales of the equipment itself and kept growing without any new investment. Similar examples are available as we see the growth around Linux, Postscript and other open-source software that allow the developers to create innovations using the available intellectual capital for communal benefit. The success of Google or Bio-Fuel or Kindle or the iPod are all attributable to the principles of transforming the unused energy to "free energy" for the benefit of explosive growth and a rapid return on energy utilized in the process.

In all the above examples the share factor has created the competitive advantage by lowering the risk and back flux. The "free energy" released from this process improvement and knowledge share in turn pushes the engine of growth. Also as these evolved enterprises move they start to attract and gravitate towards each other across multiple domains. The "free exchange" amongst these "STAR" systems will result in the fusion of knowledge and process globally; this will result in the reduction of global conflict and loss of energy for the entire system. The global lowering of resistance to growth will promote global rewards without the induction of fresh capital and the conservation of existing resources.

A prime example of the above model is the fusion reactions that take place in the Sun. The Sun generates a constant stream of energy through the process of "free exchange'. The entire process uses the principles of "free energy" to meet the needs of the entire solar system. This evo-devo "STAR" is consistently using the controlled process of the "implosion effect" to fund sustainable "perpetual" growth stored within the chaos and the entropy of the Sun itself.

The whole idea of the evo-devo of the Leadership of Sustainable Growth is to evolve a new definition of SUCCESS, as we will discover in the next milestone of our journey; this definition has to be mired in the paradigm that any SUCCESS has to be able to stand the test of "TIME". Evo-Devo "TIME" is not bonded by scarcity or paucity. The evo-devo "TIME" has to be bifurcated and degrees of separation introduced to distinguish it from the current leadership concept of time. The time of today has become one of the key issues that is constraining the culture of communalism and "perpetual" growth. The existing typical and even good leadership has turned time into a negative phenomenon by promoting its scarcity. The fact is that current leaders define success within the boundaries of time and Individual achievements. They are using individual wealth as a measure of success within a certain time frame rather than using the evo-devo of "STAR" leaders who use communal wealth, sustainability, evolution, fixation and transformation to redefine "TIME" itself. The fact is that as catalysts the "STAR" leaders will speed up the process of growth and communal benefits thus creating "TIME" for the community. The scarcity of time today is therefore an obsolete concept from the evo-devo perspective. The abundance of "TIME" that can create sustainable progress and is self-generating is the new paradigm.

The Evo-Devo of Leadership

It might be a great idea at this point to look at a timeline of events within our known universe to understand the concept of evo-devo "TIME" vs. the human leadership focuses on time.

a) The Universe was formed 15 billion years ago.

b) Light travels 9.6 Trillion Kilometers in a year.

c) The Earth came into existence 4 Billion years ago.

d) The earliest invertebrates existed 2.5 Billion years ago.

e) The first mammals came to earth 200 Million years ago

f) The first flowers grew on earth 114 million years ago.

g) The Dinosaurs became extinct 65 million years ago

h) The earliest humans were on earth 1.6 million years ago.

i) Homo Sapien Sapiens(modern man) showed up 10,000 years ago

j) Religious (hindu, jewish, etc) doctrines are 5000 year old.

k) Christianity just turned 2100 old, while Islam reached 1500 years.

l) Sikhism celebrated 500 years of "free energy"

m) The Roman Empire lasted for a 1000 years

n) The British empire only reached 750 years before it fell

o) The Sun rotates around its axis every 240 years.

p) USA became a super power less than 100 years ago

g) The most profitable companies have not survived more than 60 years with 2008 being a watershed or a waterloo for the majority of large companies of the last century.

As we review this time, energy and space line we understand that the concept of scarcity of time as a definition of SUCCESS as defined in our 24 hrs

day to day lives versus the kind of abundant Time and energy that we are discussing in the realm of long term sustainable "perpetual" growth are really two distinct and inherently incompatible "TIMES". In order to understand this even further if we eliminate the scarcity of time as a measure of success from the equation we realize that the process of "free energy", without Internal Back Flux and resistance, can provide natural capital for leadership to grow communal wealth over long periods of "Time" on a sustainable basis.

The question then that begs an answer is-" Whether it is the "Right Time" for the evo-devo of leadership of Sustainable "perpetual" growth of Communal Wealth.? ". The answer is YES. Some recent phenomenon such as the unmanaged self created chaos of the Financial Crisis, War on terrorism, A Global Meltdown, Collapse of Industrial Giants, Dollar Crisis, SDR as a new Currency Emerging economies with low ethical constraints, Global environmental issues, Cultural and Species extinctions etc., all point to the fact that this is the "RIGHT TIME" for the "Right Leadership" to follow the processes of sustainable "perpetual" growth that will withstand the test of perpetuity. Alternatively, we should prepare for uncontrolled implosions that will autocorrect the existing systems that depend on the scarcity of time.

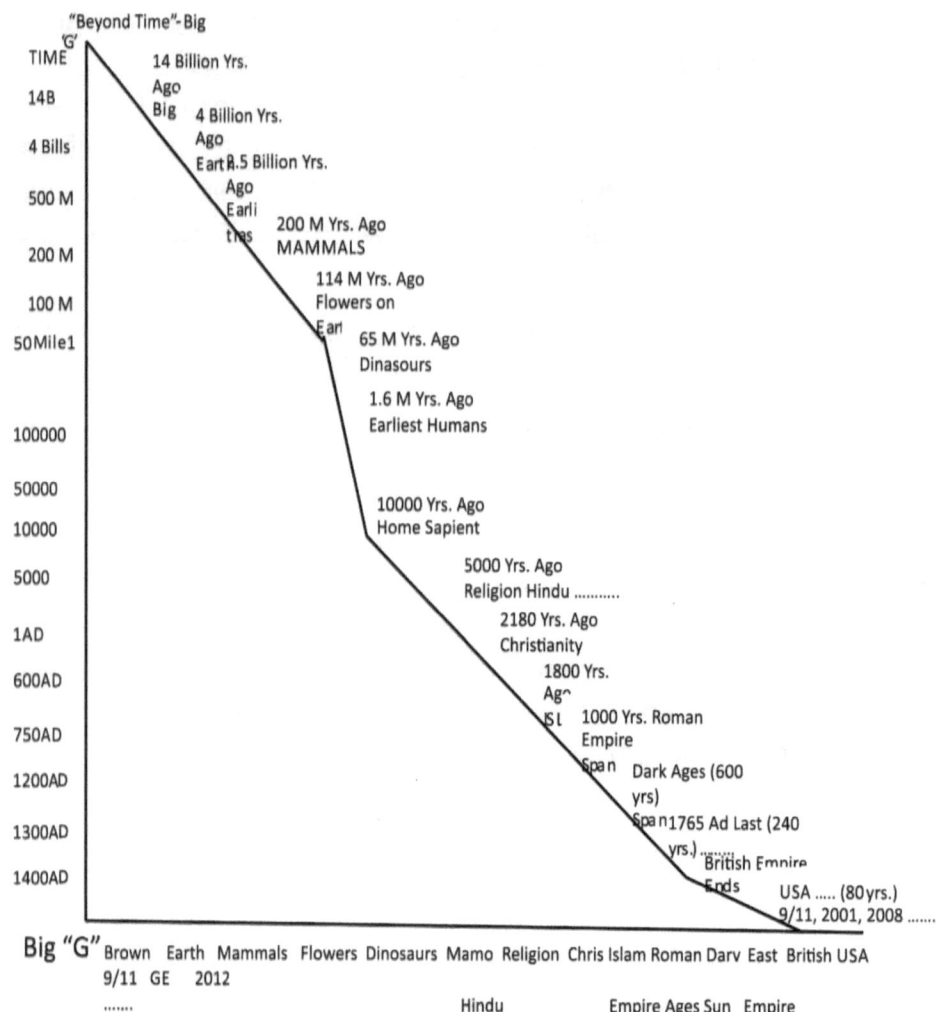

TIMELINE OF EVOLUTION – A STUDY OF CONTRASTS (Fig 13)

A great example of the uncontrolled implosion is the Ageing Process that we all go through in our lives. As our body loses the ability to create "free energy" from the entropy i.e. $\Delta G = \Delta H - T.\Delta S$ (T is the temperature in Kelvin as well as Time) and as ΔG moves closer to 0we need more energy from external sources. As we lose this battle based on the inefficiency of our bodies due to increased internal back flux and loss of energy we slow down, age and ultimately do not exist. In the sense of Time this process is limited to a period of maybe 100 years, if we are lucky. The "fountain of youth" is thus a simple mathematical equation that is linked to the entropy of our system and time. If we can reduce waste of our energy and generate "free energy" we can extend our life-span substantially. At the same time you have to be vigilant that your existing energy or Enthalpy is not wasted in an effort to fight the after effects of a decadent life-style.

The fear of mortality is the bane of good leadership as it becomes obsessed with time. In order to achieve the "STAR" focus evo-devo leaders have to transcend the barriers of individual time to the evolved state of communal "TIME". The "STAR" leaders set up the systems and processes of a "perpetual" growth engine that will allow the community to prosper even after them and will still remain in their image. The image of the Right Way at the Right Time for the ongoing competitive advantage of the community is the focus of evo-devo leaders. The community will continue to grow as it follows the leaders vision by following the path of the Right Way of Life consistently. This will ensure the immortality of the "STAR" and in turn will defy the normal aging process.

The great leaders who can master this strategy will automatically reach the pinnacle of evo-devo sustainable SUCCESS. They and their communities will be able to retain competitive advantage even in the grip of the "implosion" of chaos and adversity. The next port is the Leadership of SUCCESS and the tools that can ensure that we can attain this elusive goal consistently are going to be handed over to you. The need for leadership that can follow this goal of perpetuity as a measure of SUCCESS is essential and mandatory for our survival.

"WITHOUT RECOGNIZING THE ORDINANCES OF HEAVEN, IT IS IMPOSSIBLE TO BE A SUPERIOR MAN"- Confucius

CHAPTER 7

THE EVO-DEVO LEADERSHIP OF SUCCESS

The future of humanity and its success depends on a choice. Success and failure are both fundamental constants of leadership. Their values on the other hand are variable. The arbitrary value of success is directly linked to the leader's choices. The "Right" choice that creates a synergy where leadership potential strengths meet Communal opportunity to produce global benefits is also the true meaning of success. You, as evo-devo leaders, need to comprehend that true success becomes elusive if we try to measure It in terms of individual wealth as you will always want more. On the other hand, as soon as you evaluate success from the level of communal benefits and a shared yet sustainable growth curve it automatically becomes attainable.

The new evo-devo definition of SUCCESS is therefore hidden in its nature and culture: Sustainable Growth Under Adverse Circumstances to Create Evolutionary Transformation from Shared Sources. This is not mere word-play but a complete turnaround in your view of SUCCESS. If you can visualize the hidden meaning in the acronym of SUCCESS you can immediately see the constant of success in a synergistic, stable and sustainable enterprise. These systems use shared sources to reduce waste. The key though is that the community can continue to grow even under adversity and chaos when other's are losing focus and floundering.

In order to understand this new paradigm of SUCCESS, it is critical to acknowledge the existence and the constant of failure as well. The 6.4 billion members of the Human species question is WHY DO WE FAIL AGAIN and AGAIN?. Also, if failure is a part of SUCCESS then HOW DO WE FAIL SUCCESSFULLY OVER TIME?

The answer is an important milestone in our journey because once you can learn to fail successfully then true success is achieved. The next two illustrations will provide you with the tools to reach the above goal.

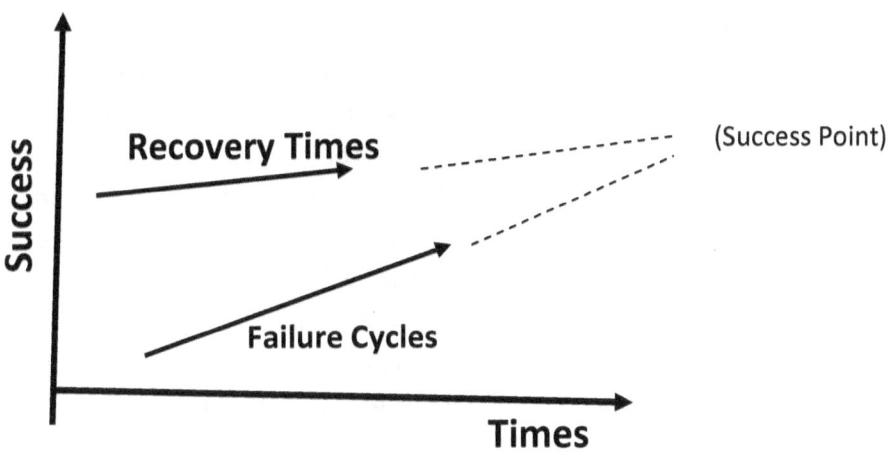

FAILING SUCCESSFULLY (Fig-14)

Too often, leaders assume a failed strategy is a wasted effort and in doing so implement changes that are radical. This is like throwing the baby out with the bathwater. As evo-devo leaders you have to understand that all anomalies are not useless. The processes that can help you illuminate the "Art of Failing Successfully" i.e. reduced recovery times and shorter failure cycles, as shown above, can be scientifically enumerated as below:

The four key ingredients of this strategy are:

1.   **Check your assumptions-"The Old Guard"**: Interrogate your hypothesis and validate your facts. Find the point of inflexion where your theory is contradictory.

2.   **Seek out the unbiased thinking -"The Turks"**: Discuss openly with people who are unfamiliar with your theories and have no bias towards the success or failure of the hypothesis.

3.   **Encourage Diversity and Create Resilience -"The Moderates"**:Find resources that do not agree with the hypothesis and the assumption.

Play the Champion vs. Challenger card to get better innovation and ideation in both knowledge and the process to plan for failure and to ensure success.

4. **Accept defeat and prevent failure blindness -"The Eureka"**: The bane of leadership that filters out information or falsifies results that contradict their perceptions is a prime candidate for failure. Elimination of bias is an extremely important phase. An evo-devo study was conducted by the group that observes scientists and their methodologies on how they fail and succeed consistently. The study used the FMRI (Functional Magnetic Resonance Imaging) to map the area of the brain associated with the perception of errors and contradictions. The area known as the ACC (anterior cingulated cortex) was observed to react differently in each individual based on their values and existing knowledge. For example if a person has never heard or seen the famous painting "THE MONA LISA" then it may trigger a null response In the ACC if the painting was displayed to him. On the other hand an artist or an aware individual would have a "WOW" response to the same stimulus while viewing the masterpiece. Thus the same truth can be perceived differently based on the relevance or Irrelevance of the reality within the observer's personal belief system. It was also observed that another area of the brain is activated to edit our reality. This area known as the DLPFC (dorsolateral pre-frontal cortex) which is located just behind the forehead is also one of the last ones to develop in young adults. The DLPFC plays a crucial role in suppressing or deleting the thoughts that do not fit in our frame of reference. The individual preconceptions and biases thus become a major issue in our evo-devo transformation.

In most cases this editing function of the DLPFC is an essential cognitive skill which allows us to filter irrelevant stimuli or false data. The "it's only a movie" or the real life vs. the reel life differentiation capability can also end up in deleting anomalies or inconsistencies that are associated with failure. At this stage the DLPFC becomes an acute hindrance. Leadership when seeing failure tends to inhibit the information and in effect is censoring the facts that do not fit their belief system. Belief, for the evo-devo Leadership of SUCCESS, is to understand the safety mechanism that is built in to our brain also distorts the truth. Therefore, all data is not equal in our eyes and we need to interpret the facts without falsifying the truth or by disregarding those facts that do not fit our hypothesis. **The practice to avoid failure blindness becomes an important part of the Leadership of SUCCESS.**

The question therefore is right in front of us: "What is that Value System that will create a belief that is needed to interpret the arbitrary values of a leader in times of adversity to be able to avoid failure blindness?

The first value that is essential for the Leadership of SUCCESS is that All Things Happen for a reason and a purpose; You have to learn and categorize the event and then MOVE ON. The function of gaining the knowledge and the process from the event and to forge an understanding of the event is a pre-requisite for evo-devo. The ability to store the learned behavior for the future is the hallmark of the "STAR" leader. The key is not to attach feelings of guilt, depression, joy or elation to the event itself; rather rationally use a "WIN-LOSS" analysis methodology so that you can modify or retain the strategy for SUCCESS.

Secondly, as a corollary to the first valuates the belief that there is no such thing as "failure". This acceptance will allow you, as leaders, to learn from your mistakes. It is a known fact that we can learn more from our mistakes than from our successes. Leadership needs failures to ensure that only the right behavior gets a chance to flourish and fixate within the genome. The evo-devo of Leadership of SUCCESS is to rise after falling and at the same time help up others who have fallen with you.

The Third value for Leadership SUCCESS is that You need to, accept the, responsibility for your actions and the outcome of your decisions, This act of acknowledgement is the key to empowerment of skills that will allow you to transform yourself and your sphere of influence. The acceptance of responsibility is not an admittance of defeat. It is also not a tool for destructive criticism but it is a positive process to replace "bad traits" with "good traits". These "good traits" are essential to lift you from being a good leader to a great "STAR" by eliminating the capability gaps wired in your processes. The specificity of failure and the acceptance of responsibility also brings objectivity to decision making rather than just generalizing an event; an essential trait for the Leadership of SUCCESS.

Fourthly, Leadership requires you to be fully aware of the fact that it is not necessary to understand everything about something to use it in an effective manner. Ambiguity, technology gaps, "risk factors" and the unknown are always going to be part of leadership choice. The ability to make the "Right" choice at the Right time for the Right reasons will depend upon the capability of the evo-devo leadership, which given enough knowledge and a built in process that lowers risk, can successfully create competitive advantage for the community even in adversity.

The fifth value that is essential for the advancement of the Leadership of SUCCESS throughout the community is to have a belief system that has complete faith in the tautology that after yourself, your people are the greatest source of Natural Capital. The community and your people provide the abundance of resources that are paramount for the long term sustainable growth even under adverse circumstances. The shared sources of SUCCESS i.e. the community and the people have a common vision and hence will share the risk and reward by providing all the necessary support for the Leadership of SUCCESS to attain the most beneficial state of advantageous selection from the competitive advantage of the "Right" choice. This does entail upon the leader to ensure that the "right" people are in the "right" place and have the necessary tools to perform their required functions. The Leadership of SUCCESS has also to develop a sense of empathy for its resources to participate in effective communication as a team through a "feedback loop". The less leadership opposes and denies the ideas and experiences of the team the lower will be the risk of "internal back flux" and higher the rewards for innovation. This does not imply that you as the leader has to be in complete agreement with the team at all times but if you listen empathically, with understanding, to the constituents you will create immediate opportunities for dialogue to explain divergent point of views. Unfortunately, the opposite is true as well that if you continually resist different point of view and persist with the "my way or the highway" methodology you will lose diversity and create a culture of conflict and the "internal back flux" will increase substantially to impede growth.

The sixth value for successful Leadership is a simple truth i.e. "WORK is Play". This is not a frivolous statement or a cliché but a "good" trait that is a fundamental basis for SUCCESS. The benefits of an environment that has forgiveness to create a spirit of trust helps in transforming a current loss into a future win. You need to move away from the process of harboring resentment and find a system to "let go" so the game can go on. **The gratification of failure**

allows the leadership to detach itself emotionally from its impact. There is no sense in the leadership behavior that lingers on the "if only" of loss rather than the process of modifying the system to the "What if" for SUCCESS.

The last and in no way the least value that can turn the arbitrary values of adversity and chaos to the constant of SUCCESS is the fact that no lasting success is possible without commitment and persistence with patience. These two virtues can assist leadership to achieve their communal goals and in turn create competitive advantage for the community. This also lowers the dependence on some outside force to come and satisfy the needs of your community in times of failure. Commitment and patience also have the added advantage of allowing the evo-devo leader to "OWN THE SUCCESS" and create faith and trust within the community to be able to implement transformation required in its sphere of influence. In the leadership of SUCCESS the arbitrary values of "setting limits" to failures will ensure that the focus is maintained on "What Works" or "What Can Work" rather than "What didn't or will not Work". These traits of commitment and persistence can then be spread throughout the community for sustainable growth.

These 7 values in effect build the character of Leadership of SUCCES and leads to contentment for the Leader and the community as the effort required has been put into the shared goals. The character of leadership strongly recommends that **SUCCESS without contentment is not worth having.** Contentment does not imply complacency or stagnation but is a transformation in perspective that the evo-devo leaders view SUCCESS as "inclusive" and not "exclusive." The character of leadership that develops a belief system that rewards virtuous behavior will meet the adage that "OLD and YOUNG we are all on our last cruise and it is the job of the leader is to construct a ship that others can have an enjoyable cruise on." This then is the epitome of contentment through "inclusivity" in the Leadership of SUCCESS.

The values and character of leadership also allows leaders to be able to visualize their SUCCESS in its entirety. This visual perception is an invaluable tool for motivation, planning and respect for Great Leadership. The capability to "SEE YOUR SUCCESS" at each step of the process with options and strategies is an excellent method to personalize your success as well as eliminate the irrational fear of failure thus making it easier to communicate. The visualization and communication that goes with it allows leadership to transform the adult-child or powerful-powerless relationship between the leaders and the community into a peer-peer relationship of equals for the achievement of long term shared success. The advantage is that once Leadership can visualize and SEE SUCCESS it will never be able to lose that perspective. As a quick example let us observe the logo below:

THE FedEx LOGO (Fig.15)

The above Federal Express Inc brand Logo contains an arrow that signifies the nature of this enterprise and its success as a "focused" forward thinking community. You cannot 'SEE" the arrow immediately as it is embedded in the logo but once you visualize this arrow you will never be able to view the FedEx logo without seeing the arrow.

Fedral Express Logo – ARROW (Fig. 16)

The visualization of SUCCESS and the use of creative imagery to communicate leadership vision to the community to generate sustainable growth will assist the evo-devo leaders in aligning their vision with that of the community. Communication, both verbal and non-verbal including the leaders "way of life", is the key to the entire dynamics of shared vision, acquiring "buy in", eliminating conflict and internal back flux as well as triggering transformation. Communication happens only if the parties concerned hear and Listen to each other and observe one another to follow the path that ends at the "WE UNDERSTAND" phase. This simple process is highlighted below;

I DO ➡ U SEE) Learning

I DO -➡ U DO) Inclusion

U DO -➡ I HELP) Mentoring

U DO -➡ I SEE) Understanding

THE WE UNDERSTAND PROCESS Fig. 17

The nature of communication needs to be consistent and constant. The communication has to be clear and concise: Both rational and factual. unbiased yet planned to the extent that it appears effortless. It should be personalized but not personal. It needs to include actions, goals, higher associations, storytelling, summaries, value statements, proofs, "leadership Way of Life", adaptations and propositions to be effective and ethical in order stimulate SUCCESS.

Communication should not be perceived as a sign of weakness or a wasted effort to achieve consensus but rather it is a strength, which used ethically, will result in a cohesive approach, the attainment of shared goals and the avoidance of the "back flux" of polarization. The evo-devo leadership of SUCCESS demands a transformation of the existing behavior of "CommuniCAN'T", a form of self-interest based Information usage, to the practice of "CommuniCAN" which believes in Information sharing and the sacrifice of time and effort to create "inclusivity" for fostering communal understanding. The "communiCAN'T" will always be a "net user" of energy while the "CommuniCAN" will be a "net generator" of energy including the "free Energy" unleashed through Information sharing.

That brings us to the next fact that **"INFORMATION" is the most valuable of all commodities** we trade in, if we are willing to understand and use it effectively, and lies at the core of the Leadership of SUCCESS. At the end of the day we are all "Info-pruners" be it economics, politics, science and relationships. The status of our "Info-prunership" depends on how effectively we use and follow the verifiable information and do not just hoard information as a source of power. For example an article that is invaluable and completely worthless at the same time (if we do not follow the Information provided) stated as under:

YOU CAN CURE HEART DISEASE: CALDWELL B. ESSELSTYN, Jr., MD. Feb 24, 2010.

In the mid-1980s, 17 people with severe heart disease had just about given up hope. They had undergone every available treatment, including drugs and surgery — all had failed. The group had experienced 49 cardiovascular events, including four heart attacks, three strokes, 15 cases of increased angina and seven bypass surgeries. Five of the patients were expected to die within a year. Twelve years later, every one of the 17 was alive. They had had no additional cardiovascular events. The progression of their heart disease had been stopped and, in many cases, reversed. Their angina went away — for some, within three weeks. In fact, they became virtually "heart attack-proof" And there are hundreds of other patients with heart disease who have achieved the same remarkable results.

What you need to know... HOW THE DAMAGE IS DONE: Every year, more than half a million Americans die of coronary artery disease (CAD). Three times that number suffer heart attacks. In total, half of American men and one-third of women will have some form of heart disease during their lifetimes.

Heart disease develops in the endothelium, the lining of the arteries. There, endothelial cells manufacture a compound called nitric oxide that accomplishes four tasks crucial for healthy circulation...

Keeps blood smoothly flowing, rather than becoming sticky and clotted. Allows arteries to widen when the heart needs more blood, such as when you run up a flight of stairs.

Stops muscle cells in arteries from growing into plaque — the fatty gunk that blocks blood vessels. Decreases inflammation in the plaque — the process that can trigger a rupture inthe "cap" or surface of a plaque, starting the clot-forming, artery-clogging cascade that causes a heart attack. The type and amount of fat in the typical Western diet -- from animal products, dairy foods and concentrated oils — assaults endothelial cells, cutting their production of nitric oxide.

Study: A researcher at University of Maryland School of Medicine fed a 900-calorie fast-food breakfast containing 50 grams of fat (mostly from sausages and hash browns) to a group of students and then measured their endothelial function. For six hours, the students had severely compromised endothelial function and decreased nitric oxide production. Another group of students ate a 900 calorie, no-fat breakfast — and had no significant change in endothelial function. If a single meal can do that kind of damage, imagine the damage done by three fatty meals a day, seven days a week, 52 weeks a year.

PLANT-BASED NUTRITION: You can prevent, stop or reverse heart disease with a plant-based diet. Here's what you can't eat -- and what you can...

What you cannot eat...

No meat, poultry, fish or eggs. You will get plenty of protein from plant-based sources.

No dairy products. That means no butter, cheese, cream, ice cream, yogurt or milk -- even skim milk, which, though lower in fat, still contains animal protein.

No oil of any kind — not a drop. That includes all oils, even virgin olive oil and canola.

What you may not know: At least 14% of olive oil is saturated fat — every bit as aggressive in promoting heart disease as the saturated fat in roast beef a diet that includes oils – including monounsaturated oils from olive oil and canola oil -- may slow the progression of heart disease, but it will not stop or reverse the disease.

Generally, no nuts or avocados. If you are eating a plant-based diet to prevent heart disease, you can have moderate amounts of nuts and avocados as long as your total cholesterol remains below 150.

The above piece of information is invaluable and miraculous in its nature but completely worthless in itself if we do not follow the recommendations of this brilliant study or do not share this information with patients or health care advocacy groups.

An evo-devo Leadership of SUCCESS would require a healthcare policy around this rather than a "disease care" strategy that requires cure but no prevention. The Information age is full of complex knowledge and processes so much so that we have now evolved a culture of "INFORMATIONISM." Unfortunately, instead of sharing the Information for mutual benefit we have developed the "ism" so that we can hoard the power of knowledge for individual benefit outside the bonds of morality and as a tool for exploitation. This "Ism" is non-benevolent as it is propagated by existing leadership globally in various "DEGREES OF TRUTH'. The degrees are achieved as each leader molds the facts or falsifies the data and results to gain control over their spheres of influence. The unethical use of the power of "INFORMATIONISM' in the end ends up destroying the leadership itself through the loss of credibility and breakdown of trust which leads to conflicts and communication barriers.

The vicious circle of unethical Information and communication continues as leadership has to expand energy to "create" truths to cover-up their earlier mistakes to avoid conflict thus leading to a further erosion of the "Natural capital' of faith in leadership as well as the fact that the actual truth is lost in the mire of falsification. The ethical use of Information and its communication on the other hand through sharing will transform ordinary people into extraordinary leaders, and therefore into a vast source of communal wealth. Information can provide the content that can enhance productivity, increase the rate of change, create innovation, lower risk, repair collateral damage spontaneously and utilize resources effectively.

Just from an infrastructure perspective, there is an extensive network of "black" fiber that exists waiting to be "lit" up with new information. The faster evo-devo leaders can use the huge potential of this shared source to disseminate ethical communication and information for "Tech Share" globally, the quicker new local content will be created for an abundance of innovation that will release tremendous "free energy" for sustainable growth. This "being on the same page" global methodology of sharing will also encourage shared goals and a focused effort to solve "critical issues" locally for competitive advantage globally. The power to touch most of the global community exists and all that is required to spread the SUCCESS gene throughout the constituents is the need for the evo-devo leaders who can provide the Leadership of SUCCESS.

Let us take a moment to reflect on this crucial question of how this cycle of information and communication can be used to solve the critical "REAL WORLD PROBLEMS"?

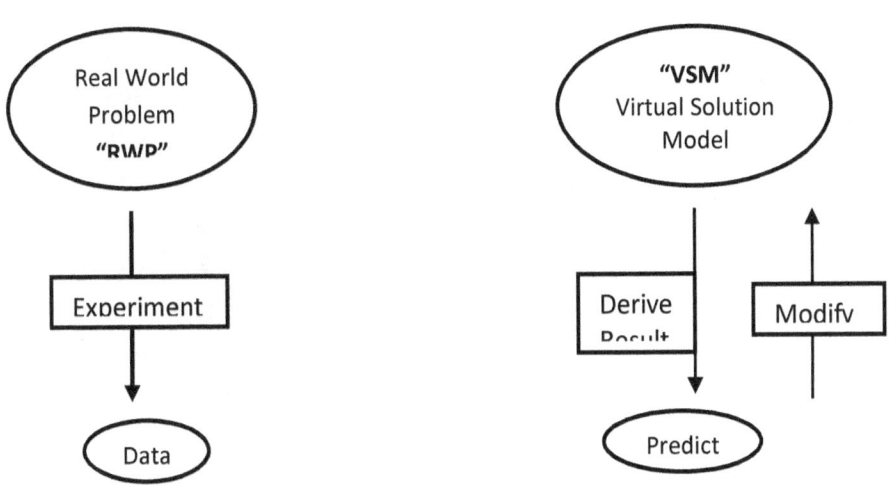

REAL WORLD AND VIRT UAL WORLD (Fig. 18)

The "Virtual Solution Models" or the VSM's are abstracted from the Real World Problems or the RWP's. The VSM's are then used to predict the outcome of leadership decisions to the RWP's. These test case scenarios are then processed via the experimentation methodology to get factual data. If the data from this experimentation matches the hypothecated results the solution can be implemented. If on the other hands the test results are not in line with the hypothesis then you need to modify the VSM. The process enumerated above is mandated for the evo-devo of leadership to be able to make the "Right Choice" consistently. This "Right Choice" can be refined further if you use the advantages of the power of shared information across multiple domains. The "Right Choice" will also ensure that the fundamental and absolute transformation that is triggered in the process meets the needs of the community. The use of communication and "feed-back loops" will move the community away from the abstractions of perceptions to the reality of accrued benefits. The element of ethical communication is demanded in the Leadership of SUCCESS. It requires the leaders to constantly, through practice, utilize communication and information in a cyclic process to reduce waste and the harmful effects of the internal "back flux" hidden in the RWP's.

The **process of using the Champion-Challenger strategy will assist you in achieving the Sigma Effect of summation of communal benefits**. The champion-challenger strategy allows you to create VSM's that may or may not be in the current arsenal of solutions. The Challenger has the right to prove the enhanced benefits of the alternative solutions within the same parameters of the RWP. This will ensure that all available "domain knowledge' is used to generate unique solutions to the RWP's. The problem we have today is that instead of trying to use the ideas of the challenger we reject them as we have fallen in love with our VSM's and are not willing to let go. You, as evo-devo leaders, need to be willing to modify the VSM's if a better alternative VSM is available for experimentation. This strategy will culminate into exponential yet sustainable growth curves. The reason this process is ethical and unique inspite of "risky predictions" is due to the fact that failure is always a distinct possibility at all times within the solution. The processes to identify and modify the solution to counter these points of failure are also built into the solution and the system. The key being that even failure is predicted and the chaos of failure becomes a source of learning and provides an abundance of knowledge for future growth. The system also lowers the chances of failure by sharing risk across the entire domain. Thus, the evo-devo Leadership of SUCCESS when combined with ethical Information and the 3 C's i.e. Communication and Commitment at the very core of its Character guarantees a faster recovery cycle from failure. The variable of failure is therefore factored into the constant of SUCCESS to accelerate the delivery of communal benefits to the enterprise. The evo-devo leaders can now illuminate the path of SUCCESS by Knowing the RIGHT WAY, Going the RIGHT WAY and Showing the RIGHT WAY consistently.

The process of specifying the objective and generalizing the subjective is the watershed that divides the simplicity and complexity of the solution. The patient endurance of the evo-devo leader to both failure and SUCCESS is a mandated character trait. These traits and values linked to a Doctrine of Sharing are critical to find the Right VSM's for the RWP's. Alternatively, as the RWP's become complex the current leadership and the communities are both caught in the paradox of mutual isolation. This mutual isolation is spread instantly across the enterprise, due to the existence of advanced super information highways thus creating a pandemic of epic proportions mired in distrust and unethical communication. The effects of information overload and the attempts to grab "mind share" further aggravates the problem of isolation. This mutual exclusivity limits the innovation needed to create a multiplicity of unique solutions. **The lack of solution diversity is a sure cause of failure.**

The only way to break this entire vicious cycle is to promote and follow the Doctrine of Sharing. You will see the economic advantages of this doctrine as we proceed further on our journey. At this point in our quest it is crucial to understand that we need to break down these "Berlin Walls" of isolation if we want to evolve. The evo-devo processes that encourage innovation and ethical communication based on verifiable facts are the key to promoting understanding within all the constituents. The need to create a dialogue between the leadership and the variegated communities is the key to the Leadership of SUCCESS. This ensures that the communal benefits of the solution from a perception and the reality basis are consistent. The deliveries of the benefits are clearly defined and the expectations are in line with the actual economic value. The same applies to the points of failure and their cause and effect: these needs to be illuminated alongside the prevention methodologies. The sharing of both risk and reward is the only way to foster trust and faith between the constituents of the leadership domain. The economic values of faith and trust are also discussed ahead. This is key to understanding the value of SUCCESS that the "free energy" stored in the elements of faith and trusts are a huge source of Natural Capital.

The principle of "UBANTU" or the spirit of humanity towards others is the breakthrough required to shift the focus of leadership from just 'preserving" what they perceive as necessary for homogeneity, a sure cause of an unmanaged implosion, to a thinking process that harnesses the principles of creating a sustainable process of "UNITY in DIVERSITY." The principles of Ubantu and the Unity in Diversity are both evo-devo processes. Both of these principles are a source of Natural Capital that can transform scarcity into abundance. The communal gain of sharing is far more abundant than the process of individual success. The abundance comes from the BREAKTHROUGH in leadership thinking that combines individual energy with communal potential to ensure a balanced approach to SUCCESS.

The "Breakthrough" required for the Leadership of SUCCESS fortunately exists in your own fundamentally self-transforming force- a force that has been established beyond doubt in studies undertaken at molecular, biological and neurological levels. With the help of this force you can disconnect those mental processes that generate the internal back flux, which hinders growth by resisting change, at the same time rewire yourself to a transformed pattern of thinking that will exponentially enhance both your integral and derivative strengths of leadership to achieve the "BREAKTHROUGH FORCE   "

It is of paramount importance that evo-devo leaders and communities become practitioners of the "Breakthrough Force" in order to lead the "Implosion Effect" for achieving explosive yet sustainable growth. In a study conducted by Yerkes and Dodson it was conclusively demonstrated that there is a direct correlation between stress and performance efficiency.

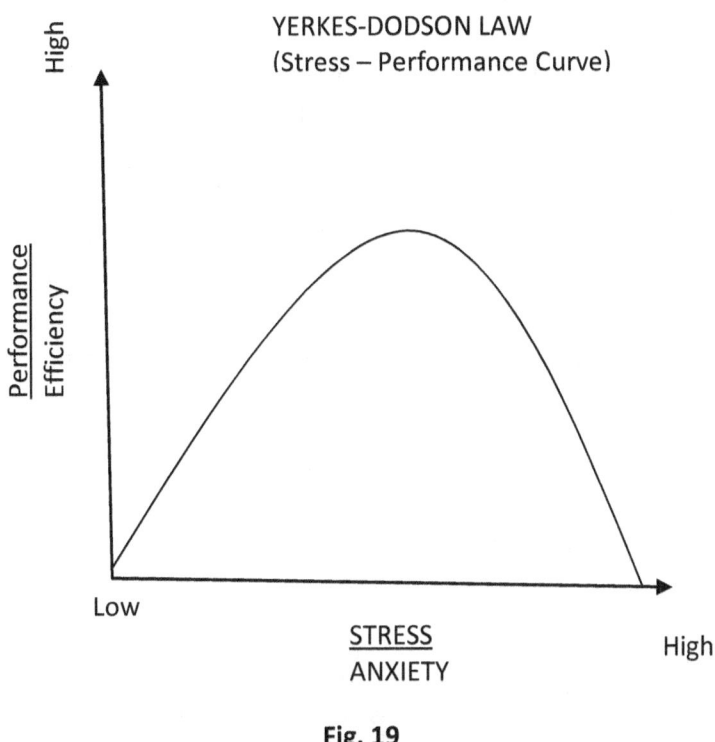

YERKES-DODSON LAW
(Stress – Performance Curve)

Fig. 19

Scientists have been observing this simple yet profound conclusion of the "YERKES-DODSON LAW" that affirms the fact that as stress increases you have an initial increase in performance efficiency i.e. you become more productive during periods of crisis but at a certain point as stress becomes too high both performance and efficiency decline rapidly This intriguing phenomenon demarcates the exact point, for each individual, at which the "Breakthrough Force" has to be applied for performance and efficiency to keep on improving even as stress increases. The trigger that we need to develop as part of the Leadership of SUCCESS is to constantly practice the evo-devo principles to find your personal "Breakthrough Point", the point at which you need to input the "Internal Breakthrough Force" as an energy spurt that will take you to the next level of productivity with an increase in performance and efficiency even in times of adversity. The "Breakthrough Point" will be varied for each individual based on their ability to handle stress but as a practitioner of the "Breakthrough Force" you can identify the point and predict rational decisions with positive results even in chaos.

In humans, the pre-frontal cortex is often associated with the responsibility of performing the "Leadership or Executive" functions. This area also controls the willpower and rational planning or action strategies including handling stress. The pre-frontal cortex area of the brain is much larger in humans as compared to other species. This factor therefore gives you an enormous potential to perform rational executive functions efficiently at all times. The issue though is that this same area has the characteristic of having an abundance of inhibitory circuits that prevent you from acting on all possibilities simultaneously including the fact that as complexity of the solution increases the inhibitory circuits become active and lower rational thought processes.

The fortunate part is that by practicing the "Breakthrough Force" one can actually exercise this area of the brain, as you would any muscle, to increase your capability to handle stress calmly, look for simple but effective solutions and retain the willpower to act rationally as well as plan for contingencies to select the best option for SUCCESS. The practice of the "Breakthrough Force" can also be transferred from the Leader to the community by training them to follow the process diligently. The new Stress-Performance curve for a practitioner of the "BREAKTHROUGH FORCE" will appear as below:

PAUL's "Breakthrough Force"-EVO-DEVO PEAKS

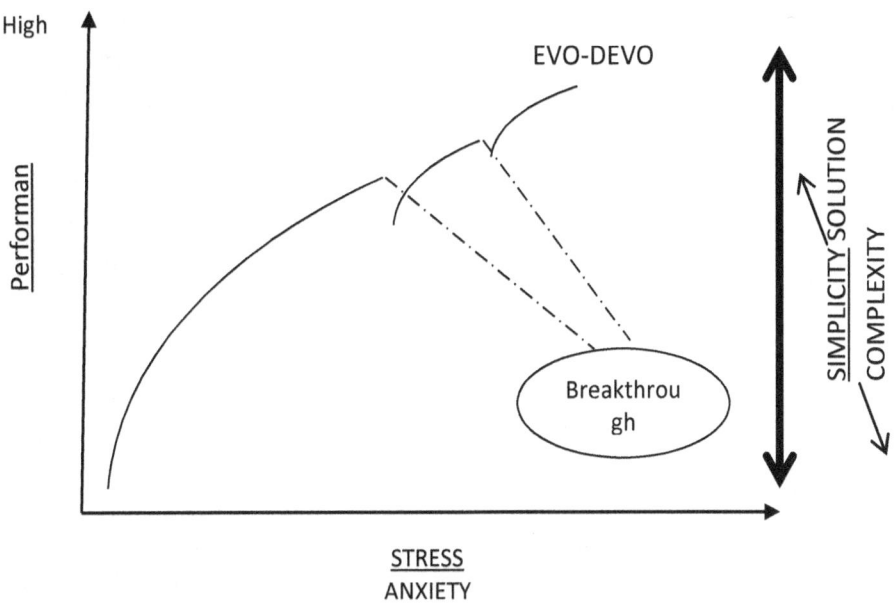

(Stress-Performance-Complexity Curve- A Practice Fig. 20)

As we observe in the above pictorial representation of the "Breakthrough Force" and its application at the correct point we observe that the practitioner of the Breakthrough Force is able to balance stress and performance by triggering the force at the right time. In actuality the evo-devo practitioner can achieve higher than normal "Peak Performance States" that allows the leader to create solutions that are successful despite stress, chaos and adversity.

The paradox here is that the evo-devo Leadership of SUCCESS under the Breakthrough Force allows the leaders to attain a higher "peak state" within the increased limits of stress while providing the continuity of a calm, rational "executive" decision making process by lowering the anxiety of failure. This inherent contradiction virtually innovates a process of acceleration of constructive activity while an overall de-acceleration or calming of physiological functions is taking place for the evo-devo practitioners. The

Leadership of SUCCESS demands this trait in the leaders since it results in the communal benefit of "more bang for the Leadership Buck" due to the competitive advantage of higher "peak states" for the leader who then delivers bigger and quicker results while using less energy.

In research conducted, using FMRI scans of the brain, to unlock the secrets behind this complex phenomenon of the "Calm Commotion" of the Breakthrough force it was found that this apparently contradictory phase is a combination of patterns a rewiring of mental circuits based on changes in the deep, intrinsic personal belief systems through mental training. The fact is that as we calm our bodies and minds under the guidance of an enhanced belief system to perform at increased levels of stress in a "peak state", as part of the Breakthrough Force process, the general brain qui alongside the slowing down of physiological functions simultaneously. At the same time certain isolated areas of the brain-especially those associated with attention to detail, space-time concepts and "executive control" functions related to problem solving and decision making- become extremely active.

The source of this "free energy" of higher peak states is still under investigation, as "out of body" experiences, as to whether it arises from within the brain or from some other collective force such as the community. There is no doubt though that a strong personal belief system and the practice of the mental skills of enhanced knowledge with benefit of sharing will result in a "Breakthrough Force" that will allow a higher "peak performance state" for the leaders to achieve long term sustainable growth for the community. The "slow down" to "speed up" paradigm is therefore crucial to the evo-devo leader and its potential for abundant energy is available to all of you at all times. The trigger to transform our performance and to alter our peak state could be as simple as "Visualizing" our SUCCESS and "feeling" the energy of enhanced capability as part of your belief system. This capability of "let go" and to forget the stress by focusing on facts and faith as a part of your intrinsic belief system will result in the benefit of the "Breakthrough Force".

In an experiment conducted by Dr. Herbert Benson MD and William Procter with the help of Dr. Lazar, as presented in the New York Times, it was demonstrated conclusively that the "Breakthrough Force" and the associated enhanced "peak states" existed. The experiment involved a few individuals of the SIKH Faith, a prime example of a "free energy" belief system, who were made to recite their prayers by repeating the words of their faith i.e. SATNAM (The True Name) and WAHEGURU (GOD is Great) while their brain functions were monitored under the FMRI scans. As the calming effects of the prayer were observed the individuals were put under stress of increased noise levels and disturbances to create chaos. It was seen that the calming effect of the intrinsic belief system was able to ensure a higher 'peak state" by achieving the "Breakthrough Force" that allowed the individuals to carry on rational thought in specific brain areas wherein normal people would have failed due the chaos and disturbance around them.

The key though to achieving the "peak performance state" using the Breakthrough Force in the presence of stress, anxiety, adversity and chaos is the practice of the evo-devo principles. The entire process is designed around the fact that with this strategy of "calm commotion" you can utilize the abundant free energy of the "Implosion effect' to fuel your higher than normal "peak state' for communal SUCCESS. Mark Hurd, CEO of Hewlett Packard (A company that has gone through various downturns successfully) said" Great Companies excel in tough times and in tough times customers turn to great companies." This here is a prime example of a higher than normal "peak state" and the application of the Break through Force because Great Leadership not only practices the breakthrough personally it also transfers the process to the community or the organization in order to create a Sigma effect of "summation" by connecting all the breakthroughs in their sphere of Influence. This Sigma Effect of multiple sources of "peak states" that are above normal evolves into the overall communal benefit to achieve the Leadership of SUCCESS and selection advantage for the constituents. Jeffery Katzenberg, CEO DreamWorks, explains the type of corporate culture required for such SUCCESS. He says "Create a haven: At the outset our hope and our ambition was to create a safe place where ideas are welcome and failure is okay. We can only succeed when what we do is original. Tell people a story about themselves. We are storytellers who are trying to give people a good laugh. Celebrate Often: All milestones are celebrated in a big way. Treat departing employees well: It is more important there be a red carpet for valued people when they leave than when someone joins."

2008 a year of corporate collapse, financial disasters and global recession has become a watershed in the process of separating the "wheat" from the "chaff". It was also a year that destroyed confidence, trust and faith including brand values not only for companies but also for countries. The latest Trust Barometer from the Edelman foundation that gauges trust in business and other institutions found a vertiginous drop in image across the board. A survey taken across 20 countries stated that 62% of the respondents trust business and government less than they did a year ago. Trust in US business is even lower than it was after Enron or the Dot.Com bust. The huge "erosion of the Natural Capital of Trust and Brand Value is an apparent demonstration of the truth that "Brand Value is directly proportional to the value of Leadership which in turn depends on Leadership VALUES." Herein lays the evo-devo of the Leadership of SUCCESS.

In the List of "Worlds Most Admired Companies; as published by Fortune Magazine, it shows that in this climate of failure, GREAT LEADERSHIP VALUES have by contrast made major competitive gains by evolving strategies that are cyclical and sustainable in nature and are thus "failure proofed". These evo-devo leaders not only protected the communal "Natural Capital" of Trust, Faith and Brand but in fact enhanced it by reaching higher than normal "peak performance states' in this chaos of an economic and financial downturn. In their SUCCESS there were "constant" intrinsic Leadership Values that were consistent and these were executed in a rational and planned manner. Organization structures and contingency plans stood the stress of recession and unlike other organizations which imploded from one structure to another losing their human resource natural capital, these Admired Companies managed to retain their leaders to create growth by leading the "Implosion Effect". This exemplifies the most powerful lesson for the evo-devo of the Leadership of SUCCESS which is the secret of not just HOW to attain success but HOW to retain SUCCESS. A time of economic crisis or political or financial adversity does not need to harm or destroy Leadership Values. On the contrary, there is no greater opportunity to stand out.**(The Top 10 Companies: Apple 1, Berkshire Hathway 2,Toyota 3, Google 4, Johnson and Johnson 5, P&G 6, FedEx 7,Southwest 8, GE 9, Microsoft 10.)**

> *The LEADERSHIP OF SUCCESS states that "WHEN SO MANY ARE SCORNED, WHAT BETTER CHANCE TO BE ADMIRED,"*

CHAPTER 8

The EVO-DEVO of LEADERSHIP OF NATURAL CAPITAL- BEYOND RESOURCE

"Evil being the root of all Mystery, Pain is the Root of all Knowledge" This saying by Erasmus is an apt description of Resources or their lack thereof as a symbol of both Evil and Pain. The Evil of hoarding and the Pain of scarcity drives the leadership of resources today. This one element of leadership has resulted in tremendous technological transformation and rapid evolutionary change, both constructive and destructive, in the past and will continue to do so in the future if allowed to dominate the nature and culture of leaders.

The problem facing Leaders and Communities is the continuously changing nature of resource as we grow and evolve. Land was not a resource unless you could "own it" legally. Fossil oil was not a crucial resource till the transportation industry made it invaluable and we found ways to extract it cheaply. Air was not a commercial resource till the communication industry found bandwidth for cellular phones and radio as well as the entertainment industry started using satellite based signaling. Uranium, Plutonium and Thorium were not resources till we had an equation that needed atoms that were "packed" so that the separation or implosion could be used to release energy through chaos or disorder and its entire energy became equal to the product of mass and the speed of light squared. Even the internet was not a resource till the content of software was added to it. These problems with resource and its transforming nature are compounded since these changes that occur rapidly modify the nature of resource itself, both locally and globally. The constant in this changing nature of resource is the Pain of scarcity of the resources. As the pain of an existing resource increase whether through availability or cost, new sources of finding, obtaining, distributing or storing fresh resources are developed using technology and operational excellence.

This "abundance" of pain within the aegis of the scarcity of resource is the final solution to move beyond resource to the evo-devo of Leadership of "Natural Capital". Just to understand this abundance of Natural Capital that can fuel sustainable growth let us look at the figure below:

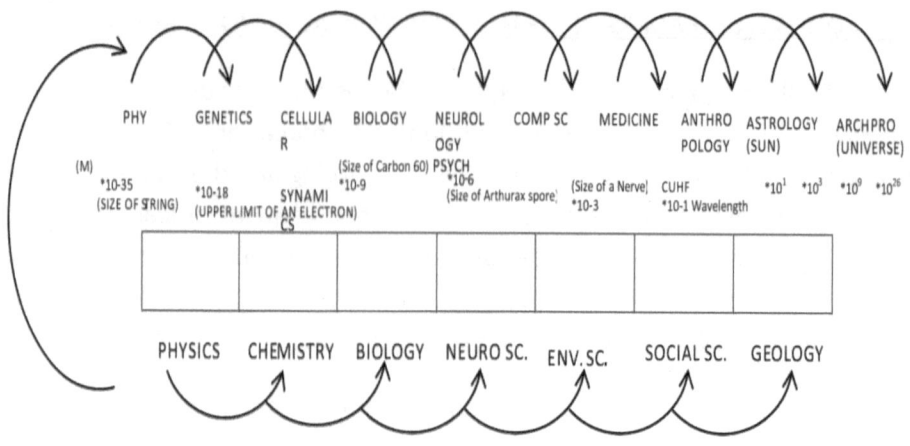

THE INTERDEPENDENT NATURE OF EVO-DEVO NATURAL CAPITAL (Fig 21)

The above scale demonstrates the sources of "Natural Capital" in its abundance as you move beyond resource scarcity. In the cyclic nature of interrelationships and interdependencies the various disciplines of science and technology merge seamlessly using the "free exchange" of energy. You will observe that there is no size small or large of mass or matter that is not a source of Natural Capital. Thus we now have the formula for ongoing growth within the paradigm of unlimited Natural Capital. The only catalyst required to start this reaction is the evo-devo of Leadership that can transform the Pain of scarcity of resources to the Joy of abundance of Natural Capital for explosive growth of Communal Wealth.

The common factor amongst the various disciplines and sources of growth is that the thread of Knowledge and Process run across the board. This Yin and Yang of Knowledge and Process linked with the abundance of sharing creates a constant supply of excellence to end the Pain. Also nature supports this interplay transference of energy between Knowledge and Process as we look at the 2nd Law of Thermodynamics that states that Entropy (a measure of the different combinations of unused energy resources) cannot be destroyed or lowered. It is amply clear that all the systems around you are thus sources of unused energy needing only the knowledge and process to unleash their potential within the chaos of pain and adversity. The sustainability of this process is ensured in the fact that as we create order in one chaos to satisfy the pain of need more disorder will be created elsewhere giving leadership a constant abundance of demands for handling the pains to release the free energy for growth.

The tautology of the abundance of both supply and demand is then the new paradigm of leadership to move beyond resource to focus on Natural Capital. The question that begs an answer is that "If there is an abundance of supply and demand through this Leadership of Natural Capital then WHY all our current strategies of leadership based on managing scarcity are?

One of the answers is the fact that your DNA is still playing catch up with these dynamic changes in knowledge and process that are taking place around you so rapidly. The human DNA was developed around scarcity from the time of inception due to the constant conflict of gathering and hunting in order to meet the basic necessities. As humans we feel "safe" in the concept of scarcity. The entire economic and financial systems under Keynes or Malthus, the fathers of modern economics, were mired in scarcity. "Bad News Sells" and scarcity is bad news and leadership is willing to use the bad news to create fear, uncertainty and doubt in order to unethically control their communities. At the same time current leadership is scared of abundance as it needs an evo-devo transformation in the nature and culture of leadership to lead this Natural Capital for sustainable long term growth.

The best example of the radical thinking that is required is shown by the evolution of the advanced "STRING THEORY" in the realms of Physics as well as other scientific disciplines. The theory is trying to reconcile the fundamental Laws of Gravity and Quantum Mechanics to reach a unified theory that would be extremely beneficial in finding multiple solutions to key global issues ranging from energy to global warming. Unfortunately, the knowledge and process required to achieve this "Breakthrough" needs NINE dimensions of space. Leadership can only see three, an evolved genius like Einstein saw four and now you need NINE dimensions (Abundance again!!) that is so minute that you will need to visualize these dimensions. The point that is being reinforced here is that the Nine Dimensions exist and prove that unlimited sources of Natural Capital are around us but we need the "eye" of the evo-devo leader to grasp the concept of connectivity or a "STRING" of these sources that are interconnected and interdependent.

The connectivity of the sources of Natural Capital, in its abundance, also implies that as we create order in one dimension there will necessarily be disorder or chaos in another connected area and as systems move between Order and Chaos and back to Order free energy is released. Global Laws mesh with local execution to sustain growth through competitive advantage. The mantra to attain the Leadership of Natural Capital is for the leaders to use both knowledge and process in the benefit of the community by connecting the dots through facts and faith within the "String" of SUCCESS. The SUCCESS though is intertwined with communal benefit and sharing otherwise the "String" of Natural Capital is broken. Thus there is a direct correlation between the Wisdom of Leadership and the Leadership of Natural Capital as well as the increase in Communal Wealth. The Wisdom-Wealth combination is the lacuna that exists in current leadership.

In fact the equation today is the exact opposite of the evo-devo desired state as wisdom is inversely proportional to wealth. This phenomenon is apparent in the existing state of capitalism which is shrouded in the mystery of hoarding diminishing returns in an economic instrument i.e. cash. Cash, which comes with the pain of an economic depression and isolationism, is now becomes the hope of sustainable growth. This elusive hope as we can see is a mathematical impossibility.

The doyen of capitalism i.e. The Americas, has pledged nearly $16 Trillion in debt (including virtual nationalization of the Financial and Automobile Manufacturing Sectors) in a desperate attempt to avoid a repeat of the 1930's "Depression." This policy of "infinite debt" is layered on top of the budget deficits, inflation, and unemployment. The lack of wisdom is even more pronounced as this debt virus is being distributed globally which will result in the collapse of financial stability worldwide. The problem is that the entire foundation of this debt is based on "unethical consumption".

The asset devaluation of the primary assets i.e .Housing and the secondary assets i.e. Financial Derivatives, both fueled by consumption, are eroding the principal itself and therefore will result in the debt itself going bad or be supported by printing the "source of diminishing returns" i.e. more Dollars. The Financial Institutions and consumers are "hoarding" this so called monetary resource in a vain attempt to safeguard their savings. This virtual resource, that is diminishing daily, is the source of a fresh complication termed as the "Dollar Crisis." If we do a macro-economic analysis of the United States economy over the last 12 years you will observe that the budget deficits and the trade deficits have remained balanced over this period. This entails that the USA has been paying the software engineer in India and the factory worker in China with the "deficit dollars" not cash. The economies of countries like China, Japan, Korea, Taiwan and the Middle East/ European Nations are now leveraged nearly 60-80% against the Dollar. As the Dollar loses its purchasing power these economies have the improbable choice of either releasing their hoarded dollars into the local economies and push inflation through the roof or reinvest back into the USA economy where a "dollar is still a dollar". The U.S. government hope is that the "Dollar Crisis" will actually result in a huge influx of the deficit dollars, paid over the last decade, back into the US economy to purchase U.S. assets thus creating a whole new wave of unethical forced consumption. The unfortunate fact is that this consumption (like the last wave) is unsustainable as the policies of "infinite debt" and varying interest rates start acting through inflation to lower the value of the assets itself thus creating a scarcity of consumption to halt the wheel of capitalism. The causes are simple-Greed, unethical use of communal resource to fund individual wealth of a few, economies of scarcity, lack of global ethics, policy of economic apartheid and a abysmal lack of leadership faith. **In all a crisis of confidence**. The solution is complex yet simple because all it needs is the evolutionary transformation of scarcity of Individual resources to the abundance of Natural Capital.

Fortunately, all is not lost!! You know that with PAIN comes wisdom, with Implosion comes free energy, with Knowledge comes new sources of Natural Capital and with the evo-devo of leadership comes transformation for SUCCESS; The abundant demand of elimination of PAIN with wisdom as an unlimited source of Natural Capital and sustainable growth. The Natural Capital itself is found in two abundant interchangeable forms i.e. Tangible and Intangible. The tangible sources of Natural Capital include: Agriculture Soil, water, biodiversity, cosmic diversity, quantum particles, fossil resources, technological advances, ocean diversity, solar, wind, air, earth, nuclear elements, entropy, chaos, enthalpy, free energy, Natural Laws of Gravity, String Theories, Symmetry, electricity, electromagnetism space-time dimensions, genetics, Right Shore Human Resource and pain. The Intangible sources are: relationships, communication, character, competency, creativity, innovation, faith, trust, culture, wisdom, Leadership Value, sharing , latent skills, beneficial traits leading to fixation, attitude and human compassion.

Your input as the evo-devo leader is to identify the abundance of these sources of Natural Capital as well as understand the inter-changeable nature of the resource. You as the leader also need to assign economic values to each of the elements of Natural Capital in order to ensure equitable sharing among the local and global community for sustained growth. In this new paradigm of shared capital the need for **"Virtualization"** is one of the main ingredients for evo-devo leadership. The ideation of virtualization is simply the fact that Natural Capital, both tangible and intangible, may be spread globally but needed locally for performance efficiencies. The leadership of Natural Capital mandates systems wherein leaders can tap into these sources "virtually" across the world to find a solution for their local chaos. These virtual sources can be utilized in multiple scenarios to solve adverse problems simply by connecting the "centers of excellence" together in an user friendly access network that is available 24/7 in a "follow the Sun approach". The idea is simple but it is important to understand that nothing occurs instantaneously without a strong medium in between the diverse "centers of excellence." The medium is you, the evo-devo leadership, that will connect these variegated sources of Natural Capital in a cohesive whole. You have to play the role of a coach, a mentor and a team player interchangeably, morphing from one role to the next, in order to lead this culturally diverse "virtual" team. This also creates the "virtualization" of the entire role of leadership as a resource available across the entire network at all times in different forms for the purpose of being the catalyst that will move this structure efficiently. You, as the evo-devo leader, cannot rely on the existing methodology of "control" or "forced leadership" but will need to develop a style that will encourage inclusivity and sharing of responsibility without loss of performance or lack of process efficiencies. This allows you to access specific leadership skills across the community which could be geographically dispersed and still be available locally when needed.

The "Virtualization" of Natural Capital without losing ownership is critical to the sustainable growth as shrinking revenues, growing global interdependence and the availability of enhanced communication networks within the parameters of a dynamically transforming marketplace requires "peak performance" across different domains simultaneously to achieve a global "breakthrough point." This elimination of duplicity of resource creates an abundance of Natural Capital through the phenomenon of "Right Sourcing".

In an attempt to understand the economic value of the Natural Capital and the competitive advantage of "domain expertise" through the diversity of the centers of excellence available to you lets once again look at a few Real World Sources of Natural Capital in abundance:

- Argon (Ar), named for a Greek word meaning "inactive", was considered inert till the year 2000 when it was found to form at least one stable compound. This gas is colorless and odorless but is the most abundant Noble gas found on Earth. It has applications ranging from Light Bulbs (as a corrosion resistor)to Geiger Counters and Medical Lasers . It may also become a source of super conductivity in the future.

- The Periodic Table comprises of 109 known elements on earth as of now. As part of various cosmic surveys and MRI scans of the cosmos it is considered that there are at least 200 more new elements available in abundance in space that never made it to earth. This combination of Astronomy, through the use of MRI scanning, and biology has been able to identify new sources of high energy as abundant Natural Capital for sustainable growth on earth.

- Dopamine, a chemical found in the brain, can create an expectation of reward and the depression of rejection based on the individuals own experiences or through relationships with others. The study of the diverse fields of Neurology, Management and Politics shows a straight line direction of how the brain functions in areas that influence business decisions or governance of nations and faith or trust among humans.

The Evo-Devo of Leadership

- The Nintendo Wii's unique wireless motion sensitive technology has not only changed the entire gaming world but has found biotechnology uses as well. The new 2009 game called Wii's Sports Resort generated over 400Million Dollars for the innovators. The total gaming industry stands at over 21 Billion dollars by current estimates.

- In a vortex atop a superconducting fluid layer of electrons researchers recently observed a 'quasi particle" with 25% of the charge of an electron. The existence of this particle and its odd charge explains the fact that magnetic and electric fields can be applied to superconducting material for multiple uses including Quantum computing. **The effect of super conduction on power generation and distribution output is expected to triple the existing capacity with nearly zero marginal cost.**

- The human race is predicted to grow to 10 billion by the year 2050. Nearly 20 countries suffered food related violence in 2010 due to rising prices attributable to increased oil prices. The need to feed the 10 Billion populace on a sustainable basis will require at least twice the amount of land under cultivation today. The "Green Revolution" of the twenty century doubled the global production of corn, rice and wheat. The new "Green Revolution" of the 21st century will come about through the combination of Biotechnology and Genetic modification.

S.Africa, 1.8   Others, 8.1   USA

China, 3.8   Argentina

India, 6   Brazil

Canada, 7   Canada

                              USA, 57.7   India

Brazil, 15   China ▬

                                                S.Africa

Argentina, 19   Others

(M- Hectares of Global Areas Planted with Biotech crops - 2007) Fig .22

GM crops currently grow on 114 million hectares of land with no adverse effects. In fact the reduction of the use of pesticides in the cultivation of GM corps is reducing ground water pollution, and increasing biodiversity. A form of rice called "Golden Rice' (rice enriched with Beta Carotene) was discovered 10 years ago but due to issues of "hoarding" gene patents it could not be released to the world for nearly a decade. Even today the GM foods and seeds being developed are for rich farmers in developed countries when in fact the need for these seeds exits in less developed countries. The advantage of "sharing" the Natural Capital of the current knowledge and innovation of this technology for global benefits will not only result in rewards for the innovators through royalties but will also save thousands of forests from extinction. If we take this a step further and add "Algae Farming" to the 114 Million Hectares under cultivation of GM crops, as rice for example needs standing water, we could solve the Energy crisis using the oil produced from the algae with a zero marginal cost to the food production.

-"Obesity is the single largest cause for the increase in healthcare costs." (USA Today- 2011). Obesity, in 2011, accounted for 10.1% of all medical spending up from 6.5% in1998. Americans who are 30 or more pounds overweight cost the country billions of dollars in healthcare.

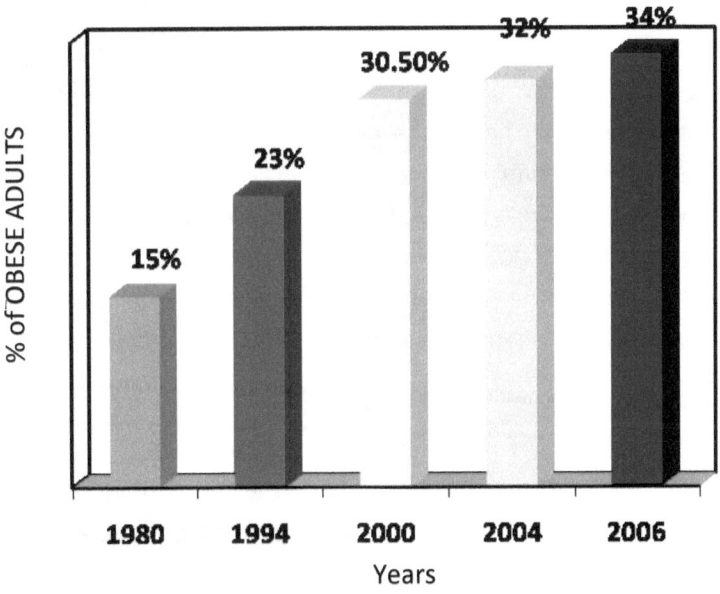

(% of OBESE ADULTS- source NCH and CDC)(Fig.-23)

About 34% (nearly 72 million) "obese" existed in 2006 as compared to 23% in 1994. The solution is simple or impossible depending on the frame of reference i.e. Exercise, healthy life style, GM food and a eat moderately-sleep moderately prescription. In the meanwhile in this recession MacDonald's and Pepsi stocks were up 20% and 30% respectively from their yearly lows.

- The Sun still produces 6000 times the energy required by the earth and all its inhabitants provided we could store and distribute it effectively. The Potential Energy of Wind is mathematically calculated as being equal to ½ (pAV) V^2 where p is the atmospheric pressure, A is the air density and V is the velocity of the wind and the "tunnel effect". As you can see the most relevant factor that influences the PE of the Wind is the velocity which triples the energy generated. The speed at which the wind blows is a direct result of the location, air density and pressure. The new source of wind energy could effectively enhance the global energy production by 30% and is abundantly available.

- BUT one of the largest consumers and promoters of energy consumption of fossil fuels i.e. the Auto Industry ended 2009 with 61% of General Motors being owned by the US Government in contravention of all dictates of capitalism and globalization. The company has not been able to turn a profit in the last few years due to their continuous rejection of the gains of "Right Shore" sourcing which is the competitive advantage demonstrated by the Kan-Ban strategy of the Japanese. In this new world Globalization is a Natural Capital as no one country or organization can excel at everything. The economic common sense is then in the principle that each country or system should focus its Natural Capital of Time, Technology and Intellectual Capital on goods and services that it can produce more beneficially than others. These goods and services then become their preferred currency of exchange to acquire resources from other centers of excellence. This give and take of excellence and efficiency is the free energy that will provide sustainable growth globally.

The Detroit Auto Industry decided to be in focused at the cost of efficiency and productivity and refused to realize the competitive advantage of "Right Source". On the other hand foreign Auto companies took advantage of the robust US Auto market to employ over 400,000 Americans at salaries that were over 20% of the national average compensation matrix. In 2010 all the foreign companies employed nearly 5.5 Million Americans, invested $200 Billion in capital within America and exported $280 Billion worth of goods from America to other countries. This clearly showed the benefits of "Right Source" that not only does it benefit the consumer it also creates a demand for the products within the sourcing destination as well as globally. GM, Chrysler and other manufacturers failed to utilize the "Right Source" capabilities thus becoming uncompetitive but also faced a double 'whammy" by missing the "Rapid Demand" in India, China and eastern Europe which in fact boosted the revenues of other non-US based foreign auto manufacturers The eschewal of the abundant Natural Capital of Globalization was the cause of the huge downfall in the US auto industry. As FIAT of Italy buys Chrysler the "Right Source' advantage will be demonstrated with Rapid ROI for the constituents of the new company but will still result in the loss of image of the leaders of Chrysler as the new image of the acquirer will be adopted. The same parameters will apply to the acquisition of Jaguar and Land Rover by the TATA MOTOR Company of India, which incidentally has also launched a mini-car named "NANO" that is available for around $2500.00 each and could actually be seen as a competitor to the motorcycle and motor scooter segment based on its pricing. The reason these brands i.e. Jaguar and Chrysler have been acquired while in the throes of an "Implosion Effect" is the fact that the entropy of Free energy and the Natural Capital of a skilled workforce, established Dealer Network, Customer Service, Loyal customer base, replacement market, infrastructure, brand value and technology were present in these companies as hidden communal wealth.

These factors when multiplied by the effect of the "Right Source" that creates both demand and supply needs will result in natural capital that will fund future growth. The new leadership becomes necessary since the current leaders, despite knowing the advantages of transformation, lack the energy and resource to fight the internal back-flux to increasing diversity through sourcing and shoring. The current leadership is focused only on the absence of capital and its scarcity rather than the abundance of natural capital available within the globalization phenomenon.

Leadership that has recognized these advantages have done extremely well even in this adverse economic scenario. Apple stock was up 88%, Google 45%, IBM 40%, Amazon-70% and Dell 34%. Apples iPOD and iPAD linked to the iPhone / iTune transformed Apple from an Information Technology enterprise into a key player in the entertainment vertical. Google has become the largest information and transaction provider in the world. It has also connected social and business needs to innovate a networking amongst all its constituents. IBM morphed from being a hardware vendor to the leading provider of services. 66% percent of its revenue and manufacturing come from outside the USA. Amazon has become one of the largest retailers in the world destroying the entire myth of "shelf space". All these companies have used their technological edge to develop services around them in the "SERDUCT" (a combination of services and products) environment. The strategy also includes a global reward system for its stakeholders through the competitive advantages of "Tech Share" and the free energy of globalization.

- Another key example of abundance hidden in the entropy of waste is the area of health care records. The US government is going to spend nearly $70 Billion over the 3-5 years to digitize health records. This process will not only assist the consumer of the services but will create a demand for efficient storage, retrieval and access functions. Telemedicine and sharing medical data across multiple domain experts will also be increasing by over 60% in the same time frame.

- The USA Today in its New Year Breakthrough's Review in Science - talked about the following:

- Genome Mapping gets personal: "Nature" Magazine reported that the age of personal genome, an entire genetic map of a single individual, began in Harvard University researchers hope to pioneer a field of personalized medicine.

- Finding how stem cells multiply: A crescendo of discoveries pushed stem cells from the lab dish to the news headlines. This "Breakthrough of the Year" was compounded when two teams, for the first time, created pluri-potent-cells - unspecialized cells derived from specialized cells - from patients suffering from 11 different diseases. The goal is to create an immune-system friendly transplant tissue for patients.

In all these examples we are finding new energy that is locked up in our existing processes that can be a huge source of fresh Natural Capital. The currency market is another key area that breeds the virus of scarcity. The IMF and the global financial industry are focusing on a new medium of exchange called the SDR. The SDR (Self-Drawing, Rights) has the potential to unleash the Natural Capital locked within the single currency i.e. the Dollar. The SDR is a measure of the country's economy comparative to other countries. It is also a measure of its innovativeness and evo-devo of communal wealth. At this time the SDR is pegged only to the dollar, pound and the Yen. If the proposal to add the Rupee from India, the Yuan from China and the Rouble from Russia is accepted the shared risk of these major economies will immediately release fresh natural capital. The energy that is currently trapped in the global hoarding of dollars will be freed. The free exchange of currencies linked to the inherent strength of all the global players is an excellent replacement for the current single currency methodology. The only country that does not agree to this is naturally the USA.

The idea behind the SDR, a currency now quoted in the Wall Street Journal Currency trading segment, is to create a more equitable "exchange benchmark" as well as release the free energy that is built up in the dollar due to the entropy. This entropy is a huge source of Natural Capital since the dollar has become a source of PAIN as it is only a measure of the resource known as CASH and is scarce as well as provides diminishing returns. On the other hand the Natural Capital of KASH, Knowledge linked with Attitude, Skill and Honest Effort, with its culture of abundance and a fair measure of resource of any entity is available to you as a source for sustainable growth.

The best part of this move from CASH to KASH and from scarce resource to abundant Natural Capital is the fact that this transformation comes at "zero marginal cost" due to the free energy released in the process of evo-devo of Leadership of Natural Capital. The competitive advantage of "zero marginal cost" is a tremendous gain that if applied with Knowledge and Process can eliminate the PAIN of adversity and create sustainable "perpetual" growth. The PAIN of adversity in areas such as lack of education, poverty, hunger, pollution, power, diminishing physical resources, financial systems, Ethical lacunas, energy Crisis, over population, loss of diversity, cultural gaps, technology gaps, inefficiencies etc. are all sources of abundant demand for KASH through the adage of zero marginal cost. These PAIN's, which are a clear indication of a leadership gone bad, need to be eliminated through the

Leadership of Natural Capital utilizing the competitive advantage of innovation under the aegis of zero marginal cost.

This new benchmark of KASH and zero marginal cost should be employed across all entities if sustainable growth and subsequent benefit of survival is the goal. This benchmark will change the parameters of services or products to the aforementioned concept of "SERDUCTS". Serducts move beyond the narrow confines of resource to the visualization of the abundance of supply and demand in the business of eliminating Pain, internal back fluxes, sharing benefits, sharing risks, zero marginal cost and sustainable growth through competitive advantage. You, as the evo-devo leaders, need to understand that the competition is not from other supplier of the same resource but emanates from the efficiencies of the process itself. For example you need to realize that United or Continental are not only in the business of running an Airline but are also in the Logistics and Transportation business. The competition is not from just Delta or Southwest but could come from the Telecommunications industry through Video Conferencing which is trying to eliminate the need for business travel by employing the zero marginal cost phenomenon. The question to the Airline industry is not just limited to reaching economies of scale through higher efficiency and productivity but HOW to eliminate the PAIN of commuting or vice-versa enhancing the benefits of face-face interactions rather than just electronic communication. The key to this game of Leadership of Natural Capital and the selection advantage of a zero marginal cost scenario linked to KASH not CASH is the focus. The elimination of PAIN would also mean the promotion of the concept of Leadership of Ethical Consumption. The benefits accrued from the ideas of ethical consumption as a net generator of Natural Capital is visualized in the next chapter as we move forward to the next phase of the evo-devo of Leadership.

"TODAY's HERESAY IS Tomorrow's DOGMA"   PILZER.

CHAPTER 9

THE EVO-DEVO OF LEADERSHIP FOR ETHICAL CONSUMPTION

Consumption, in the modern world, provides not only sustenance to life but is also a source of angst and conflict. This is primarily due to the constant indulgent use of available resources without ethical considerations. The existing edifice of wealth and success is based on the weak foundation of unethical consumption and virtual scarcity. Ethical consumption, on the flip side, would provide a sustainable growth model through the satisfaction of needs by the elimination of PAIN and an ongoing incremental satiation of wants through the aegis of professional selling, communication, ideas, innovation and technical civilization. This should lead to an abundance of communal benefit and competitive advantage that would be spread globally. If you, the leader, can jump out of the traditional consumption box that is CASH based and see the unlimited boundaries of ethical consumption based on KASH you can understand the advantages that are derived out of this model. The pressure to "sell" refrigerators to Eskimos is no more true than cutting the branch that you are sitting on. In order to follow this natural course of evolution that leads us away from "forced consumption" to "fact and need " based utilization you have to learn HOW to lead and practice this concept of abundant Natural Capital. The Leadership of Ethical Consumption requires a credo of practice that is trained in the art of processes that ensure the alignment of the right "Natural Capital" with the right "Need and Want" to fulfill the abundant demand of PAIN elimination. At the same time it mandates abhorrence for over consumption, waste and unethical promotion that focuses on CASH but not KASH.

The figure below represents the nature and culture of ethical consumption that uses KASH to fund sustainable growth and mandates the practice of Professional selling that ethically links demand to the right source to ensure that the benefits of the consumption are shared globally in an equitable manner.

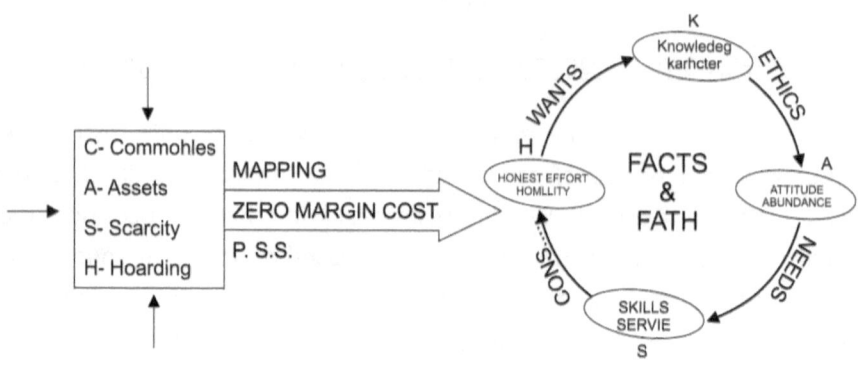

THE PRACTICE OF KASH vs. CASH (Fig. 24)

The rudimentary connector of Cash-Kash, demand-supply, goods-services, features-benefits, seller-buyer, and provider-user, is the sometimes ignored role of Professional Selling. This Professional Selling, a practice, is one of the key links that uses the power of knowledge and process to promote "SERDUCTS" that will not only meet needs but also fulfill wants in incremental steps. Professional selling also ensures that the communal benefits of the consumption far outweigh any individualistic benefits. The benchmark of Professional Selling is measured in the value to the consumer rather than the value of the good or service itself. The benchmark also provides for the zero marginal cost of process improvement so that the investment is self- funding in terms of growth and is sustainable evolutionarily.

The definition of CASH as a diminishing resource of Commodities, Assets, Scarcity and Hoarding , is a promoter of unethical consumption vis-à-vis KASH, a source of Knowledge with compassion, Attitude of abundance, Skills with process and Honest effort with humility are linked directly to the art of PSS (Professional Selling Skills) with the adage of zero marginal cost for "perpetual" growth. The art of PSS can be summarized in the following words of Ralph Waldo Emerson, "A great man is always willing to be little. Whilst he sits on a cushion of advantage he goes to sleep; When he is pushed ,tormented, defeated he has a chance to learn something; when he has been put on his wits on his manhood he has gained facts, learns his ignorance and is cured of the insanity of conceit." The art of PSS can eliminate PAIN at the same time ensure sustainable growth by lowering the risk, increasing value, enhancing Digital iQ, creating a Rapid Return on Investment and filling the existing gaps of both knowledge and process.

There are only three kinds of gaps that can exist in any consumer of knowledge and process for the need and want of ethical consumption:

A) CAPACITY GAPS

B) CAPABILITY GAPS

C) VISION GAPS

The Capacity Gap can simply be defined as the "consumption of more" of the same at maybe lower cost and slightly better efficiency to meet the existing conditions of growth. It is a horizontal level of consumption that is required for day to day sustenance and some incremental growth of the system.

The Capability Gap is the need for consuming "better" goods and services that meet the requirement of substantially improved performance from existing processes for benefits of higher productivity, lower cost, Quality improvement etc. This is more a vertical level of consumption that is intended to improve the overall efficiency of the system to create rapid growth.

The Vision Gap" is the need for consumption of civilized technology, ideas, innovation, process improvement and enhancement of knowledge that will benefit the leader and the community by ensuring both a competitive and a comparative advantage for the entity as a whole. The Vision Gap fulfillment also ends up completing the capacity and capability gaps by meeting the needs and wants of the community on a sustainable basis. The benefits to the community as well as the related spheres of influence will include **LOWER COST, HIGH VALUE, RAPID RETURN ON NATURAL CAPITAL, RISK MINIMIZATION and an EVOLUTIONARY SELECTION ADVANTAGE for the system.** The VISION GAP is a cyclic process of consumption.

The GAP paradigm is that all three levels of consumption i.e. horizontal, vertical and circular need fulfillment as all three gaps exist in the knowledge and process domains of the entity creating PAIN. The identification of the GAP and the subsequent solution, using the right set of Natural Capital or resource in the right quantities, is the evo-devo of Leadership of Ethical Consumption. The benefits of the elimination of PAIN will be threefold:

a) In the case of Horizontal consumption the community will get the benefit of higher productivity to meet the existing demands at lower cost.

b) The Vertical consumption pattern will satisfy the need of higher productivity at lower risk due to better quality assurance.

c) The Circular consumption will create a constant demand for ongoing consumption through risk share, ideation and redefinition of the process for competitive advantage. This in turn will ensure sustainable growth.

PAIN is the P̲enalty of A̲dversity and the I̲dentification of N̲eed . The practice of elimination of PAIN demands a professional who can create the value proposition that will ensure the appropriate consumption of Natural Capital for the cure of the cause of the PAIN not just a symptomatic relief.

There is an old saying that advises us to "stop digging when you are in the hole". Unfortunately, leadership today feels that it can eliminate the PAIN of unethical consumption by encouraging more consumption i.e. dig a deeper hole while in the hole. The evo-devo of the Leadership of Ethical Consumption on the other hands demands Professional Diagnostic Skills from the leader to eliminate the PAIN through the Identification of the gaps that are the cause of the adversity. The diagnostic skills for a leader, a professional in the art of ethical consumption, is no less than those of a doctor in finding the underlying cause of your disease, for the lawyer that collects all the evidence to prevent a wrongful conviction or a CPA that has all the proof required to get you through the pain of an IRS audit. This Professional "FACT" based diagnostic process is currently lacking in the leadership today and is by itself one of the points of failure you observe in the systems of Politics, War, Business, Religion, Science, Culture and Community.

The relationship between the USER and the Provider has to be one of, mutual benefit with, the balance tilted in favor of the USER. **This mutually beneficial exchange of energy based on facts and faith, where the user acquires the needed benefits and the provider guarantees he ethical delivery of these benefits, is the foundation of ethical consumption**. This requires a professional approach to both the buying and selling process in order to avoid any misuse of Natural Capital. The "process improvement" in the areas of buying and selling is not a one- time initiative but is an ongoing and motivated trait transforming program.

The concept of Ethical Consumption seems simple but in this world of excesses and virtual consumption the entire idea is doomed for failure. Just as an example: Why do most Weight-Loss programs fail? Why do efficiency "process improvement" strategies such as Six Sigma and Lean manufacturing, which encourage ethical consumption, end up not delivering the benefits envisaged?

The concept of "process improvement" starts off well but under increased day to day stresses of the expectation of short term unrealistic results these valuable ideas fall on the wayside. These initiatives react in much the same way as would a rubber band when it is pulled with increasing force. There is the initial "stretching" and the subsequent "yielding" phases before it fails entirely or reverts back to its near original shape. This "stress train" curve and its time period is a major cause of failure of the ideas of "process-improvement" that would result in the Leadership of Ethical Consumption for sustainable communal benefits. The problem and the solution again lies with leadership and their core values.

The Question: How do you, as leaders, then motivate this "process improvement" from consumption to ethical consumption both within the user community and the providers so that the abundance of Natural Capital can be harnessed effectively?

The transformation of consumption in its nature and culture with the introduction of ethics, alongside the abundance paradigm of Natural Capital, is an inclusive seeding process that must be planted by embedding procedural and behavioral modifications to prepare the foundation for the change <u>before</u> the transformation begins.

Let us look at our elastic rubber band again. In the "stretching phase" the effort is well planned and executed as we have an objective that is defined and monitored. As leaders you monitor the initial phase of consumption of energy diligently to lead it to success of the initial goal i.e. stretching.

Unfortunately, this is not success. (Who does not remember the American President George W. Bush declaring the end of the "War on Terrorism" more than 10 years ago while we still have the ongoing hostilities in the region!!!). As we continue to expand and consume more energy to keep pulling the rubber band the goals and objectives are now less well defined and the rubber band "yields" to the unnecessary changes by becoming permanently deformed as its basic structure is now impaired. The tactical stage of implementation and execution is now faltering and management of day-to day functions start taking priority and the change stops delivering benefits in line with the consumption of resources. As we keep using more energy to pull the band, the band itself starts narrowing at the edges and weakens. This "bottle neck" then is unable to withstand any pressure and it fails subsequently. This "failing phase" is also the stage when most unethical consumption takes place and falsification of results starts occurring to indicate some success while hiding the failures. In the end the consumption pattern is back to being a net user of energy rather than a net provider of energy and the Natural Capital of the Leader and the Community is expanded in leading to the "Implosion Effect' and the entity is now broken into small pieces as is the rubber band.

The lessons learnt from the above experience clearly indicate one fact i.e. FAILURE is painful, embarrassing, public, shocking and predictable. The solution: If the points of failure are also planned tactically the adversity will make the process stronger rather weaker by eliminating the "bottle necks." The idea of reinitiating the SUCCESS of the "stretching phase" as we reach the "yielding phase" will ensure ongoing sustainable growth with the minimum use of Natural Capital using the abundance of free energy of the Implosion itself. The only way you can achieve the above cyclic consumption results are by acknowledging the failures of the capacity or "stretching" phase and the capability gaps of the "yielding" phase at the same time leading these points of failure to become points of inflexion for new growth by the addition of Natural capital and transformation at these points in the "vision" phase. This then is the essence of the Leadership of Natural Capital.

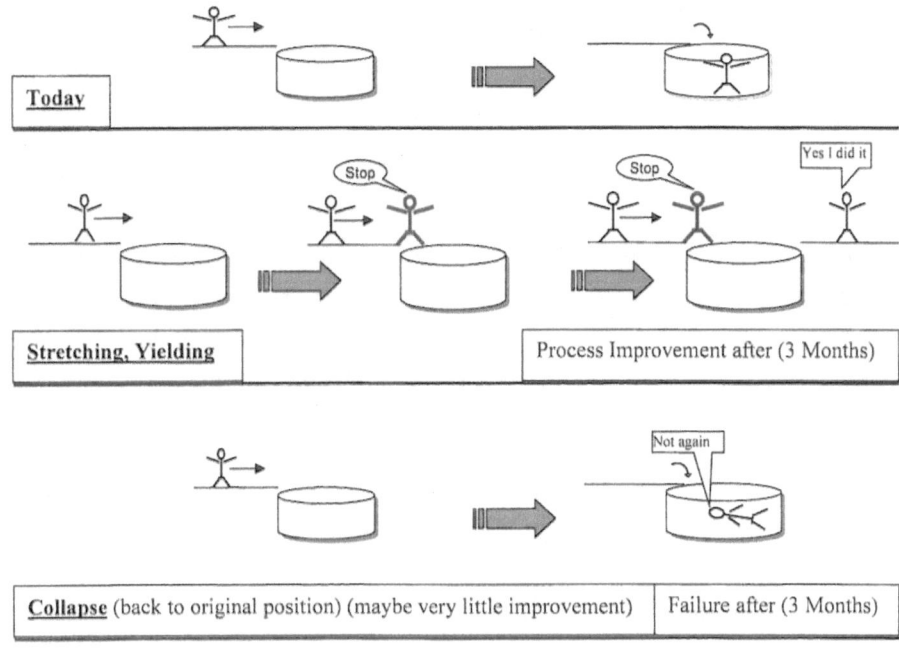

THE RUBBER BAND Fig.25

The solution to acquiring the trait of ethical consumption within the leader and the community is four fold:

a) **Professional Approach and Practice**: The leader and the community need be trained in the art of professional selling/buying and demand fulfillment with tools and resources that can both enhance as well as monitor the practice and the results.

b) **Incentive and Reward Linked to Practice**: The ethical use of Natural Capital and the enhancement of Communal Wealth has to be adequately rewarded on an ongoing basis. Process Improvement that promotes and leads to ethical consumption has to be directly tied to the performance incentive as a key motivator.

c) **Think Big with Small numbers**: Goals should be realistic but not SMALL the teams should be small (no larger than twelve members) but be thinking BIG. This not only helps in lowering the 'Internal Back Flux' but also ensures a efficient use of the Natural Capital of human resource.

d) **Leadership Participation and Enduring Patience**: Leadership has to a part and parcel of the process not just "support" it. The "implosion effect" and its associated energy needs a practiced approach and personal commitment with enduring patience for results and there is no better source than the leadership itself. By living and breathing the 'stretching; 'yielding' and failure points first hand leadership vision can make adequate change at the appropriate time based on facts.

FAILURE CANNOT BE DELEGATED BUT SUCCESS CAN BE. Ask Alexander, Gandhi, Mandela, Machiavelli, Bill Gates, Warren Buffet, Ratan Tata, Mukesh Ambani, Guru Nanak, Jesus Christ or Mohammed and you will get the same answer to the Leadership of Ethical Consumption.

The relationship between the user and the provider is one of trust and faith. The USER uses facts to identify the PAIN and the provider should be assisting the user to lower the penalty of the pain by the best use of Natural Capital. The USER needs to follow the methodology as below to gain the maximum benefits of the ethical consumption of the provider's solution:

V - Visualize the existing processes employed within the community.

A - Analyze the Gaps- Capacity, Capability or Vision-for owned and acquired assets.

I - Identify risks, assumptions, contingencies, goals and failures.

B - Benefits need to be planned for both quantitative and qualitative metrics.

P - Plan SUCCESS and FAILURE with goals for both as well as customizations.

E - Execute and Implement flawlessly through the profession of "BEST PRACTICE".

M - Monitor constantly and Evaluate the need for new sources for SUCCESS

This process is to be employed whenever a use of Natural Capital is warranted. In the current scenario as consumption leaders you are aware that technological advancement and "user remorse" will kick in as soon as a cycle of consumption is completed. **The competitive advantage of ethical consumption is derived since the expected benefits of the expense of Natural capital are identified in advance and once these benefits are achieved the cycle ends.** A new cycle is then initiated to reap further benefits of process-improvement which is built on the foundation of SUCCESS of the initial consumption cycle that was completed beneficially; This ensures that each cycle of consumption delivers the required results hence eliminating the PAIN at each phase before starting the next phase. Thus VAIBPEM ensures that he Leadership of Ethical consumption can Visualize, Analyze and Identify both Pain and Benefits at the same time and Plan, Execute and Monitor for SUCCESS.

Simply put:

USER + VAIBPEM = SUCCESS

USER + CONSUMPTION= FAILURE

On the other side of this equation are the **providers** of Natural Capital, including ideas for Process-Improvement, who are not only redefining individual processes but are focused more on an industry wide or global PAIN elimination. These providers of Natural Capital, in the Leadership of Ethical consumption, need to be aiming at the "Global Best Practice" scenarios. In order to create "centers of excellences" that are adaptable for Individual consumption by the user group. These best practices should deliver both tangible and intangible benefits with minimum customization. The best practices should be aligned with the needed value proposition that is personalized into a long term "reference site" relationship of **that** user with **this** provider for the ongoing transfer of mutual benefits. The best practices should create a global competitive advantage but executed locally both for an individual entity or community.

The Professional Practice in the proviso of Ethical Consumption requires the providers to visualize the needs of the users in a "Global Best Practices" strategy by mapping the existing processes of the user against the ideal standard and identifying the points of failure and the gaps. This personalized solution that meets the gaps and enhance the process from a sustainability perspective is then proposed to the user. The proposal should include a detailed value proposition and an "opportunity cost" and loss of benefits analysis due to delays in the decision making and execution of the solution.

The foundation of the edifices of the proposal are entrenched in the detailed analysis of the facts that are acquired from the users processes, assessed from an efficiency and optimization of resource matrix, assimilated into the value system of the entity, arbitrated to remove any inconsistencies and include any contingencies with adherence to the basic principles of sustainable growth with communal benefits with a shared reward system. The Professional Skills of Provision (PSP) that are required for the Leadership of Ethical Consumption include the complex process of diagnosis of the PAIN; understanding the process gaps; building faith in your solution approach; creating trust in the user-provider relationship from a guaranteed transfer of the value as proposed and needed by the user; and finally the fulfillment of the consumption for provision of the ultimate benefit of competitive advantage to the ethical consumer. The PSP process can be divided into the categories as enumerated below:

a) **Expecting**: The in-depth understanding of the processes, available resources, needs, wants and expectations as well as motivations behind the expectations from a typical industry or global "best practice" trend is the first step in the PSP process. The act of acquiring the available public information and initial questioning of the consumers allows the professional providers in identifying the right targets that can benefit the most through the ethical consumption of the solution, by the satiation of their expectations, that is being provided.

b) **Targeting**: Mapping the individual consumer by assessing the obvious and hidden expectations with the facts of costs, risks, benefits, time productivity matrix, competitive advantage vis-à-vis the proposed solution is the second-step. Targeting is not only the identification of the entity but also the "MAN" within the entity. The MAN is the combination of the Money, Authority and Need within the user for the acquisition and ethical consumption of the solution. The facts provided by the MAN and the points of failure indicated are then translated to a visual transfer of the vision gap between the MAN and the provider.

c) **Approach**: The gathering of facts and the analysis of the process with mapping it to the expectation of the target leads to the third-step that defines the approach to solving the PAIN of the MAN. The Approach has to be one that brings the maximum benefits to the user with the minimum expending of Natural Capital in the fastest possible time to lower the risk and cost of the target. The Approach has to guarantee a Rapid Return on Natural Capital adjusted to the Internal Rate of Return or "Hurdle Rate" of the user.

This "Hurdle Rate" is the benchmark a Professional Provider needs to meet in order to make the consumption of the proposed solution ethical compared to the use of the Natural Capital into other areas that would give a better rate of return to the client. The Approach has to be user focused rather than solution focused. It needs also to include the facts that have been gathered through the expectation and targeting process as well as "proof" of the benefits of your solution with reference sites that have achieved competitive advantage using the proposed solution. The Approach will necessarily have well defined process-improvement goals with penalties associated with the non-performance of the recommended path by the provider. This Approach has to be directly communicated to the MAN and should include the loss of competitive advantage and associated "opportunity lost costs" that will accrue if the proposed approach is not implemented at the right time. The Approach should be sustainable and include the ongoing costs of customization with intellectual capital transference and the benefit of competitive advantage at each stage of the solution consumption curve.

d) **Negotiation**: The Negotiation process is an important fourth-step in the process of ethical consumption and the PSP. The Negotiation step is the point at which most unethical consumption takes place and can result in the user selecting the wrong solution if the foundation of expectation, targeting and approach have not been completed professionally. In spite of having the 'right Fit" from a solutions perspective entering the Negotiation phase without the facts is a sure way to promote unhealthy consumption that will not benefit the user or the provider. The give and take nature of the negotiation process requires "tradeoffs" on cost vs. benefit, opportunity vs. resource, and risk vs. reward. This "trade off' has to be fact based on both sides in order to ensure that the user does not end up trading off a part of the solution without understanding the corresponding loss in benefits or delay in accrual of the benefits or a loss of competitive advantage required for sustainable growth. The Negotiation phase needs to be evolved to include the "zero marginal cost" scenarios in order to be realistic and sustainable especially in the times of financial crises and adversity. The phase also emphasizes a shift from lower cost to lower risk including the guarantee of the benefit accrual. The Negotiation phase is one of the most dynamic areas of ethical consumption and its fulfillment. This point in the cycle of ethical consumption is also the point that will lead to strong relationships for the future and the ongoing consumption of your ideas by the consumer.

e) **Close**: The Close step is the fifth-step in the process and requires the unconditional acceptance from both the user and the provider that the proposed solution meets the "expectation criteria" to provide the advantage of the elimination of PAIN and a satiation of needs and wants from a sustainability standpoint. If the process has been done ethically the cycle of consumption can now begin. Unfortunately, if all objections have not been met and facts have been falsified this is the point at which these errors will come back to haunt you. The reason is that the point of a close for you the provider, is also the first point of execution of the PLAN for the user. This "go-no go" switch is one of the points of failure in the Leadership of Ethical Consumption and mandates leaders to be professional in their practice of the entire process. The faith in your own solution once you factually see the benefits it will bring to the user community and the individual consumer makes it much easier to close the transaction for the mutually beneficial exchange of energies.

f) **GO FORTH AND EXECUTE**: The final stage of the PSP process will be the order to execute the PLAN as proposed with the user for the provider to deliver the solution within the guaranteed time and cost. It is important to note here that the Leadership of Ethical Consumption demands that the cycle is considered complete only when the proffered benefits start accruing to the user. This evaluation phase should lead into the evo-devo Leadership of Relationships that are a consequence of the PSP process.

USER + VIABPEM = SUCCESS = ETANCO + PROVIDER

USER + Consumption = FAILURE = ETANCO + PROVIDER

PROVIDER + Selling = FAILURE = USER + VIABPEM

As indicated in the above equations the process of Professional Skills and their practice is necessary to ensure the Leadership of Ethical Consumption both from the viewpoint of the user and the provider. This paradigm is true not only in the business world but also applies to Politics, Religion, Social, Personal, Governmental or Aggression as all walks of life face the adversity of PAIN and have expectations for SUCCESS. The more you, as the evo-devo leader, train yourself in the art of Professional Skills to understand the motivations of the recipient and discover their "HOT Buttons" the chances of your SUCCESS are virtually guaranteed which in turn will benefit the constituents of your community.

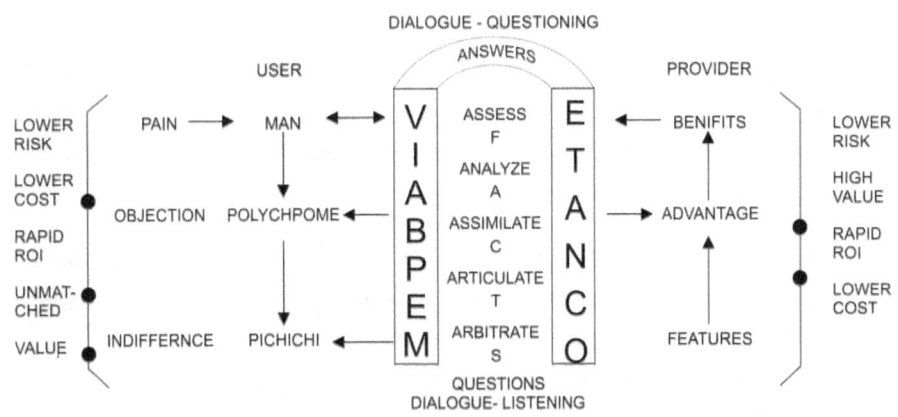

THE ART OF ETHICAL CONSUMPTION (Fig 26)

The secret to the practice of the Leadership of Ethical Consumption is fact based DIALOGUE. The real secret to fact based communication or DIALOGUE is "QUESTIONING" and "LISTENING". The art of questioning and listening to ascertain facts and in turn using the facts to handle the objections or indifference to the process is the end game. To ensure the objective of the DIALOGUE as well as to achieve the objective of SUCCESS the cycle of Questioning, Listening, Objections and Acceptance is wholly depended on the players of the game. The USER has the MAN but also has the "Polychromes" and the "PICHICHIS". The Pichichis and the Polychromes (i.e. glorified Pichichis with a title) have no ability to say "YES" but do have the capability to say "NO" by raising objections and if not handled restricting access to the MAN. It is extremely important to handle these objections as part of the practice of VIABPEM and ETANCO to create a path of "least resistance" for the MAN and the PSP to look at ideas in a free exchange of energy. This will assist all the constituents to reach the acceptance phase and the successful implementation of the solution to attain the accrued benefits in a low risk environment.

The basis of handling objections and eliminating the "back flux" of the Pichichis and the Polychromes is to gather facts through Questioning and Listening to initiate the DIALOGUE using ethical communication. **The five pillars of the factual dialogue is to <u>Acquire</u> the facts through questioning and listening, <u>Analyze</u> the facts vis-à-vis both Knowledge and Process, <u>Assimilate</u> the facts using the best practices and ethical value system, <u>Articulate</u> the PAIN and the solution from a visualization and planning perspective and finally use facts to <u>Arbitrate</u> against any delay to the process of ethical consumption and subsequent "opportunity lost cost".** The current situation is one that uses unethical communication in order to create a "PUSH TO CONSUME" for LIKE TO HAVE consumption rather than an ethical representation of facts to create a "PULL TO CONSUME" for a NEED TO HAVE focus.

The DIALOGUE of ethical communication using the 5 A's will eliminate any indifference to facts or objections to the changes needed for the proposed solution. The DIALOGUE allows the facts to speak for themselves without personalizing the objections at the same time uses the facts to map the solution to the gaps and the pain points to create a strong, highly defendable situation for the peaceful ethical consumption of the benefits. Once the benefits start accruing and sustainable growth with the added advantage of competitive advantage is achieved the Leadership of Ethical Consumption is realized and leads to the Leadership of Relationships as we will see in the next chapter.

"TALKING USES ENERGY DOING CREATES IT. THE PRACTICE OF DOING "RIGHT" MAKES PERFECT RELATIONSHIPS."An Evo-Devo Statement

CHAPTER 10

THE EVO-DEVO of THE LEADERSHIP OF RELATIONSHIP

Leadership has its own gravitational pull relative to the community. The community in turn creates a similar pull on the leader. This gravitational force between the leader and the community is Relationship. The force of relationship is a huge reservoir of Natural Capital and free energy that can be used for sustainable growth. The community absorbs or emits SUCCESS that is directly proportional to the leadership's gravitational field and its potential in which the community is situated. The strength of the relationship is built on trust, faith, mutually beneficial exchange, sharing of risk and rewards of the competitive advantage of SUCCESS. The unmatched value proposition of relationships, especially in times of chaos and adversity, is an important part of the tangible benefit of the evo-devo of Leadership.

The paradigm of the Leadership of Relationships is hidden in abundance in the relationship itself and is a source of impetus to both growth and the enhancement of the Natural Capital. As Faulkner once said "There is no such thing as was--- only is. If was existed there would be no grief or sorrow." This phrase is the foundation of the Leadership of Relationships since the force of the relationships are based on trust and faith over time and in the past but have to be maintained in the present for the future. You, as evo-devo leaders, cannot take a relationship for granted because it existed in the past but you have to nurture and sustain it constantly if you expect this "force" to assist you in times of the "Implosion Effect" and adversity.

The Leadership of Relationship is also one of the best routes to populate the community or the sphere of influence of the leader with the right evolutionary transformations so that the evo-devo of Leadership can spread towards fixation and the potential of the community can be full realized. Individual perceptions of exploitation will need to be handled whenever there is a clash between individual expectations and communal success. The evo-devo communities that are "fixated" with the culture of the Leadership of Relationships will automatically gravitate and attract each other. This conference of evolved communities across the globe will induce the exchange of free energy that will fuel the universal "explosion effect" of sustainable growth. The ethical use of Natural Capital and a lowering of conflict are by-products of the Leadership of Relationship.

The other considerable advantage of this phenomenon is that the force of relationships abounds infinitely. The infinite nature of this force is limited, in its use, by the leaders thus making it finite. This tautology can be explained further if we look at an experience from our material universe. The relationship that exists amongst the various constituents of our universe, such as the stars is similar to our own leadership domain. The stars are spread all across the universe. These stars are of variable densities, sizes and compositions but essentially are still the same in their nature. In principle however far you might travel through space, you will find an attenuated group of fixed stars that are related to each other in various ways. The common factor though is that each of these star systems is unique yet similar to the other systems around it. Each system has its own center of excellence around it. This universal phenomenon is conclusive evidence of the evo-devo theory that it is more efficient to have multiple, even infinite, centers of excellence connected to each other rather than one finite material center that governs all the relationships. A single finite center, however large, is destined to become gradually but systematically impoverished and scarce due its very nature that is centralized. The nature of attraction and its force within the universe of relationships is also defined by the similarity of their focus wherein "centers of excellence" in one domain will attract other "COE"s in the same domain to become mutually beneficial yet remain independent. This concept will be explained further when we reach the destination of Global Interdependence in our quest. At this point it is prudent to understand that we need to modify the generally accepted principles of relationships that are currently followed. These practices are mired in the scarce nature of resource and within it the seeds of conflict.

For long leaders have searched for the "silver bullet" that can resolve conflict without physical aggression and still allow them to retain control over their sphere of influence. The fact is that the Leadership of Relationships gives you the tools to be able to adapt and yield to transform chaos into harmony. The tools give you the alternative that is validated by the process that uses the power of the natural human conditions that instinctively repudiates conflict to solve problems. The strength of your relationships permit you to take advantage by moving with the basic human instinct rather than resisting it.

It is the epitome of wisdom to utilize your strategic relationships to reduce conflict and confuse your detractors by giving them the dilemma of the "Right" response. The Leadership of Relationship that applies the wisdom of communication to avoid the waste of unnecessary conflict is the evo-devo required for SUCCESS. This strategy is comparable to clearing a wider or new canal to stop a flooding river rather than trying to build a dam against its natural flow. The first strategy that opens new or wider channels of communication creates abundance while the second creates scarcity because you are constantly depending on your size as a source of strength instead of using the wisdom of relationships as the tool. The problem is that we have been forced into a belief system that is focused on the principle of scarcity that favors the "BIG" and its associated perceived advantage of size and its consequence of FUD ie Fear, Uncertainty and Doubt to unethically control any relationship.

The transformation for the evo-devo of Leadership is the concept of multiple connected "centers of excellence" relatively associated on the principle of mutually beneficial exchange of Natural Capital in a cycle of ethical consumption. This connection of multiple Leadership domains in a cohesive whole also assumes that these "centers of excellence" are independent but still interdependent based on the gravitational force of Relationships inspite of great distances thus being free of any "forced domination" for exploitation based on size or mass alone.

The freedom from the distasteful conception that the universe of relationships needs to possess something akin in nature to a single large center in order to exist is the foundation to the evo-devo of the Leadership of Relationship. The ideation of various leaderships and communal domains, each of those sustainable on its own, associated under the natural laws of global sustainable growth through the aegis of the relative effect of relationships is an evolutionary change that is desperately needed to gain the selection advantage.

The selection advantage of "perpetual" sustainable growth is achieved through the Leadership of Relationships since in the interplay of a fair exchange of energy no single entity is singularly dominant or indispensable. This fundamental shift in the relative culture of leadership from one that is finite due to its predatory and controlling nature to one that is infinite due to its abundance of respect and shared risk-reward is the transformation needed within yourself and the community.

The concept of this relative exponential nature of the evo-devo of relationship that are decentralized, infinite yet finite and independent yet interconnected can pictorially and mathematically be represented as below:

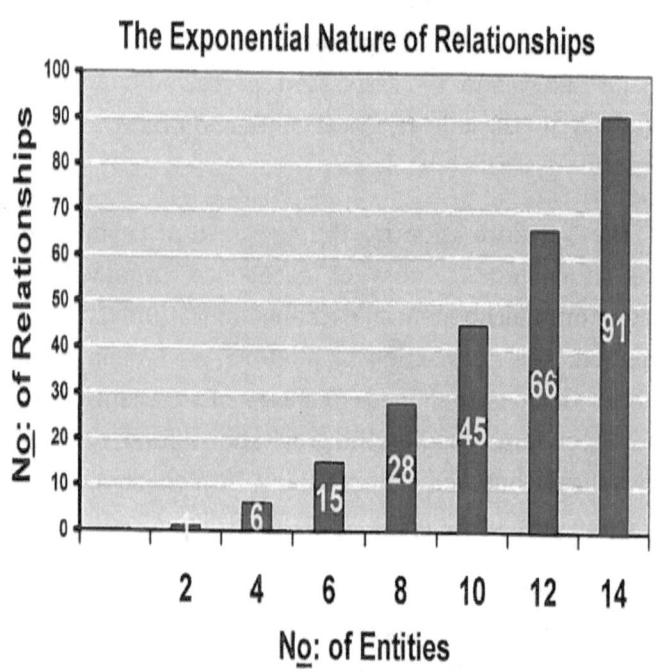

= No. of people in the Relationship

= Preceding No. of Relationships

= 0 when single

N	N	R = N + n − 1
⚇⚇ 2	0	1
⚇⚇⚇ 3	1	3
⚇⚇⚇⚇ 4	3	6
⚇⚇⚇⚇⚇ 5	6	10
⚇⚇⚇⚇⚇⚇ 6	10	15
⚇⚇⚇⚇⚇⚇⚇ 7	15	21

The Exponential of Relationships – Fig. 27

The pictorial representation you see above is not a one to one increase in relationships as we would see in a finite centralized culture. There is an exponential and abundant network of relationships that is available to you as a powerful source of Natural Capital if lead in an ethical manner. The formula for the calculation of this surge of Natural Capital of relationships is as below:

$$R = (N) + (n-1)$$

In the evo-devo world where R is the total number of relationships and n is the number of individuals or "centers of excellence" involved in the relationships and N is the existing No. of relationships. You will observe that the relationship curve increases or decreases exponentially with every addition or subtraction. For e.g. If you have twelve (12) entities in a relationship universe then the actual number of relationships, based on the above equation, ends up at 66. This demonstrates the abundant Natural Capital of the Leadership of relationships that can be harnessed for success. Also it is apparent from the above equation that the introduction of one additional person in the existing relationship domain adds a whole plethora of complexity to the structure.

The huge potential of relationships as a store of unused energy is directly linked to the gravitational force of these relationships based on faith, trust and a shared risk-reward scenario with the elements of domain expertise. If these elements are missing in the owned or acquired relationships then the whole gamut of relationships and their interdependent nature becomes a source of negative energy and chaos due to the large numbers involved. In its negative energy state, as is occurring today, the effort expanded to manage these numbers results in a tremendous waste of resources. The sole reason: The current unethical nature of leadership. On a global scale the fact that leadership is focused on wealth accumulation, without the benefit of equitable distribution, has created an atmosphere of conflict and mistrust. The solution is to move from the "I" factor to the "We" factor in order to re-establish the relativity of the natural balance of relationships.

The current "Oppressive" nature of the relationships is detrimental to growth since it is against the natural laws that exist in the universe. The oppression of leadership that takes away the **worked for gains** of the people in terms of property, dignity, justice and a sense of recognition and distributing these communal benefits to himself or herself and the small band of "loyal supporters" is the cause of hatred and contempt for leadership itself. The fact is that in the time of need it will be the community and the people, in their abundant natural capital, that will be of use to the leader than the few loyal supporters who will be running for the hills to save themselves. The nature of the Leadership of Relationships in the above case also indicates that relationships that are not ethical but bought by power and money do not sustain under the force of adversity resulting in isolating the leader from the real source of power of the relationship i.e. the community and the people who are the ultimate stakeholders.

At the same instant if a leader is fair and just in the awards of both risk and reward linked to performance of the individual domain experts he or she will create a foundation for sustainable growth even in times of chaos using the entropy of the loyalty of relationships in their incremental predispositions. The predisposition of the masses will be towards the leaders till they break the bond of trust. The predisposition of the few, gained through nepotism or bought by greed is to hoard power for themselves even to the extent that it may harm the leadership or the community. Also if the leader has the support of the community and the domain experts, the few will not dare to harm the leader fearing the retaliation of the masses.

In this era of instant gratification it is similarly true that it is possible for the leaders to lose the leadership of relationships even when doing perceived "good". If the community and the domain experts do not see some gain or growth but are all waiting for some future reward then disenchantment sets in against the leader. Thus it is important that as evo-devo leaders you ensure even a modest distribution of reward to the masses or provide ways of taking less from the people in order to assuage the feelings of the community and to keep the relationship strong. It is key that the leaders communicate the causes and remedies of adversity to the constituents at all times and especially during adversity. There is no such commodity as "Less" communication. The abundance of communication between the constituents of the relationship will always lead to the abundance of the Natural Capital of the Leadership of Relationships. The "feed- back loop" has be strong so that the leaders can understand the situation on the ground floor. The need for a leader to be in constant touch with the community is necessitated from the fact that the sustenance of the people comes from the leaders and the survival of the leader comes from the community who own the Natural Capital.

The communication loop, as a foundation of the relationships, emanates from the cyclic nature of the **Faith-Belief-Value-Feelings-Thought-Action-Results-Ethics-Relationship** paradigm. The belief and value System of the leader is the basis for the right feelings, resultant thoughts, subsequent correct actions, and planned results. The ethics are reinforced with the results and the right relationships are created that will benefit the community and the leader. In the absence of the communication loop in relationships, actions without thought of the community will result in negative feelings and subsequent destruction of the relationships with associated loss of Natural Capital. Also the impact is not limited to the immediate relationships but has a cascading, $R = -N + (n-1)$, effect which implies that the destruction of free energy will be widespread.

The double edged sword of advanced communication and super information highways currently makes it easier to build relationships with sources of Natural capital and the community but at the same time the disadvantage is that the community has multiple avenues of information that may create ambiguity. It is crucial that the leader has the relationships based on faith, trust and facts with the sources of information and the community so that the words of the leader are accepted over other sources. This will also ensure that, over time, the value system being inculcated is in line with leaders' core values and vision. In the diagram below you will observe that the deep relationships connect right down from the perception to the schema while the shallow relationships end up at the perception level alone in the Thought-Action Cycle.

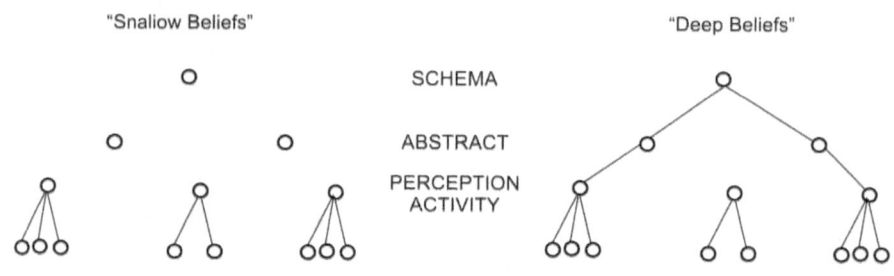

THE THOUGHT - ACTION CYCLE (Fig. 28)

The Leadership of Relationships is also dependent on the nature and culture of the leader as demonstrated by his or her "WAY OF LIFE." The action of the leaders cannot be diverse from the words or the communication. This puts an onus on the leaders to practice and demonstrate a "Way of Life" that they want the community to reciprocate. The integration of a beneficial "Way of Life" will result in the Leadership of Relationship as well as the evo-devo of the leaders themselves. As an example let us look at the universally pure relationship between the Earth and the Sun. Tie Earth gives back the same amount of energy that it receives from the Sun. The only difference is that the energy from the Sun is communicated in a much higher frequency with lower entropy to the Earth. The Earth uses this lower entropy (due to the lesser number of photons in the light from the Sun) to create photosynthesis in plants which in turn lowers the plants entropy at the same time the community eats the plants or the animals who eat the plants thus lowering their entropy and using the oxygen released by the plants to create energy. The energy is used to create all that we see today and have a relationship with. This energy is transformed to heat which in turn is reflected back to the sky with much higher entropy that is then used to create the gravitational plug that formed the Sun. The Leadership of Relationships also envisages similar beneficial exchange of energy between the "STAR" leaders and the community.

Let us take another example that would explain the current global financial and economic crisis and the results of unethical relationships. The Roman Empire rose about 2000 year ago. Its demise can be attributed to a crisis of confidence in the leaders within their relationships. The Roman Empire started with the right idea that immediately created empathy of relationships between the leaders and the masses. The strength of the masses is what gave the Roman leadership the impetus for acquisition which transformed the weak and vulnerable Roman leaders to become the Caesars. The ongoing acquisitions and their assimilation into the Roman belief system enhanced the relationship of the Romans as they created new laws and communal wealth for these new constituents which were fairer then the ones already in place. At the same time the original constituents of the Roman empire i.e. the masses received the rewards of the growth of the empire. The problems started in the 3rd and 4th centuries when the leadership became corrupt and unethical by continuing to expand by acquiring new territories without a real need other than satiating their own ego and sense of power. The new territories did not have the required relationship of faith and trust with the Roman Emperors as the process of assimilation was ignored by the leaders in Rome and in certain cases seconded to the corrupt leaders locally.

The Leadership of Laws was now changed to a Leadership of Force which was not only unjust but also believed in hoarding benefits for the leaders to the detriment of the community. These corrupt leaders now became the "Agents of Power" on behalf of the Caesars. These agents of power had a relationship of convenience with the original constituent's i.e. the Romans and slowly started shifting the balance of power in their favor to commence building their personal empires.   The chaos created by this unmanaged growth started to impact the masses in Rome and they started to suffer due to the excesses of the agents of power and a weak Caesar. This chink in the armor of relationship between the Caesar and his constituents was further aggravated as the Roman leadership used force and oppression to control the original constituents which created the "Implosion Effect" that wrought havoc in a long, slow and violent end to the Roman Empire. As expected the Agents of power did not help the Caesar in any way. The worst was not over, the prolonged demise of the empire and its fall due to lack of faith and trust of the community created a crisis of confidence that pushed the whole world into the 'Dark Ages" from nearly 450 AD to 900 Ad: an era of extreme fear, poverty and loss for the vulnerable.

The "Way of Life' of the Roman Leadership was one of the main causes for the fall of the empire and the "Dark Ages" but it did not just effect the immediate community or the leaders alone, the Law of Relationships R= N + (n-1) was triggered and the entire evolutionary development of mankind was pushed back. The parallels to today's economic Imperialism are astounding: overstretched forces, domestic greed, declining values, foreign enemies, lack of leadership faith, no protection for the weak, and a continuous push for unsustainable growth through force with a complete lack of conscience.

Adrian Goldsworthy, .the famous historian, said" That empires are no more immune from human stupidity than anything else". Size is no guarantee against failure. In fact when leadership with absolute powers errs, the result of their errors of judgment grows exponentially. We can only hope that the mistakes of today i.e. self-interest, self-Aggrandization, success only measured in cash or dollars based on a strategy of "infinite debt and unchecked market forces pushing unethical consumption will not end up in a slow, long and violent death of economic Imperialism, founded on the basis of economic apartheid, to push as into another 500 years of a new Dark Age.

What then is this WAY OF LIFE that can lead to the evo-devo of the Leadership of Relationships? The Answer: A leadership that avoids oppression and discrimination in relationships and fosters bonds that thrive in adversity. Let us study one of the purest, long standing relationships of man with a higher Power. This relationship has stood the test of time especially when faced with adversity for leaders and community alike. The SIKH ("Sikhi" is a continuous process of learning) community founded by Guru Nanak Dev (1469-1567) is based on the principles of following a "way of Life" that leads to relationships and free energy for growth of self and the community. G4r4 Nanak was a great leader, philosopher and thinker. He based the Sikh "Way of Life' on the principles of the removal of discrimination as followed by the Hindu caste system and the oppression of the Muslims perpetrated by the Mughal rulers.

The idea: a free, casteless society living in peace and harmony without the Laws of Force to attain a good quality of life. The communication of these ideas (through The GURU GRANTH SAHIB- The Living Guru) was simple, relevant and straight forward. The three tenants of the "Way of Life" that inspires constant transformation were- Kirit Karo, Nam Japo and Vand Chako- Honest Effort, Effort including Worship without expectation, and a policy of First share then partake.

The ideas of Guru Nanak, in terms of the community, are propagated through the aegis of: a) "SAT-SANG", a congregation or formation of relationships with like-minded people with a similar way of life, b) "LANGAR" or Shared Kitchen which is open to all without any discrimination, and c) The concept of a single higher power or creator (SatKartar) who is universally present in everyone. In all this Guru Nanak Dev has, in the words of writer Kushwant Singh, created "the ideal that gave birth to Punjabi Consciousness and to Punjabi Nationalism." The community has survived and prospered over the last 500 years and in-spite of being decimated multiple times (at one time only 30,000 Sikhs were left to live in the jungles) by the likes of the Mughals, Hindu kings and other invaders, has come back each time to become stronger and flourish after each "Implosion". Today it has over 80 Million Punjabis; a vibrant growing and learning community.

The Leadership of Relationships whether as a spouse, parent, president, prime minister, pastor, pope, teacher, scientist or king is about "connecting the dots". Only when you, as the evo-devo leader, can connect the dots in the right sequence will you be able to see the holistic scenario. In order to connect the dots or at times even being able to see some of the links you need understanding, enduring patience, facts, truth, knowledge and faith. The power unleashed through connecting the dots correctly to form enduring positive relationships is immense. The paradox is that this process is occurring at both ends i.e. the leader and the community simultaneously. The communities the family, the wife, the children, the nation, the congregation, the student or the business associates are forming their own holistic picture of you while you are trying to form one of them. This process also occurs both at the conscious and subconscious level. Our belief systems, biases and values are all being utilized in this process. It is therefore necessary that we not seek for reason in a specific pattern or scattered arrangements of traits or objects instead look for a deeper universal order in way the people behave and manage their relationships.

The traits that will form the enduring relationships between a leader and the community or "sphere of influence" is relevance to each other. This relevance is a key factor for connecting the dots in an attempt to visualize the whole picture and is again based on sustainability rather than an immediate gratification of unethical wants. For example if we form an alliance based on the notion that a relationship with a larger company or nation will be beneficial to you based on size alone then it is not a relevant relationship. The larger company or nation in times of adversity will sacrifice the smaller entity to gain power since it may consider that relationship to be irrelevant.

You may also have heard of the 7 second rule that dictates that we judge people and relationships in the first 7 seconds of our exposure to them (e.g. the myth of LOVE at First sight). The 7 second response is not a precise measure of the relevance of a relationship since it is built on preconceived biases and values that may not be appropriate. The next step to the 7 second rule is to get facts that may or may not make the relationship relevant and at the same time connect the dots to understand the nature of the relationship that is being built. If done rightly this, process of connecting the dots to attain relevance will create a strong relationship that will stand firm during adversity and will lead to evolutionary growth for both the leader and the community.

The power of relevance, connecting the dots and relationships can be observed in the famous equation $E=mc^2$. This one equation changed the world. The power of this relationship only occurred when the dots were connected that Mass and Energy were really the same and were directly connected at the speed of Light Square. The connection that created the relevancy of the Laws of conservation of Mass and Energy thus released tremendous power from small amounts of matter that could fuel explosive growth sustainably. Herein lies the explosive power of the Leadership of Relationships that is based on facts, trust, and relevance. These relationships can transform the nature and culture of mankind through the Leadership of Faith as we will see in the next chapter.

"MEMORY IS THE GAURDIAN OFALL THINGS" Cicero

CHAPTER 11

THE EVO-DEVO OF THE LEADERSHIP OF FAITH

"Ehyeh aster eyeh" this puzzling phrase commonly translated as "I am so I am" or "I am that I am" is also translated in the Greek language as "I am being". The essence of this saying in the evo-devo of the Leadership of Faith is: **"We are so I am."** This transformation that puts the community first is essential to the dialogue that will lead to the Leadership of Faith which describes leaders as one who can take the "I" of self and through faith create a "We" of the community through trust. The community then becomes the embodiment of the leader and the leader becomes the presentation of the community. The goal of leadership is to serve the community by unleashing the potential of the community through faith in the leader for creating the competitive advantage for the community. It is also paramount that the leaders inspire the same Leadership Core Values in other leaders in the relationship to create the power of fusion and in turn evolutionary growth.

As you are aware FUSION is the source of tremendous free energy as is faith that fuses the leader and the community. Faith and fusion need to work hand in hand to create an environment of low resistance to growth and a high degree of flexibility to change. The Age of Fusion where the leader is the servant of the community and the community has the faith in the leader to serve them is the fundamental solution to lead the chaos of adversity to explosive growth and reducing the negative effects of the "internal Back Flux" that deters positive change. The circles of energy, as we fuse together relationships between communities based on faith can then create an engine that will generate enhanced communal wealth and act as a source of Natural Capital.

At this point it is important to differentiate between the easily confused natures of Faith and Religion. We are discussing Faith not Religion. As leaders you understand the ambiguity of the statement "Facts are True but the Truth can be fluid."

The above statement is the fundamental difference between Faith and Religion. Faith has to be based on facts hence has to be true while Religion is based on the Truth as perceived and communicated therefore it is fluid. The reason: Faith mired in the process wherein Religion is a combination of rituals. The ritualistic nature of religion provides a "promise' of relationship between Man and God without following the "way of life" as required by the faith in the relationship. Religion has been used by leaders to bolster loyalty to them through the rituals to avoid change and preserve the identity of the community against allied influences. Some of the most abhorrent leaders regularly fulfilled their ritualistic duties. Faith on the other hand is entrenched in the concept that the Leader looks after the well -being of the community and its stakeholders as the small "g" with the assistance of faith in the BIG G or higher power without the need for any rituals among the "beings".

The Leadership of Faith as a store of free energy through entropy, in this Age of Fusion, is meant to be a relevant relationship between the community and the leader built on interdependence that fuses the two into a universal whole. This whole then needs to fuse with other such communities to form "trading" relationships that are mutually beneficial. This process enhances the positive effect of the faith itself to transform into Trust. This trust will ultimately lead to the evolution of a new belief system of ethical values that will transform the leadership and communities simultaneously.

Religion is based on the fact that there is no interdependence between Man and God. God does not need Man while man an can achieve "Godly" status by following the rituals and fulfill his need for a GOD. Religion also makes the promise of "the meek shall inherit the earth" without creating the necessary circumstances that allow the meek to attain the luxury of trust while the strong and aggressive are using Religion as a lever to dominate them.

The evo-devo of the Leadership of Faith is necessary in order to inculcate the trait of a **Leader of Laws rather than a Leader of Force**. A leader of Laws will own its resources and Natural Capital through the aegis of trust. A leader of laws will need to be all merciful, faithful, humane, honest and patient while a leader of force could be Religious without having any of the other required characteristics. A leader of laws will enhance faith and trust instead a leader of force will use power to enforce unethical laws for his own benefit thus losing the trust of the community. The leader of laws will work transparently while a leader of force will work covertly and apparently. The leader of laws will use force to protect its constituents from oppression and discrimination while the leader of force will use laws to oppress and discriminate.

The defining lines are clear but the "catch 22" is in the execution of the strategy. In order to become a leader of laws and acquire the characteristics of mercy, faith, honesty, humanity and trust a weak or new leader may be tempted to act against these qualities to get a quick start or unsustainable growth. The Leadership of Faith thus necessities that the leaders not succumb to this temptation because this initial unethical approach will mar the foundation of trust required for SUCCESS. The solution is that in the times of adversity leadership should fall back on the Natural Capital of faith and trust of the community and use this interdependence to gain strength of knowledge and process to achieve SUCCESS. This interdependence will assist the leaders to survive the temptation of moving away from the trust of the community to the slippery slope of unlawful behavior that encourages unworked for gain and greed.

The fixation of this trait that encourages faith and trust through sharing and interdependence in leadership values will slowly start replacing the "greed' gene thus innovating an evolutionary change in the constituents of the Leadership of Faith. This process of permeation will reach maturity as it spreads beyond the immediate sphere of Influence to other Leaders and communities resulting in a global "ripple effect' that in turn will provide further benefits to the innovators. The circle of faith-belief-values-ethics-trust working in harmony is one that has contributed to evolutionary growth in the past and will continue to do so in the present and the future. The foundations of faith lie in the three processes of learning:

1) Faith through Others

2) Faith through Ourselves

3) Faith through neither Others nor Ourselves.

The first two processes are good in the sense that these are based on observation, facts and experience. The third process is bad since it is based solely on perception. As leaders of today meander through the cycle of "FAITH BUILDERS" i.e. parents, teachers, peers, media and portals, the influence of the adage "Perception is Reality" is reinforced at all points. The faith in the system is built on the shaky foundation of a perception of facts rather than actual facts. This would not have occurred if the "Faith Builders" had followed a "way of Life" that would teach the facts based on tested and proven experiences or from their own findings.

Another example that reflects on the major impediment to the evo-devo of Leadership of Faith based on perceptions rather than facts leads to a value system that selects hoarding over sharing for growth and scarcity over abundance. A recent spatial survey of various school going children within the ages of 6-10 years was taken using the photographs of various leaders. These included pictures of Abraham Lincoln, Albert Einstein, Gandhi, Mandela, Bill Gates, George Bush, Barack Obama, Jesus Christ and Ronald McDonald. The result was a higher than 98% recall of the McDonald mascot (Ronald McDonald) and a less than 40% recall of the other leaders. The question: How do you create a Leadership of Faith that rests on the shoulders of Ronald McDonald which represents a lifestyle that if followed in excess would lead to obesity and ill health?? This is not to vilify the McDonald brand. The same principle is applicable to the ads promoting smoking in the 60's in the USA and now in the Asian countries or extensive cell phone usage being hyped today. The answer: The "way of life" that teaches children to drive safely while we as parents drive over the speed limit when we can get away with it, are all reasons for the belief system that selects a Ronald McDonald over a Jesus Christ in terms of a leadership role. We have to adopt a new way of life

In another survey of graduate MBA's from leading management schools on the issue of the Top 5 management skills required for a CEO saw the propensity of capabilities that were focused on Competence, Self-Reliance, Effort, Innovation and Execution skills. Honesty, ethics, loyalty, sharing, relationships, faith and trust did not even make the grade in the top 20.

In a world where some of the Global Multinational Corporations have revenues higher than the GNP of 96% of the world's nations, the CEO's of such corporation are in fact more powerful than the ,leaders of most nations. These huge corporations are therefore replacing trading relationships that existed on a nation-nation basis with a new corporate-nation equation. Wal-Mart is the 4th largest trading partner of China far ahead of other leading nations. The political equation is being shifted to CEO's who will be governed by their key motivators and their belief in controlling technology and resources in order to create wealth for themselves. Also since these leaders are not elected representatives of the people they are not governed by the accepted political ethics of morality.

The domino effect of the mortgage and economic crisis that has spread globally due to the unethical practices of U.S. based financial institutions has lead to unemployment in Europe, China and India. The collapse of the economies of Greece and Spain and the fall of the global stock markets with the huge loss of associated wealth is prime examples of the type of impact corporate leaders have on nations today. The effect of this global financial crisis cannot be attributed to a world war or global pandemic of disease as in the past but is the cause and effect epidemic of leadership founded in greed.

`The relationship of nations and corporations demands that corporate leadership needs to have the same trust and faith of the people as do governments when dealing with the issues of morality such as honesty, loyalty, risk, reward, ethics and benefit sharing in an equitable manner. These new "Kings" of the world need to learn about mercy, faith, humanity, religions, honest effort, process of communal wealth and a leadership based on the evo-devo of faith and facts. In all they need to accept that they carry a Universal Service Obligation as well.

These "Corporate Nations" have to gain the knowledge and process on handling the balance of power that can affect the lives of the common man both domestically and globally due to their actions. In effect the corporate nations and the trading nations have to develop a "Consciousness' based on Truth, Symmetry and Morality, for all the constituents to lead a collective consciousness of being just as a measure of real SUCCESS.

Let us question this concept of "reality" of SUCCESS without any bias about "consciousness" or a discussion of unachievable states of utopia or "justice for all". The **First Truth** is to attain a state that creates an evo-devo leadership that is mired in the reality of a "Leader Positivist" A leader positivist is one who puts forth the appropriate questions to the system to create the reality as desired for the SUCCESS of the community by having answers that are in line with observational facts. Curiosity is an essential trait as a foundation for the leader positivist, A reality that is greatly removed from your classical picture as taught to you should not force you to give up on the new reality. The Leadership of Faith demands that reality is to be viewed as a ubiquitous phenomenon based on Entanglement.

The **Second Truth** the Leader Positivist has to understand is the paradox of independence under the chaos of entanglement and relativity; As the independence of the system grows so does its entropy of entanglement. Within this entanglement lies the key to sustainable growth. The entanglement includes also the three consciousnesses of the Physical, Emotional and Faith World that are intertwined with the reality of SUCCESS.

The **Third Truth** is the fact that each of these worlds, though separate, work together in an entangled and relative state. Each of these has their observable elements that are apparent to the Leader Positivist as the ultimate observer These observations will create the leadership consciousness and the real world for the leader and the community. The entangled nature of the real world and its associated free energy will provide the Leader Positivist with a broad spectrum of tools to powerful and rapidly change the physical, Emotional and Faith Entities to create attainment of the desired results in terms of real SUCEESS.

A leader positivist who achieves the evo-devo of a collective consciousness is able to attain the Leadership of Faith. This leadership is underlined by the entangled nature of the leader with the community. The Leader Positivist does not have to hold a position of power to gain faith. He does not need to be a King, CEO, President or Prophet to become a leader positivist. He does need to be humane, patiently enduring, and merciful.

A simple example of a simple man is that of Bhai Puran Singh of India. He was awarded the highest honor of the country, "The Padma Shree", as well as the International "Harmony Award" in 1990. Puran Singh, was born in Amritsar, India, in 1904. His Profession- Helping the needy, the ill, the injured, the homeless, the handicapped, the lepers and the other members of the human species whom society had rejected. His Legacy - Free Hospitals, Free

Outdoor Medical facilities, Free education and Homeless Shelters. His Personal Assets - Two sets of clothes, one pair of shoes, a turban and a shoulder bag. The shoulder bag contained the items of personal hygiene and small pebbles or stones. These stones and pebbles were picked up by Puran Singh from the road so that these would not injure or hurt somebody. His motivation -- "I promised my dying mother that I will help the poor and the downtrodden all my life." A true Leader Positivist.

The Three Consciousness's as demonstrated above and in the next illustration are defined as below:

THE PHYSICAL ENTITY: This is the physical reality that is created as a consequence of the observance of the Laws of Nature and our physical universe.

THE EMOTIONAL ENTITY: This is the combination of the beliefs, values and your current patterns of focus including physiology. The Emotional Entity is also the basis of your emotional well-being. The Human Species has over 3000 words to describe our various emotional states but as leaders you experience less than 1% of these in our practice. The 1% (14-30 words) used are mostly in the negative domain of the Emotional Entity.

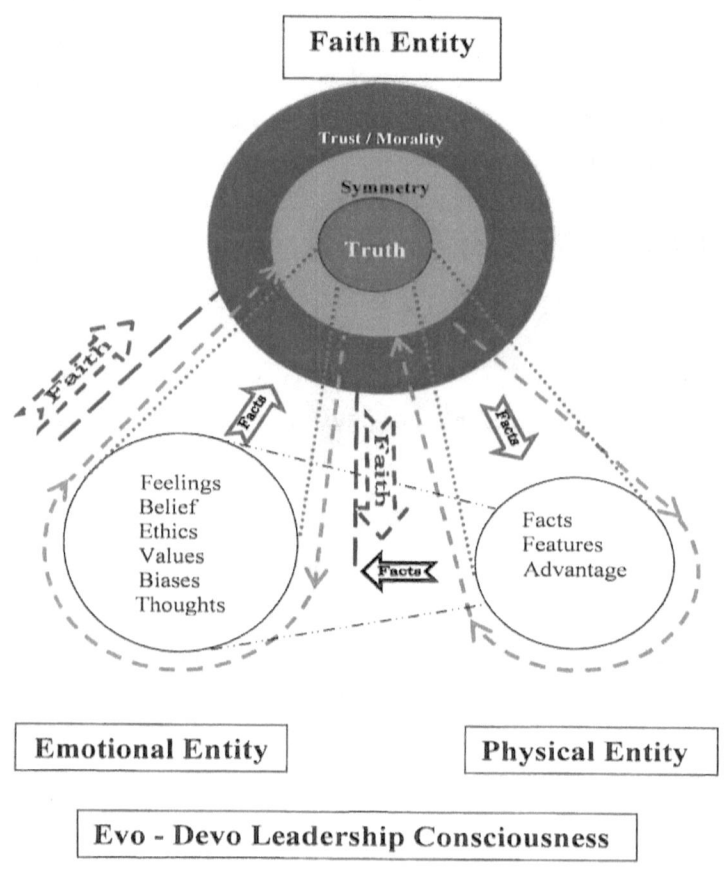

(Fig 29)

THE FAITH ENTITY: This entity is a combination of the Truth, Symmetry and Trust/ Morality domains of the leader The eternal Truths, the Symmetry of Beauty and Chaos, as well as the Trust of Moral Hope all join together to create the entity of Faith. The very nature of this entity is designed to act on both the Physical and the Emotional entities in multiple different ways. The dimensions of Faith i.e. the Truth and Symmetry are entangled and act on the Emotional and Physical entities. The Symmetry dimension is even more entangled into the Beauty and Miracle areas as it brings about the beauty of both the emotions and the sensual nature of the consciousness. Thus resulting in what we sometimes call the miracles of Leadership.

The faith dimension of trust and its entanglement with morality works on the emotional entity alone to create the Moral Consciousness of desired behavior i.e. mercy, sharing, wisdom, motivation and loyalty with the community and promotes the concept of real SUCCESS through just decisions for the Leader Positivist. The beauty of this entanglement is also the facts that these entities are "real things" at the same time are dynamic and variable depending on the Leadership of Faith to create the appropriate reality.

The Three Entities and their constant entanglement while trying to retain independence is the ambiguity that exists in the leadership domain and can be effectively and productively harnessed by the power of ethical, moral and just behavior. The definition of justice in the paradigm of evo-devo behavior is one that will promote strong relationships between Nations and Corporations in Trading, Nations and Nations vis-a-vis Culture, Weak and Strong through respect, Wealth and Communal Wealth through ethical consumption, Aggression and Oppression for the elimination of discrimination and finally between Intellect and Wisdom to create sustainable growth. The justice has to be based on certain global laws and has to execute ethically to develop the local potential in line with the global needs and wants of humanity.

The current focus of leadership that exudes an appearance of a justice system based on global laws but in effect utilize it as a tool to implement a Leadership of Force is in direct contradiction to the Natural laws. The problem with appearances is similar to the issue with perceptions since both are based on non-truths and hence easily refutable when arbitrated thus lowering the faith and trust value. The signs are all in front of you as when you see a leadership recall of Homer Simpson higher than Bill Gates; Media belief systems built around "Bad News Sells"; 9% of a civilized nation's population is in prisons or under probation; unemployment in a "wealthy" country is over 10-12% on a capacity gap basis and 25-30% on a capability gap; 33% of the global population is living below the poverty line; justice is only a word based on the perception of lawyers and a lose-lose paradigm; aggression and war are mired in strategies like MAD (Mutually Assured Destruction) and WMD's (Weapons of Mass Destruction) and economic policies of MAI, IMF, OECD etc. are pacts between powerful nations to exploit the weaker "partners"; and one species can impact the "well-being" of 65 million other species on the planet moving some towards extinction; the realization hits that our perception of justice is a failure because the above facts present a picture that is not in line with the desired consciousness.

The first good news is that you are now aware of the consequences of the absence of justice and the associated chaos. The second piece of good news is that you are also aware that Justice has to be linked to conscience morality and faith otherwise it will sans a conscience. The third good news is that some of the best nation states and corporate consciences have developed from some unconstitutional and immoral beginnings only with sole purpose of acquiring power and are willing to transform.

The problem is that once power is acquired the motivation to change is diminished so the morality required to build an equitable justice system is lowered in value. The examples are also in front of us if we study the Roman Empire, The British Empire and the Spanish Empires wherein acquisition of power for the sake of power leads to lower moral values and a lack of leadership faith. At the same time the fear of loss increases thus leading to the collapse of the empirical structures under chaos. The fact is that the absence of justice in the actions of leadership triggers the Laws of Nature and Natural Justice. The entangled nature of the Physical, Emotional and Faith entities are then invoked in their infallible nature to invoke order.

In this phenomenon of nature also lies the solution to the enigma of the Leadership of Faith. If the reality of the leader and his community can reflect the values of the Laws of Natural Justice without corruption, you can create harmony and growth perpetually within the variables of chaos. The Key being that the morality of justice has to be mired in the trust of the community through the execution by the leader. The evo-devo leader can use this opportunity to build a global reputation of faith by instituting new Wise Laws and creating an atmosphere of Moral Hope. Such a reputation will be a tremendous source of Natural Capital for the evo-devo STARS. The STARS have to base this reputation on the constant practice of just behavior not just an outward conformance to justice for the sake of appearances.

In this new paradigm of entanglement the evo-devo STARS, will need to be all merciful, all religious, all faithful, and all honest. This nature of leadership will ensure that it provides the modest complement of resources that each individual in the community needs to develop the potential. The Formula for representing the above paradigm will be as below:

INDUCTION   + ANALOGY   + HYPOTHESES = WISE LAWS   +MORAL HOPE= Leadership of Faith.

INDUCTION is the study of events and the ratios of entanglement to evolve the Physical Entity and the derivative principle for probable success.

ANALOGY is the probability of similar causes leading to similar effects as in the Emotional Entity.

HYPOTHESES are the symbol of the Faith Entity as it eliminates all causes that can be excluded to lead up to the true cause and effect.

Induction, Analogy and Hypotheses are all founded upon facts and grounded in truth which are connected in a "perpetual" loop of modification and rectification in line with new observations in accordance with Natural Laws while being tempered by the fires of experience and learning to arrive at the epitome of the Leadership of Faith through Trust. **The point to be noted here is that there is a tendency of Natural forces to impose order on even the most chaotic system as soon as Wise laws and Moral Hope vanish.** The guarantee of evo-devo leadership of Faith is that it will continuously endeavor to provide Moral Hope within the parameters of Wise Laws.

This wisdom of leadership mandates that in spite of all the prejudices and the associated fears of Loss, as are mired in your belief system as well as the physical and emotional entities, even when reason dictates otherwise, you continue to perform repetitive acts of faith. This faith and the Natural Laws related to it will ensure sustainable growth even under the "Implosion Effect" of adversity. The competitive advantage of collaboration that is innovated as part of this process is elaborated In our next mile stone of the Leadership of Global Interdependence.

"Truly it is a very Natural and Ordinary thing to desire to acquire."

Machiavelli- The Prince

CHAPTER 12

THE EVO-DEVO of LEADERSHIP of GLOBAL INTERDEPENDENCE

It is an unwritten fact that Young Nations are passionate; Middle Aged Nations are full of pride while the Old Nations are prejudiced. This Three P's of nations apply similarly to leadership as well and are closely linked to the concept of Interdependence. Globalization is not a new phenomenon. Trading has been and will continue to be an avid source of evolutionary transformation. Trading evolved from a predominantly Individual pursuit between artisans and consumers in the olden days to the Imperialism of controlled trade of today to the economic advantage of large conglomerates in the near future. The trend though is that it will naturally evolve to the exchange of services between local areas of specialization based on economies of scale with the collaborative processes of competitive advantage between the experts and the global consumers irrespective of geography.

Essentially, the above strategies all represent the common goal of "interdependence" through the Integration of abundant Natural Capital that exists across all domains. This invisible "STRING" of Interdependence that connects the innovation and expertise of individuals or a community with the expectations of other individuals and communities is in essence the Leadership of Global Interdependence. The overwhelming reason that leadership in this key area of human civilization is necessitated is the widely distributed nature of Natural Capital and the rapid demand for it across the globe but the customization, of these demands has to be personalized and fulfilled locally. The entire process is prone to unethical behavior hence the current prosperity for controls and structures that are restrictive not progressive. Recent progressive advances in supply-chain processes i.e. JIT, Kan-Ban and the evo-devo Just in Case, which promote the concept of Just in Time linkage of supply/demand and individual customization as well as alternative sources, if required in an emergency, have been made possible due to the global growth of technology, communication and logistic infrastructures. The problem associated with this connectivity and globalization is that the linkage of POS (points of Sale) and POP (Points of Purchase) for global consumption in real time based on the interdependence "STRING" has also resulted in the real time distribution of failure alongside benefits.

Let us look at some examples to understand the powerful force of global interdependence and its entanglement with ethical behavior.

-The "WE 32" virus took **7 hours** to bring down global networks and created a complete data blockage across all information highways.

-The "swine flu" virus took **7 weeks** to move from Mexico to Australia and mutated nearly 70 times in this process of jumping the animal-human barrier. The normal process of the "flu" virus vaccination production used to be an annual process. This allowed the last years vaccine be available to the last country in the cycle and the next years mutation be vaccinated for the first country to the opposite end of the globe. This entire process is now disrupted as the "flu" virus completed its cycle in 7 months instead of 12 months as expected.

- The greatest coordinated growth and subsequent decline of the world's economy only took **7 years** i.e. 2001-2008 to complete its cycle. This virus started after the"dot.com" bust in 1999-2000. The 2001 start of the boom was initiated by the US Federal Reserve which increased the that total credit available in the market at a growth rate that   was nearly 5 times the GDP between 2001-2007. This credit limit was increased by not only lowering the interest rates but also by increasing the money supply. The increased consumption of money was backed by debt linked to the housing and mortgage markets. This resulted in the boom in the USA as well as pumped nearly $ 10 Trillion in liquidity across the globe. The effect of this boom of unethical consumption was felt globally across the supply chain. The supplier nations triggered their own local boom by pushing capital spending in infrastructure such as plant and equipment from the USA to meet this "virtual" demand. The resultant pressure of this boom was felt on resources such as oil, energy, transportation, real estate, wages, etc. which created a surge in prices of these commodities. The global demand for goods and services and its associated expansion of the production cycle between 2001-2007 turned out to be the most extensive coordinated boom in the economic growth curve of all times. The increased credit and liquidity also pushed the US trade and budget deficit from 2% of GDP in 1999 to 7% of GDP in 2006.The rising "virtual credit" linked to the virtual "asset values" connected to the virtual "demand" leveraged the financial markets in the area of commercial and consumer lending.

Nearly 80% of this leverage was against the US mortgage backed securities. When the real estate market collapsed in 2006/2007 the world's most devastating and extensive decline started and spread across the globe in real time. The Financial crisis in the USA created a economic crisis worldwide as consumption came to a halt and unemployment jumped thus resulting in a crisis of confidence between the leadership and the community. The greed virus reached full circle in 2008 and since then has destroyed over 15 trillion dollars in "communal wealth". Every child born in the new world will carry the burden of this loss.

These are some examples of the entangled aspects of the Leadership of Global Interdependence and the "String Theory" of globalization that can now rapidly impact us harmfully and beneficially depending on the leadership.

In an attempt to establish some ground rules in this crucial area of leadership evo-devo let's try and understand the constituents and the characteristics of interdependence. For instance what constitutes an American Company? If a company is headquartered in America but 2/3rd of its revenue and costs come outside of America is that the definition of an American Company? If we have a Chinese or an Indian company that generates 80% of its revenue in the USA and Europe is it an Indian or a Chinese company? If a product or service is built with an overseas content of close to 100% but is designed and branded in the U.S.A is it an American product? If one country's economy is leveraged to the extent of nearly 75-80% with another country's growth and policies then is that country a free and democratic nation? If a nation's entire financial structure and GDP is leveraged 98% with a global fund i.e. IMF or other financial institutions can we call it a sovereign entity? If a traditional U.S. company destroys over 100,000 jobs and over $1trillion in equity capital while a "foreign company creates 50,000 jobs and builds nearly $300 Billion in U.S. financial capital which company is more beneficial for the local economy?

The answer is simple that there are really no traditional barriers to any entity in this current scenario of global interdependence other than self-imposed political barriers. If you, as leaders, can accept this fundamental principle of the Leadership of Global Interdependence we can now start analyzing the real substance behind this entanglement and the knowledge and process required to succeed in this dynamic world with an abundance of Natural Capital.

The paradigm of Global Interdependence is directly related to the effectiveness of the leadership and the community. In reality the effectiveness value of an entity is the measure of its Global Interdependence. The duality of independence and interdependence co-existing ethically is the transformation of short-term success to long-term sustainable growth. This paradox is further highlighted due to the nature of leadership that can only see itself in an independent state without seeing the entangled nature of the whole.

The need to understand the cohesive nature of the leader and the community with other leaders and their spheres of Influence is the key to conservation of Natural capital and explosive growth. The example below created by Schrödinger, a great leader and a physicist, clarifies the above paradox of independence and interdependence that exists both in the physical and emotional worlds (Light for example exists interdependently as a particle and also behaves interpedently as a wave!!!)

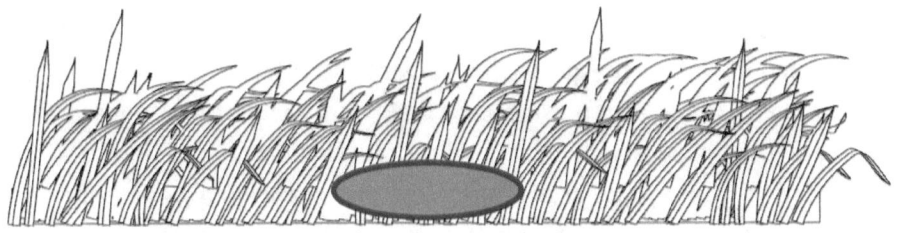

ROCK AND THE SEAWEED - REALITY (FIG. 30)

In the above diagram if we begin by throwing our rock, the one that created all the ripples of energy earlier, into a pond then the rock will start impacting the immediate ecosystem by becoming a stable area for life within the ecosystem. At the same time the weeds will start to grow around it and entangle with it. The rock and the weeds are now an interdependent system but our nature of leadership will see the rock as independent from the weeds. If we remove only the rock from the ecosystem, it will collapse and destroy the seaweeds around it and visa-versa. In its collaborative nature both the rock and the seaweed are beneficial to each other and will be able to create a sustainable environment for growth effectively.

In the preceding diagram, that depicts the Maturity of Interdependence Effectiveness, you see the correlation between leadership growth and productivity as you move up the value chain. The maturity that occurs as you move from a dependent to globally interdependent results in the transformation from being a learner to becoming a collaborator. This evolution is the true essence of SUCCESS and the Leadership of Global Interdependence.

In Analyzing the internals of this powerful effectiveness tool called Global Interdependence we observe the following: The two pillars of Global Interdependence from the perspective of maturity, its efficiency, and its effectiveness are "SOURCING" and "SHOREING".

SOURCING: The pillar of Global Interdependence known as sourcing is a comprehensive mapping of all the processes within the leadership domain for the purpose of analyzing their operational, economic, and quality efficiencies. The key is to remember that "NO PROCESS IS SACROSANT or IMPERVIOUS to change." The role of mapping within the maturity matrix of interdependence is essential to identify the gaps as well as the redundant or broken processes. The idea of Sourcing has to be applied to all these mapped processes to reduce the waste and gain effectiveness. The mapping tool should also model the entanglements within the processes so that the effectiveness value of each process is enhanced. At the same time the global value of the cohesive whole is increased as duplicate or repetitive processes are replaced or abandoned. The question to in source or outsource the process to gain global efficiencies and effectiveness has now to be transformed to the evo-devo principle of "RIGHT" source.

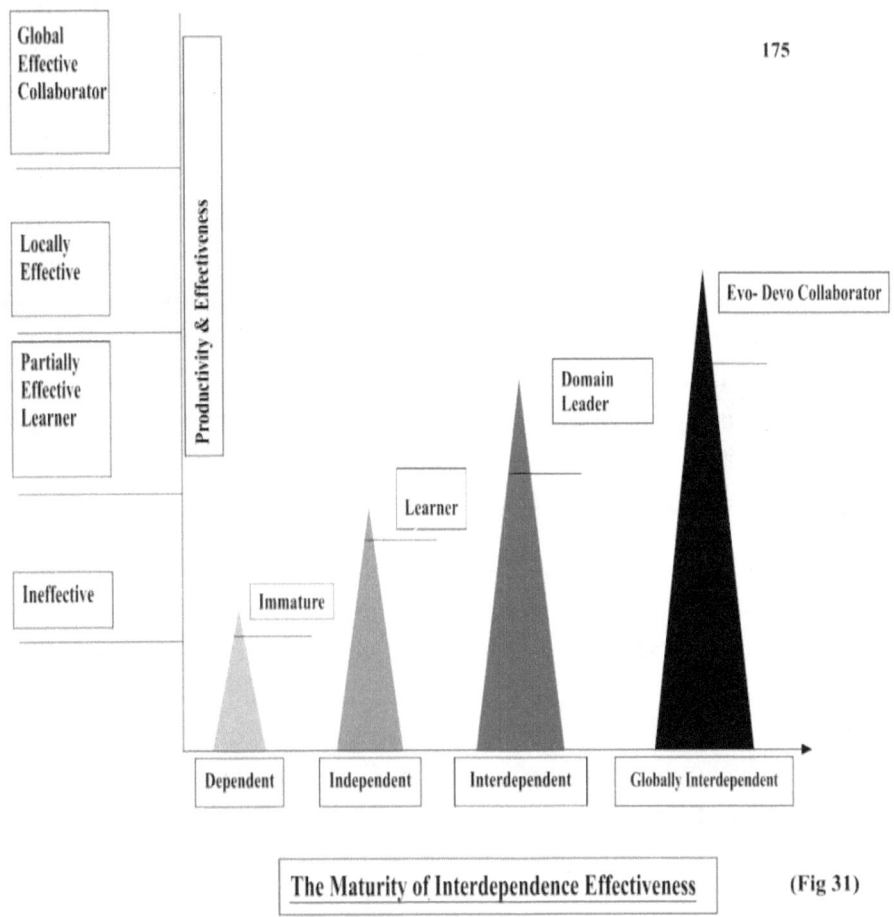

The Maturity of Interdependence Effectiveness   (Fig 31)

"RIGHT" Sourcing based on domain expertise is the first step of interdependent collaboration. The collaborations could be partially owned, acquired or shared in their nature. The above relationships allow the leaders to attain adequate leverage to mitigate risk. It also allows leaders to integrate "best practices" across the enterprise. The Y2K process is one such example. The transformation of the software and databases to incorporate the Year 2000 standard revealed hundreds and in some cases thousands of entrenched and hidden processes that were being used without any mapping. The good companies used the Y2K opportunity to reduce the waste that had accumulated in the years. The great companies used this opportunity to create global effectiveness by reducing waste while implementing best practices based on the domain expertise of Sourcing and "Shoreing".

SHOREING: The next step is to match the sourcing with a strategy of shoreing. The "Right" source without the "Right" shore is ineffective. The selection of the "RIGHT SHORE" is an extremely important decision and includes domain knowledge and vision matching of similar values between the shorer and the shoree. The sources could be onshore, near shore or offshore but the key is that the integration of the sources with the shore has to enhance capacity, capability and vision of both the parties. The "centers of excellence" and domain expertise that will be created will become huge reservoirs of Natural Capital. At this point it would be appropriate to warn the leaders that SHOREING should never be an attempt to transfer waste without reducing it. The idea of sourcing and shoreing is not to pass the buck to another company or a different shore. The key to successful sourcing and shoreing is to "FIX IT before YOU SOURCE IT or SHORE IT."

In the Global Interdependence paradigm this mistake is the biggest cause of failure. In this regard technology can be a major boon. The processes can be mapped and any waste or inefficiencies can be eliminated initially by removing the Technology Gaps. You, as leaders, can automate manual processes or even convert automated processes to manual by unbundling them. Once the task of mapping, automating, and unbundling has been accomplished and the process is "fixed" only then do you attempt to shore it. The gain is multiplied manifold if you follow these steps rigorously across the entire system. The unbundling phenomenon may seem surprising in this atmosphere of Technology but certain processes e.g. CRM can be more beneficial when de-automated. It is also true that other manual processes are candidates for technology to increase productivity and effectiveness. In both these pillars of Interdependence i.e. Sourcing and Shoreing you have to be vigilant that new avenues of waste and duplication do not creep in as a part of this strategy. One of the crucial areas is the training and Domain Knowledge efficiencies amongst the parties. The cost of training and retraining as well as transferring Domain Knowledge can become prohibitive if not mapped correctly at inception. The need to map the cultural divides as part of the management process and the diverse value systems is another cause of angst and failure if not planned properly. The idea is to not become complacent but constantly continue to map the effectiveness and efficiency of the processes.

The two processes that are crucial to the health of any enterprise relative to SOURCING and SHOREING are the SUPPLY SIDE and the DEMAND GROWTH. The Supply side processes can be benefited from the Global Interdependence leadership in five key areas:

a) FIND

b) OBTAIN

c) CREATE or MANUFACTURE

d) STORE

e) FULFILL or DISTRIBUTE

The common factor in sourcing and shoreing all the above is that the benefits are similar. The supply side sourcing and shoreing should automatically generate the competitive advantages of LOWER RISK, LOWER COST, HIGH VALUE and RAPID RETURN ON INVESTMENT. We will elaborate on these advantages as we progress into the Leadership of Economics, but it is mandatory to mention these benefits so that the effectiveness and efficiencies of the enterprise with regards to sourcing and shoreing can be monitored and measured consistently.

Once the supply side mapping is completed it is very useful to complete the next step by aligning the Demand Growth with the supply source or shore. The advantage of the integration of the "RIGHT SOURCE" and the "RIGHT SHORE" with the Demand Growth will unleash a huge source of energy for ongoing sustainable growth for all the participants in the maturity index.

The supply side and demand growth are entangled in the evo-devo process. The Demand Growth linkage with the Supply source or shore will result in an explosion of demand in unexplored, new, emerging and traditional markets. **This interdependent nature of the supply side and demandside economics can be better understood if you view the supply chain as a "SOURCING OF COST and the Demand as a "SOURCING of REVENUE".** In effect the "cost" of one entity becomes the revenue of the other in a sourcing relationship. The domain experts get revenue by improving the supply chain processes. The other party that is using the domain experts gets a foothold in the market through their relationship with the source. The law of Global Interdependence in its evo-devo avatar now comes into play and states that "THE SUM OF THE PARTS WILL BECOME GREATER THAN THE WHOLE." This interplay between the supply and demand sourcing and shoreing is one of the fastest ways to enhance communal wealth and achieve sustainable growth.

Though imperfect, we can still see multiple examples of this phenomenon and its associated competitive advantage in diverse industries such as manufacturing, financial services, Business Process Outsource (BPO), Legacy Modernization, Object Oriented Technology, Architecture and Design as well as Legal services. The principle is common the "centers of excellence" are using the existing costs of the enterprise or community to create effectiveness by lowering cost and risk. At the same time these center of excellences also become ethical consumers of the processes that are migrated i.e. the entangled nature of the "ROCK and THE SEA-WEED" working together independently in an interdependent nature.

The word imperfect is necessary since the current level of maturity in this area of evo-devo is lacking in trust and collaboration. The key causes of failure today are:

a) The tendency to create a fixed class of workers or a hierarchy of inequalities and

b) The practice Intellectual Capital Hoarding.

These two causes have the effect of classifying certain processes as "untouchable" and certain resources as "un-source-able" not because they are not available elsewhere but because you, as leaders have decided that these processes are too important to be given the advantage of domain expertise; that these resources have to be in house even if they create waste- a violation of the evo-devo principles of Interdependence.

In the nature of Interdependence if you bar one segment of the entangled structure i.e. the Rock or the Seaweed, to a lower hierarchy of domain you create an inequality in the process of integration based on class not on expertise. This results in developing a class of specialization that is limited in its growth thus becoming un-sustainable in the future.

The evo-devo of Interdependence desires that you share knowledge and process across the domains irrespective of shore or source with the objective of fostering innovation. That strategy will help in creating multiple self-sustaining "knowledge domains". The cumulative effect of these "knowledge domains" will be a self-replicating and seamless link between supply and demand as the purchasing power of the knowledge domains increases. This enhanced purchasing power in each knowledge domain will become a source of ethical consumption of the goods and services or "SERDUCTS" that they are producing.

This multiplier effect of the Leadership of Global Interdependence is demonstrated as below:

Let us assume that you have a Chinese or an Indian company providing the Right Source and Right Shore services for you at $4 per hour. This may be an advantage of lower cost to the tune of 40-50%. You have the power to continue this relationship without any change till it loses its cost arbitrage advantage. On the other hand as part of the evo-devo process you share knowledge to increase the capabilities of the domain experts to provide a higher level of service at $5 (a 25% increase in rate) an hour, the effect will be two-fold:

a) Your cost savings will be substantially higher (70-75%) since you are now sourcing an advanced process that costs you much more originally. Also you are lowering your risk since you have an alternative source of supply for an advanced "in demand" service.

b) The 25% increase in wages for the domain expert is a huge jump. This new revenue will automatically be used to buy goods and services from your markets creating a new global source of revenue.

On the macro-level the interplay of the evo-devo of global interdependence is clear that it is a source of abundant demand while helping create efficiencies in the process itself. The multiplier effect of this paradigm is apparent when you match the global resources such as telecommunication, transportation, knowledge share and logistics with both labor arbitrage and process arbitrage to create "Best Practice Knowledge Domains." The exponentially enhanced yet diverse skills focused on innovation and performance of the domains will create rewards that will be distributed on excellence rather than class. This focus of developing performance excellence instead of a "class of service" is the evo-devo needed today.

The collaborative nature of the interdependence scenario is marred by the unfair practices of a special class of developed nations on the lower class of developing or less developed nations. These policies can be attributed to the common ailment of "INTELLECTUAL CAPITAL HOARDING". The unfair nature of this exchange is implemented using unethical tools as below:

a) Intellectual Capital is withheld from sharing through Technology Ownership and "need to know" biases even amongst interdependent entities.

b) The unethical use of a single branded currency that the emerging markets require to purchase, acquire or upgrade technology and intellectual capital.

These two factors have resulted in the practice of Intellectual Capital Hoarding which becomes a major barrier to global interdependence. The barrier of "economic apartheid" has resulted in the current trade imbalances. The lack of acceptable branded foreign currency i.e. Dollars and the extensive learning curve of technology is forcing the developing or underdeveloped nations to buy profitable finished Hi-Tech and capital goods from the developed nations while providing the raw material resources to them at a cheap cost. The policy of economic apartheid has created distinct classes of trading i.e. the low margin commodity class and the high margin finished goods class. The problem is that these classes are not based on any type of specialization or domain expertise but are created out of the scarcity of resources and investment capital. The actual fact that these classifications have no correlation to performance is another major issue.

The policy of economic apartheid is based on the simple principle of hoarding technology and branded currency to create artificial scarcity in an attempt to control the competition. This strategy has resulted in an erosion of faith and trust. The evo-devo benefits of global interdependence have been negated resulting in the "Blue Collar" vs. "White Collar" and "First World" vs. "Third World" type of nomenclature. The enforcement of these unfair global practices are currently imposed through Trade agreements, Laws of force and Intellectual Property Rights that are not based on innovation but more on aggression. This aggression is furthered by the advanced weapon systems or "attack" strategies of the developed nations, if opposed. These self-imposed technology barriers result in the loss of Natural Capital through hoarding, exploitation and oppression.

This exploitation and the associated superiority complex of the developed nations results in another form of loss of Natural Capital for the less developed nations, known as "Brain Drain". The natural instinct of the domain experts of third world nations to gain knowledge forces them to immigrate to the developed countries. This pushes the less developed nations further into the hole as not only does it lower their Natural Capital of human resource but economically as well. The Third World countries spend a large portion of their resources in education to develop these domain experts but end up losing them to the developed countries in their quest for knowledge. In effect the third world ends up subsiding the education expenses of the developed countries through "brain drain" and also suffers the additional loss of the benefits of the most productive years of their resources. The negative effects of this "Brain Drain" are not limited to economics alone but are cultural as well. The resources face cultural disorientation which becomes a barrier for social assimilation leaving them without roots.

The current state of globalization is therefore comprised of "economic classes" segregated by their status as Third, Second or First worlds with the added confusion of ethnic profiling, brain drain, sweat shops, technology barriers, terrorism, discrimination, and oppression. These unfair practices are not limited to the developed nations alone. The lesser developed nations, in an attempt to gain an edge, have created their own unethical practices for globalization. These include dumping goods, local exploitation of resources to lower costs, corruption, Intellectual Capital Rights infringements and violations to create a level playing field. The problem cannot be generalized by using these classifications but has to be objectively identified as one of leadership. A leadership that is unwilling to trade selfish short-term gains for the long-term strategy of sustainable global success through sharing the communal wealth is the cause of this malady.

In the evo-devo Leadership of Global Interdependence the solution is very simple. At the macro-level the solution revolves around the ideation of "centers of excellence" linked to domain expertise and performance. In order to achieve this balanced approach of promoting global "Best Practices" you will need to create self-sustaining processes that are lead by the sharing of intellectual capital across the entire gamut of domain experts to promote innovation. At the micro-level trust, faith and wisdom have to be evolved to counter the perceived "loss of control". These falsified perceptions of globalization can be dissipated using the two evo-devo principles listed below:

a) Intellectual Capital Retention

b) "Sunk Cost" recovery

a) The strategy of Intellectual Capital Retention increases trust, faith and wisdom by providing the existing domain experts to retain the seeds of the knowledge and process that they are transferring. As the process of knowledge transfer occurs from the local founders or champions to the "centers of excellence" or challengers, the basic tenets of the business logic is retained with the founders. This acts as a tool for disaster recovery if the challengers fail to deliver the pre-agreed benefits. Also even if the challengers are successful the founders can continue to monitor and control the quality of service (QoS) of the "centers of excellence". In effect these points of Intellectual Capital Retention become the key drivers of lower risk in the whole process of Intellectual Capital transference and interdependence.

b) The second strategy of "Sunk Cost" recovery is a huge saver of economic investments. This process allows the retention and enhancement of business logic alongside the development of new processes without duplicating resources. The "sunk cost" recovery principle allows you, the leaders, to utilize the benefit of the "entropy" stored in the existing technology to generate free energy for growth by the reduction of waste. The process of "sunk cost" transference takes place when the existing "knowledge domains" transfer the processes to the "Right Source". At this point they can jump the technology gaps by investing in the current best practices including the capital infrastructure. The "Right Source" and the "Right Shore" migration to lower cost areas allows the source to enhance its technology and infrastructure since the low cost areas have limited investments in the latest technologies.

The new "centers of excellence" therefore pay for the up-gradation of the entire process and the existing domain experts don't lose the "sunk cost" investment and still receive the benefits of better technology, knowledge and processes. The fact is that the enhancement of technology in the lower human resource cost areas will allow the "double benefit" of labor arbitrage and process improvement simultaneously. The existing infrastructure that is available to the domain experts becomes a "disaster recover" site in the event of a failure. This process increases the Digital iQ and Technical Civilization of both the parties. **(This principle is further expounded in the next book: "The evo-devo Guide to Failing Successfully"- Expected date of release 15th December 2013).**

The above cycle of transference and retention of sunk cost and Intellectual Capital can be repeated cyclically as the "Right Source" evolves with time. The Digital iQ and Technical Civilization keeps increasing thus creating an ongoing process of improvement.

The advantages of these two evo-devo principles of globalization ensure that synergy is created whenever Natural Capital is spent. As an example, if you look back to the 16th/17th centuries the two largest trading nations were India and China. The "silk route" and the "spice route" were the two destinations of choice for Europe. As these nations traded with the western world the consumers took advantage of new technology and better processes to migrate these businesses to Europe. The Western nations continued to improve and innovate through technology to retain their competitive advantage over the last 175 years. The 20th and the 21st century are seeing the resurgence of India and China as they use the benefits of both the labor arbitrage and technology up-gradation to recover their lost competitive advantage. There is no reason for alarm in the western world as the cycle will repeats itself. If this ethical nature of exchange is treated with trust, faith and wisdom it will result in the Leadership of Global Interdependence which will conserve Natural Capital, create abundance of demand and new sources of supply with innovation.

The evo-devo required is in the area of leadership that is willing to share intellectual capital linked to the benefits of best practices to enhance the Digital iQ and increase Technical Civilization of the community. The rewards should also be shared equitably through the aegis of a "global trading currency" that is available to all equally.

The combination of a global exchange currency in line with performance and growth linked to a pool of intellectual capital supported by individual domain experts; the entanglement of independence and interdependence through the process of following the available "best practices" while evolving new ones through the diverse "centers of excellence"; is the solution to the Leadership of Global Interdependence.

In Vienna, a thin green line of a beam of entangled photons pierces the night skies in a "free space" quantum experiment. Since the photons are entangled they do not have any individual states, but each photon has its own energy value and function. The fact though is that when energy measurements are made on one of the photons in an entangled pair, the information of the other is instantaneously known. This experiment proves the working of the quantum level interdependence and functioning of individual particles over long distances. This phenomenon has tremendous advantages for future usage in areas of telecommunication, energy and medicine.

In terms of our quest this experiment is a prime example of the Leadership of Global Interdependence wherein the Individual domain experts connected are an entangled medium of technology and trust with the consumers to deliver global benefits. The concept of SUCCESS without Conflict is the next port of evo-devo of leadership as we learn to avoid conflict at the same time be prepared for it as a source of battling unethical practices that destroy communal wealth.

"IDEAS ARE CONNECTED IN CIRCUITOUS WAYS, AND YOU NEVER KNOW

WHEN A DISCOVERYIN ONE AREA WILL SHED LIGHT ON ANOTHER-" STEVEN

PINKER-"The Stuff of Thought"

CHAPTER 13

THE LEADERSHIP OF CONFLICT and AGGRESSION

Conflict, is an extreme form of communication. When backed by Aggression it transforms into a symbiotic relationship between fear and anger. Conflict due to its inherent nature is a "net user" of energy. In its virulent form i.e. combined with aggression it can easily trigger the "Implosion effect" by acting as a catalyst as it magnifies the existing inefficiencies within the system resulting in the collapse of the system itself. In the same vein, as leaders you are aware, that conflict is inevitable hence managing, planning and leading it are crucial to the evo-devo of leadership and essential for the long-term growth and success of the community. The Leadership of Conflict can result in creating both strong and ethical relationships that will become sources of Natural Capital in the future.

"PEACE and LOVE"- The slogan of the 400,000 music lovers who streamed over the huge span of Bethel, NY on the rainy weekend of Aug 15, 1969 (incidentally 15th August,1947 is also the Independence day of India) was a response to the conflict of Ideology that existed at that time. Even the symbol as below:

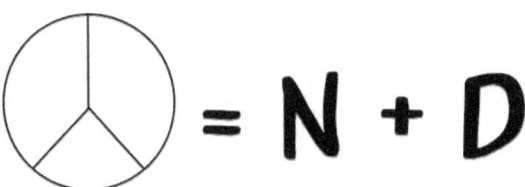

"PEACE" (FIG. 32)

Which represented the idea of "Peace" is a combination of the letters N and D i.e. Nuclear Disarmament. The nature of that response and its leadership built a society that commands the world in the form of the so called "baby boomers". This generation of leaders has created more communal wealth globally than any other community in history.

September 11, 2001, NY World Trade Center, was another conflict of ideology that was mired in the wrong response. If you were one of the billions who watched this disaster on television or the millions who were trapped in the chaos in NY, you realized the nature of the symbiosis between FEAR and ANGER. The response to that fear and anger was the hell of "SHOCK and AWE" that not only destroyed nations, cultures and faith it also resulted in the near economic destruction of global financial markets creating the "depression" of 2008-2012 just 40 years after the "PEACE and LOVE" phenomenon.

John Steinbeck, in his famous novel the "Grapes of Wrath" said- "Whenever there is a fight so hungry people can eat, I'll be there. Whenever there is a cop beating up a guy, I'll be there. I'll be in the way of guys yelling when they're mad. I'll be in the way when kid's laugh when they're hungry and they know suppers not ready, and when the people are eating the stuff they raise and living in the houses they build- I'll be there too". The constructive anger of this piece of literature enumerates some of the areas of conflict that exist in this age and there are many more that can be added to this list such as- bio-diversity, pollution, global warming terrorism etc. All these conflicts are looking for a resolution that can only be provided by the "right" response from the Leadership of Conflict that not only provides a solution to these issues but uses them to create a holistic, environment of faith and trust.

In an attempt to understand the nature of the correct response and to prevent an overreaction that will intensify the problems we need to analyze the process that creates this symbiosis between fear and anger. The concept of SYNERGY, even under the chaos of conflict and aggression, to retain the evo-devo leadership paradigm of SUCCESS is the only "Right Response" to the issues facing us today. The response that can turn the nature of conflict as a net user of energy into a net generator of energy through the aegis of SYNERGY is represented in the thought processes shown in the next diagram:

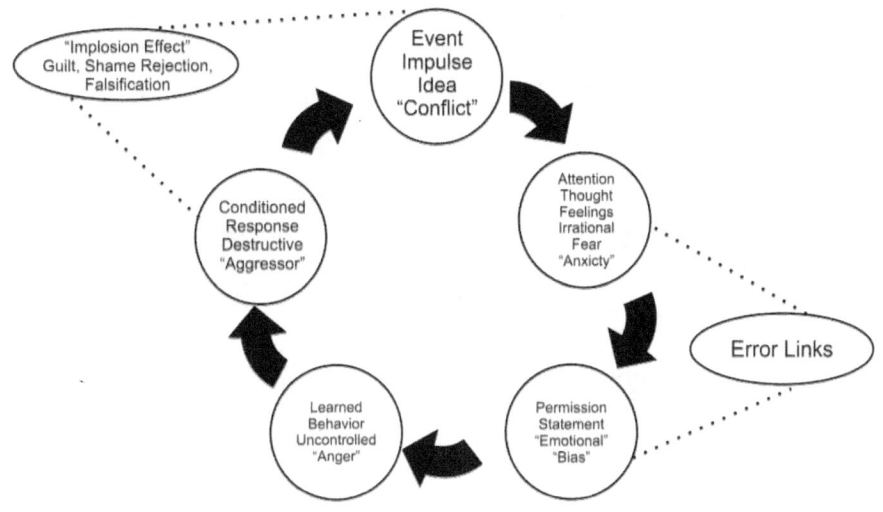

THE EVENT-RESPONSE CYCLE of CONFLICT AND AGGRESSION (FIG 33)

The cycle of an event to its response is one that can be applied to all levels of leadership behavior whether in business, family, community, war, or politics. The event triggers various different thought processes including fear, uncertainty, and doubt and discombobulating. We seek justification or acceptance of these thoughts based on our "feelings" that form the basis of our emotional biases which in turn depends on our belief system. As we delve deeper into this thought-feeling-belief-value phenomenon we will realize the in most cases our thoughts are based on the faith of the "whatever worked before" syndrome. These learned or acquired behavioral traits include fear, aggression and revenge that further the conflict by enhancing its nature and scope. This also includes guilt, shame, loss, regrets and ongoing justification of these thoughts and subsequent actions predicted on these thoughts.

The conditioned or learned behaviors are founded upon the "Error links" between fear and anger which result in the aggression response that is irrational in nature. Fear and Anger are key emotions and are used both for constructive and destructive purposes. The conflict though arises from the "emotional" bias that is embedded in our belief system that has been developed over time based on experience or "peer to peer" learning cycles. The stronger our emotional bias the higher our propensity for sameness and our rejection of differences in ideology. This current global aggression epidemic of sameness is the root cause of most conflict and aggression that we see around us because the laws of nature seek diversity not sameness. The only option to end this cycle to create synergy or unity in diversity is to move away from the "emotional" bias to a "factual" bias in order to arrive at the "Right" response.

The transformation from emotions to facts is based on the process of factual response of the 7 A's that encourage planned behavior:

1) Acquire all the facts

2) Assess all the acquired facts

3) Analyze the assessed facts.

4) Assimilate the analyzed facts into the event response cycle.

5) Articulate the assimilated facts and look for synergy.

6) Arbitrate to handle objections, indifference and conditioned behavior.

7) Accept the final solution after arbitration and implement effectively.

The above process will result in a fact based permission statement that will result in synergistic "planned" behavior based on prepared responses. **In the evo-devo of the Leadership of Conflict the "Right" response is the prepared response that has taken into accounts all the facts and the competitive advantages of the response for all the constituents of the community.** It is the primary objective of evo-devo leaders to prepare and plan responses for the protection and well-being of the community and to guard against the loss of Natural Capital and communal wealth under various contingencies of adversity. The Leadership of Conflict requires the leaders to be both a visionary and a connector of synergistic behavior. As the evo-devo leaders gain the faith and trust of the community as a guardian of their "communal wealth" further synergy will automatically be established to foster the effectiveness of the "Right" response. The transformed process based on the above learned behavior through an evolved belief system will now be repressed as under:

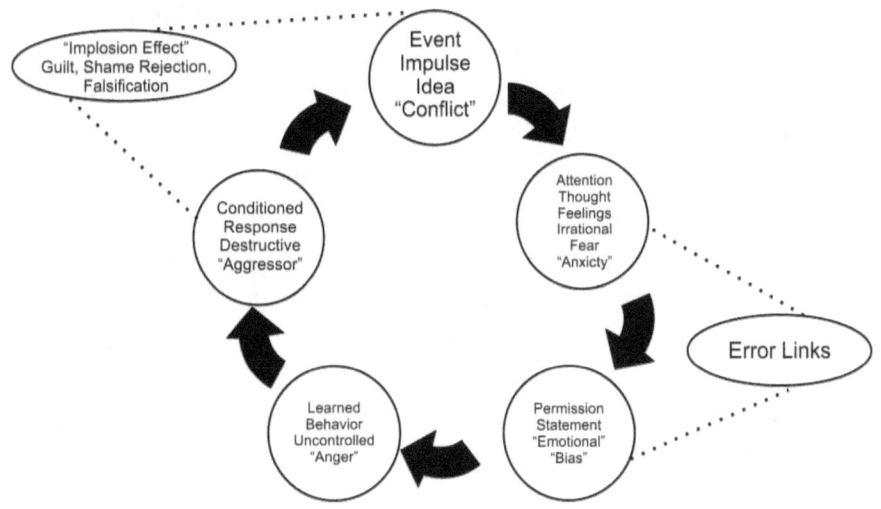

THE EVENT-RESPONSE CYCLE of CONFLICT AND AGGRESSION (FIG 34)

The key difference in this new event-response cycle is the elimination of the "error links" that lead to irrational aggression and conflict. These error links are now replaced by the synergy links that reduce conflict and increase communication. The point at which the conflict is resolved and synergy and communication are established is the point of inflexion in the Leadership of Conflict as it will result in the formation of new relationships that are formed under adversity and hence will stand the test of time and chaos. The strength of these relationships that create synergy from conflict will be a source of Natural Capital for all the constituents.

The global conflicts of today are caused by the constant emphasis of leaders on the communication and behavior that **"objectifies the subjective and generalizes the specific"**. The reactionary process that is based on the subjective nature of the conflict rather the objective nature of the problem results in the dilemma of ongoing crisis management. As soon as the leaders emphasize synergistic behavior by focusing on the paradigm that "Objectify the specific and generalizes the subjective" we will immediately move away from crisis management to planned leadership that will eliminate the root causes of conflict i.e. economic inequality, cultural misunderstanding, resource and consumption apartheid and replace these destroyers of SUCCESS with the energy of diversity.

Diversity is a huge store of free energy that can be utilized for the sustainable growth of the community since it enhances synergy and the "resilience" of the constituents to withstand conflict. The conflict that arises out of the creation of the barriers to diversity is mired in the Leadership of Force that uses its policies of scarcity and apartheid to get the sameness of culture, strength, resource and consumption. This uniformity that developed nations impose on the rest of the world is the ultimate cause of conflict today. The fallout of this strategy is not merely an assault on the economic, aesthetic and ethical values of society but is resulting in the destruction of the diverse knowledge base required for cultivating the process of sustainable growth. The destruction of the Natural Capital of diversity through conflict is lowering the selection advantage of the entire human species which needs a large gene-pool to survive and evolve.

The United Nations Food and Agricultural Organization warned that most of the global food supply had dwindled down to just a dozen crops and only 14 animal species. According to the FAO three-quarters of the world's food crop varieties have disappeared in the 20th century. This conflict of differences based on just an emotional bias without the necessary accompaniment of a factual and synergistic approach has resulted in a severe compromise of the global food supply due to a lack of diversity. The same phenomenon can be observed across other area of physical resource and social behaviors.

As an example let us look at another key indicator of the lack of leadership of conflict and the "knee-jerk" responses that demonstrate the vicious loop of "Fear-Anger" linked to an emotional bias. This example deals with the area of crime and fraud in global society today. In the USA alone the spend on corrections in 2008 was over $50 Billion. Nearly 25% of all households are touched by crime. The real cost of this conflict is borne by the private sector which is currently spending over a Trillion dollars on recoveries and securitization on this area of the failure of leadership. The government is focused on the "knee-jerk" response linked to the emotions of retribution and control while the private sector is focused on minimizing their risk and expense of crime. Neither the government nor the private sector is concerned about the prevention of crime and the factual biases that define the nature of crime and fraud as well as the erosion of ethical values that support it.

The judicial system is focused on the uniformity of sentencing and incarceration without understanding that 66% of the prison population returns back to prison in less than 3 years. The flip side is that society is becoming desensitized to crime as the government projects a sense of false control through prolonged incarcerations and the insurance companies pay the individual loss. For example we have become so used to the crime of auto theft to view it only as an inconvenience since the risk of loss is passed on to the insurance companies. In this abyss of conflict the auto-theft problem continues to fester and grow.

The "Right Response" in this area of chaos would be one that should lower the number of car thefts and its growing economic loss to society. Synergistically, it should also create economic value from the productivity of the human resources that are currently involved in the perpetration of this unlawful activity. The evo-devo solution therefore would be to reduce or eliminate the demand for stolen cars. This can be achieved by using technology like QR codes and penalty on the buyers of these vehicles. The current insane alternative that warrants the incarceration of a large segment of the population that steals these cars for their livelihood is economically and socially inefficient. The community spends more than the value of the car in "corrections" and the insurance company still pays out the value of the car to the insured. The social effect of this conflict is the loss of the economic value of the incarcerated felon in terms of his communal wealth as well.

The evo-devo solution appears simple so why cannot we implement it?. The answer goes back to the basic fact that our unethical values that promote greed and unworked for gain override the synergy of the "Right Response." The insurance companies increase the premiums to recover their costs; the government gets revenue from sales tax of new cars i.e. 2 million cars at an average cost of $ 5,000 per car is $10 Billion in sales and the sales tax @6% would amount to $600 Million; and the car dealers make a huge margin on these stolen cars. Similar examples of this sort of behavior can apply to stolen laptops, cell phones and other electronic equipment that can easily be tagged or QR coded for identification. The area of crime and fraud is a prime example of a sector that can attain synergy through the Leadership of Conflict.

The interconnected nature of laws, justice, human psychology and technology are the factors that we need to consider when evaluating the advantage of synergy to achieve the goal of the Leadership of Conflict. Conflict exists on several levels. Evolution is a conflict. Competitive advantage is a conflict. Politics, Business, Arts, Science and Technology have all become arenas of conflict not synergy.

The only solution to conflict and aggression for the attainment of Leadership goals is via the road of synergy. Synergy comes through planned strategies and tactics. Strategy comes from the Greek word meaning Generalship or "strategika". The leader creates the strategy. The tactics evolve from the efficient and effective employment of the resources that are available to the leader or "ta-taktika". The Greeks may have been instrumental in the evolution of these words but leaders across the globe have and will continue to use strategies and tactics to win. When faced with conflict that is inherently evil the fundamental steps of a successfully strategy for the Leadership of Conflict are listed as below:

a) **Identify your enemy to the lowest common denominator**: Get all the facts about your opponent: Moral, emotional and physical; motivations, drivers and wants. Do not believe perceptions and theories but collect real hard facts. Perceptions may have been deliberately created to mislead others. Your enemies strengths and weaknesses need to be known in their naked state without any hidden secrets.

b) **Measure your enemy's actions**: Judge your opponent through his deeds not his acts. Do not judge their strategy from their words or the words of others. The deeds of your enemies will guide you in the tactics you need to employ against them. These planned maneuvers that defuse the expected actions of your enemy can win wars without even fighting the battle. It is also important to understand that your opponent is also taking his measure of your strengths and weaknesses. Therefore, it is of paramount importance that you understand yourself and your past actions so that you can confuse the opponent.

c) **Isolate your enemy**: The art of utilizing communications, alliances and rationality to bind the hands of your enemies is an excellent strategy to win.

This process is highly effective when dealing with an opponent who may be stronger than you in terms of assets. In order to isolate the enemy you can use wisdom, morality and ethics to prevent him from gaining the advantage of his size. By isolating the opponent and guiding him into your comfort zone to deal with you at your terms rather than his will get you the desired results.

d) **Destroy your enemy but transfer his alliances**: When faced with conflict that is unavoidable always be a true enemy. A true enemy can never be a friend. Eliminate him from your sphere of influence. Do not leave an empty space or a backdoor for his return into your domain. At the same time transfer the alliances of your opponent to yourself. This will serve two purposes; One, it will make you stronger and Two, it will ensure that your opponent remains weak. The alliances that you acquire should be those that were important to your enemy.

e) **Own your Strategy and Tactics**: You should become a champion of strategy and tactics through practice. Innovate your own plans, tools and methods that are best suited to your resources. Strategy is a way of life for the evo—devo leader and is mandatory for the Leadership of Conflict. It cannot be borrowed or loaned it has to be your own. At the same time be a true friend and gain the moral high ground with your actions. This is the most effective deterrent to conflict and aggression against you.

You, as leaders, have to be responsible for the community and yourself in conflict with destructive forces. It is also desirable to understand that conflict is not all evil. Conflict is required for a species to evolve as adversity is an essential part of diversity. Natural conflict has resulted in major changes for society in terms of evolutionary growth and the attainment of the balance between chaos and order. The primary issue is the unethical nature of man-made conflicts which occur for the wrong reason and hence create illogical outcomes due to their unethically biased nature. The negative energy of man-made conflict and wars are a major source of loss of Natural capital since the fundamental differences are not ethical but mired in the cause and effect of gaining power for oppression and discrimination.

The question for the evo-devo Leadership of conflict is apparent-"HOW DO WE ATTAIN LEADERSHIP of CONFLICT AGAINST NEGATIVE FORCES THAT NEED THE SYNERGISTIC RESPONSE OF WAR?

If we understand the advantage of conflict and wage war against negative forces that destroy Natural Capital i.e. poverty, crime, oppression, discrimination, pollution, etc. and tackle these issues on a global "war footing" we can attain the synergistic values of aggression and positive anger without the fear of loss.

Most developed countries today are spending nearly 6-8% of their GDP on defense. This nomenclature of a defense Budget is in reality more appropriately defined as an attack budget. This budget is higher than the overall annual GDP growth of the countries. In its negative effect these attack costs are creating a deficit in the Natural capital of "communal wealth" across the world. The justification is presented as a necessity to protect the community but is actually a representation of the irrational fear and anger of a leadership that protects its populace through war. The wars of today are trying to eliminate "differences" without any moral hope of synergy. The effect of these wars is to lower the diversity and relationship values of all the participants.

Inspite of this gloom-doom scenario there is a tremendous amount of entropy and free energy locked up in this area of man-made conflict and aggression. The transformation required is to implement the Leadership of Conflict to create synergy by destruction of the causes that necessitate the man-made conflicts at the same time getting rid of the effect negative forces have on the Natural Capital of the community. The key advantage is that both these facets of the Leadership of Conflict are the same. The unused energy locked up in the defense or attack systems in terms of technology alone could be a solution for prevention of crime, fraud, medical disasters, ecological calamities and even negative human relationships. The negative energy entrenched in the Leadership of Force can be unleashed by accepting diversity and creating synergy through the aegis of Ethical Communication and sharing of Natural Capital. The managed "Implosion Effect" on the elimination of differences while resolving the global issues facing the community will immediately result in the explosive growth of both cultural and economic diversity. The result will be felt in a substantial enhancement of communal wealth as the resources locked up in the man-made conflicts are released to fight the natural conflicts that exist thus creating a synergistic beneficial effect on the global community.

At the same instance the Leadership of Force will be utilized against certain elements of society that will not communicate ethically or share for the communal benefit. It is necessary to be prepared for these sources of "internal Back Flux" and conflict who will be a threat to the overall evo-devo of the Leadership of Conflict. The advantage here is that the response of the Leadership of Force against these elements will be of a preventive nature and a well-planned strategy the will negate in any irrational response based on fear and anger. The controlled Leadership of Force and Positive Aggression against the negative forces will result in enhancing faith and trust amongst all the constituents and further the cause of ethical communication and synergy.

In an attempt to explain the advantages of ethical communication and its direct link to synergy and growth we should study the AND-BUT paradigm as below:

As you observed the current focus of leadership to spend huge amounts of Natural Capital in the area of defense or more appropriately attack strategies is akin to building huge fortresses and castles in the past that may look good but have no value if the leadership that resides in these fortresses is unethical and hated by the community. The idea of a leadership that is founded on the faith and trust of the people is synergistic in nature and provides tremendous energy for sustainable growth by eliminating conflict by using ethical communication rather than force. Herein lies the secret of the AND-BUT paradigm and its synergy.

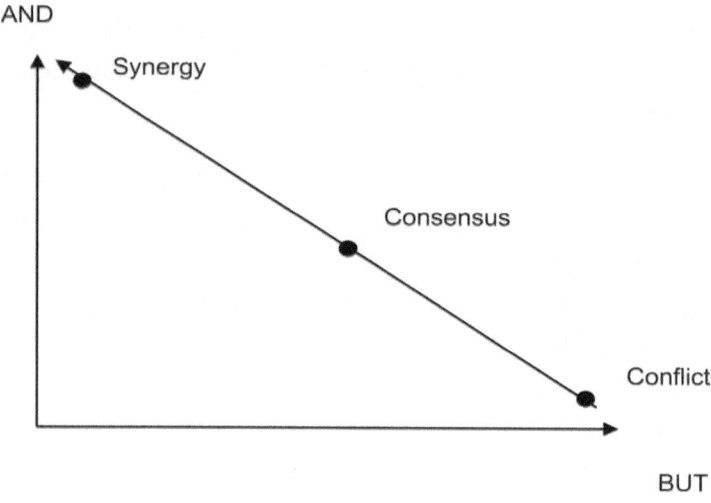

THE AND and BUT SYNERGY (Fig.35)

Ecology is the science that connects organisms and their interrelationships with the environment. AND and BUT are both strong members of the human ecological system. Culture on the other hand is the communication of beliefs, knowledge, process and wisdom that transforms the nature of human ecology. AND and BUT are also strong cultures that influence the nature of leadership individually and as a combination thereof. The culture of AND is communicative and synergistic to illuminate the wisdom of a new path. The culture of BUT is divisive and conflicting mired in the MYOTH syndrome. (MY WAY OR THE HIGHWAY). The culture of AND-BUT is the middle-path of the consensus builders.

In the human ecology and culture all three natures of leadership coexist with the most predominant being the AND-BUT consensus builders. The differences in characteristics of their leadership nature are tabled below:

	AND	AND-BUT	BUT
1.	SYNERGY	CONSENSUS	CONFLICT
2.	WIN/WIN	LOSE/LOSE	WIN/LOSE
3.	COLLABORATIVE	COMPROMISE	DEFENSIVE

4.	ETHICAL	COMMUNICATION	FALSIFICATION Communication
5.	TRUST	RESPECT	ANGER/FEAR
6.	MORAL HOPE	HOPE	ANXIETY
7.	DIVERSITY	SAMENESS	SELF/EGO
8.	EVO-DEVO LEADER	PROBLEM LEADER	Leader

The concept of great leadership in its evo-devo nature is to transform the BUT to AND in order to free up the unused energy stored in the BUT to create a unique culture of Human Ecology. This culture is founded in the competitive advantage of the combination of energy rather than the neutrality of the equilibrium of sameness or the disadvantage of the division of conflict. The advantage of the AND-BUT paradigm can be easily demonstrated in our day to day lives if we start replacing the BUT permission statements with AND permission statements. Please observe the three different statements below:

A) You are giving some good advice BUT I want to...

B) You are giving some good advice and we can look at them but I would like to modify...

C) You are giving some good advice AND we will combine these together with...

The AND culture needs tremendous preparedness, planning, restraint and humility to succeed. The precision required in the AND operation and it's practice is akin to a surgeon removing a tumor without harming the healthy cells around the tumor. The practice of the synergistic culture in the Leadership of Conflict is to acquire all the available facts, plan all the scenarios for success and failure, execute effectively and monitor the recovery of the relationships. The above process will also prevent any future conflict.

It is important to recognize at this stage that there will always be certain circumstances in which conflict is inevitable but the evo-devo leader will still try to plan for synergy in the future by handling the conflict with the faith and trust of the community. The tips to breaking the AND-BUT cycle can be achieved by 5 simple strategies that can be used in your daily evo-devo:

1) AWARENESS: Awareness is the first step towards stopping the behavior cycle that leads to conflict. The more you learn and acquire facts about different events and contingencies the more control you have over the results.

2) HONESTY: Once you have seen the behavior that encourages conflict and promotes irrational fear and anger you must evaluate the risk factors or triggers that set up the error links.

3) MOTIVATION: Motivation, Dedication, Practice and Precision are components of this strategy that will ensure that the BUT cycle is interrupted before it starts or even when it has already started. The process of challenging the negative thought process is a key tool in eliminating the thinking errors.

4) THOUGHT ARREST and TRANSFORMATION: Awareness, Honesty and Motivation will help you in the Thought Arrest of conflict and aggression. The strategy is to use your prepared plans rather than then spur of the moment emotional response being allowed to guide your actions. If you can transform the negative thought to a fact acquiring or questioning action rather than acting on the irrational thought you will immediately break the cycle of conflict.

5) EVALUATION: As the negative thought-action is transformed into a positive, synergistic and advantageous outcome the actions need to evaluated and stored into the belief system for ongoing evo-devo of the individual. It is also necessary to communicate and inculcate the successful behavior with precision amongst the leader's sphere of influence for fixation.

The constant emphasis on precision is due to the fact that this is the key differentiator between success and failure of the Leadership of Conflict. In conflict rarely are you given second or third chances to create synergy once the negative thoughts have translated into aggression and subsequent negative results. Leadership becomes great when leaders overcome adversity and conflict that is in opposition to the communal well-being. When faced with extreme conflict the leader has to have the discipline to focus on the objective to WIN and create synergy using all the resources at his or her command. The required resources should be prepared in advance to be able to execute the "Right response" at the Right Time.

In order to be prepared for conflict and synergy requires you to understand the model and dynamics of the entire equation. The model of conflict as discussed earlier has both a negative and a positive overtone depending on the objectives. The negative conflict is characterized by the objectives where one leadership attempts to maximize the minimum expected "pay off" and the opposing leadership tries to minimize the payoff to the first party. The process is adversarial as it is based on one party gaining advantage over the other without realizing the "zero-sum" nature of conflict. This "zero-sum" nature in essence does not provide the necessary pay-off expected when evaluated holistic-ally. It also ends up lowering Leadership Core Values though it may sate the leader's ego temporarily.

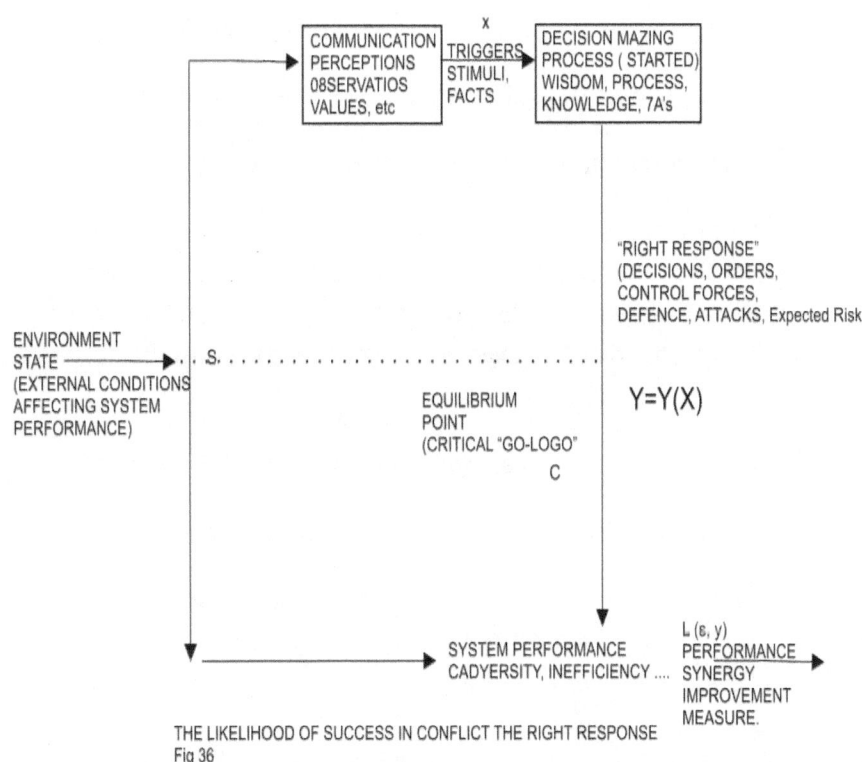

THE LIKELIHOOD OF SUCCESS IN CONFLICT THE RIGHT RESPONSE
Fig 36

The positive conflict that eliminates the "barriers" to sustainable growth and releases the free energy stored in the system is extremely beneficial to the communities involved and also assists in raising the faith and trust values of leadership. The entropy in both the above types of conflict is the measure of the expected uncertainty in the probability of success, the involved randomness of process, the expected risks of the leadership decision and other such risk factors. The inherent real-time nature of leadership decisions during conflict exponentially increases the negative or the positive impact on society. The factors that are crucial to the process of decision making in conflict and in the minimization of the expected risks involved which in turn maximizes the chances of achieving the "Right Response" to have a high likelihood of SUCCESS are as under:

a) The External Conditions affecting the system and its performance i.e. ENVIRONMENTAL FACTORS- (S)

b) The observed facts and stimuli for response- TRIGGER FACTORS (x)

c) The time and "go-no go" equilibrium points - CRITICAL FACTORS (C)

d) The responses, forces, tools used in the decision- DECISION FACTORS (Y)

The Expected Risk (E) is therefore a function of the environment, triggers, equilibrium, critical and decision factors. The Leadership of Conflict requires that any "Right Response" cycle include at least one equilibrium point to minimize the expected risk. The exact parameters of the critical factors and the equilibrium point (C) are two-fold :

1) The added impact of False Acceptance of the response - FALSE ALARM (FA)

2) The added impact of False Rejection of the response – MISS (M)

The determinations of the above impacts are required to define the equilibrium point and the critical factors for each event during conflict and the response to the event. The advance planning, preparedness, fact acquisition and Leadership Core Values are all invaluable in the identification of the added impact of the False Alarm (FA) and the Miss (M) to substantially increase the Likelihood of Success (L) via the "Right Response" (R) through the minimization of the Expected Risk (E). In a simple mathematical representation of the above strategy the above function will appear as follows:

R= L greater than E where E= FA divided by M, and the environment factors are equivalent to the response and decision factors or Y=Y(x)) at the equilibrium point.

$$R= L>E \text{ where } L= +S.C.Y(x) \text{ and } E= -S.(-x).FA/M$$

In order to achieve the likelihood of SUCCESS in conflict you need to also deal with the ambiguity and estimates of facts and truths. You can have two scenarios here as well:

a) If an **efficient estimate (facts are known and observed** i.e. +S and −S with C and x are well defined) exists the Likelihood ratio of SUCCESS and the "Right Response" will appear as a synergistic solution with a unique equilibrium point.

b) **If only a sufficient estimate (observed and known facts   unknowns)** exists then the Likelihood ratio of SUCCESS and the "Right Response" will be dependent on the unknowns and the estimates. In this situation you will be able to define an equilibrium "region" and a "worst case" or "best case" response for the maximum likelihood of SUCCESS.

For simplicity let's look at a "real-life" conflict scenario. You are in your office preparing to rush to the conference room for an important dissatisfied client meeting. You suddenly experience a strong pain in your chest. Lets also assume that there are only two responses available to you which are D0 and D1. D0= Do nothing, ignore the pain and go to your meeting OR D1= Call 911. The factors surrounding the decision are enumerated below:

a) Environment Factors: 1) AGE - 46 years

2) Family history of heart attacks

3) High Cholesterol observed during the last medical check-up.

4) High Blood Pressure

5) Dissatisfied Client

6) Client Retention

b) TRIGGER FACTORS: 1) Severe Chest pain on the left side

2) No breakfast in the morning

3) Lots of caffeine

c) CRITICAL FACTORS: l) Pain increasing to around 7 (scale 1-10)

2) Casualty rate after the first 30 minutes in a heart attack increases exponentially.

3) Relationship of the Account Manager with the client.

d) DECISION FACTORS: 1) LOSS of BUSINESS

2) LOSS of LIFE

3) LOSS of TIME

4) LOSS of FACE

5) UNKOWNS

Both D0 and D1 have four options: Let's assume you prefer the D0 response:

a) D0 is true and accepted by the facts.

b) D0 is false and rejected by the facts.

c) D0 is true but rejected by facts. (MISS)

d) D0 is false but accepted by facts. (FALSE ALARM)

The "Right Response" that maximizes the Likelihood of SUCCESS and minimizes the risk for the above preferred choice is mapped out graphically as under:

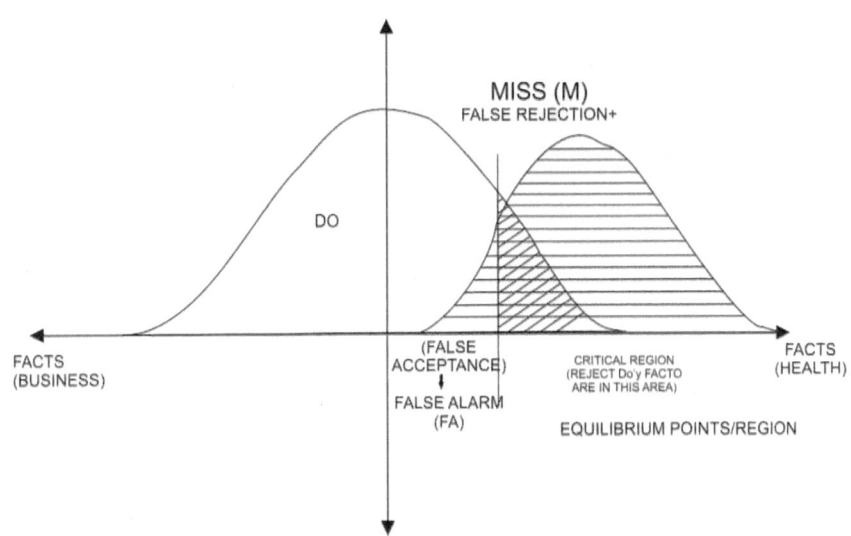

THE "Preffered Choice" Validation for Conflict Response (Fig 37)

The above graphic representation of the various facts clearly indicate that the "preferred. choice" Do is not the right response and should be rejected. The D1 option of calling 911 is the "right response" with the maximum likelihood of SUCCESS for the leader and the community. The synergy of the "Right Response" can be enhanced by using the equilibrium region by calling the client to explain the circumstances and a request to send your account manager to the meeting to gather all the facts and a quick response if so desired by the client. The "Right Response" demands the minimization of the expected risks of the leadership decisions while maximizing the communal benefits by selecting the optimal choice. The Equilibrium point between conflict and synergy has to he attained for the transition of the entropy of conflict to synergy for SUCCESS.

The BP "Oil Spill Disaster" triggered by the series of cost-conscious decisions of the leaders lead to the April 20,2010 rig explosion that killed 11 personnel and touched off the biggest oil spill U.S. history. The few critical decisions made by BP in designing and implementing the new well i.e. 6

stabilizers instead of 21 in the well before cementing (saved 100-150 hrs in the process), a pipe that ran from the bottom of the well to the floor of the sea (saved approx US$10MM), not allowing the cement in the well to bond properly (saved another 9-12 hours delay in opening of the well), not allowing the heavy drilling fluid circulation to test for any gas leakage (saved another 8-10 hrs) and finally the decision of the leadership to allow the trade-off between cost and safety. The current law states that the maximum penalty that could be awarded in the case of an offshore oil spill is capped at US$75MM.The cost of $75MM vis-à-vis the trade-off on safety may be the "preferred choice" that went into the decision making process that selected to open the well before all the risks were minimized.

If the leadership had taken into account the environment factors, the equilibrium point between safety and cost, the randomness of the process and finally the overall impact of the decision including the "False Alarms" and the "Miss" and being fully prepared to fight the expected "failure" then the "Right Response" would have been to delay the opening of the well as the other option did not meet the critical point criteria for the Likelihood of SUCCESS.BP has signed an agreement to pay US $ 20 Billion to cover the costs of the disaster. BP is lost nearly 30,000 barrels of oil a day that flooded into the Gulf. BP share price hit its lowest point in 40 years. The total cost of the decision will probably end up close to a $100 Billion. They say hindsight is 20/20 but if we follow the right process in the Leadership of Conflict we can minimize the expected risk and create a uniquely synergistic solution for adverse situations such as wars (WWII), natural disasters (Katrina) or ideological conflicts (Iraq, etc).

The other aspect of the Leadership of Conflict from an evo-devo standpoint is to always plan around your weaknesses. This is the area that the opposition will exploit to gain advantage. Secondly, you need to absorb the understanding and knowledge of the failures of great leaders, not just the successes, in order not to repeat those responses that lead to their failures. Thirdly, the ultimate test of any decision is in the nature of its benefit and its IF and THEN characteristics, **All decisions have consequences. The decisions that stand true on the foundation that states-"If this decision benefits the community more than the leaders or a few then it is most probably the**

"right" choice. The practice and professional approach to the Leadership of Conflict is a sure way to success in this crucial aspect of evo-devo leadership.

The reason that you need to constantly hone your leadership skills to succeed in adversity is to transform your natural responses in conflict to become the "Right Response" consistently. The natural response in times of fear, anger and other violent emotions that are apparent in any crisis are stored in a segregated area of the brain known as the "AMYGDALA". This part of the brain lies just behind our forehead and stores responses to crises that have been built over a long period of time going back to prehistoric times. The "AMYGDALA" does not store learned or acquired memory which lies in the cortex. The "Right Response" may at times run contrary to our natural instincts that still requires further evolution or fixation. In the attainment of the evo-devo necessary for the Leadership of Conflict we need to "rewire" our brain circuits by training our intellect to acquire facts and communicate ethically to move away from conflict to synergy. The assimilation of these new behavioral traits into our belief system will ensure the leadership ability to create sustainable growth.

Mahatma Gandhi, also known as the Father of India, stood against the all-powerful British Empire to attain independence for India. After assessing the strengths of the Empire and the weaknesses of the Indian populace, he combined the two in a synergistic approach of "Ahimsa" or non-violence and "Satyagrah" or the "Path of Truth'. The timing of the "Right Response" in line with the British focus on World War-II resulted in the August 15, 1947 declaration of Independence by India. Nelson Mandela, the architect of the South African nation, used these strategies to end the war against oppression and apartheid. Both Gandhi and Mandela are well-known figures who have achieved the Leadership of Conflict by using synergy over aggression and ethical communication over war. The key to their wisdom and unique path that was in contrast to the natural instincts of survival was founded on the principles of moral hope and law as well as the concept of communal service before self. The facts and preparedness of these leaders was no less than any general going to war. This included the need to motivate millions of people to follow their lead without the discipline of a trained army which is available to the Leaders of Force. Despite the conflict and adversity involved in both the above examples the truth is that Britain is one of the leading trading relationships for India and South Africa is growing faster than any other African Nation thus benefiting all the constituents irrespective of color.

The mutually beneficial nature of the Leadership of Conflict that unleashes the huge stores of energy trapped in adversity, anger, fear, aggression, war etc. for transformation of the communities to gain competitive advantage is the "Right Response," The power of fission or fusion can be used to kill millions at the same time it can solve the world's energy conflict. The power of hunger can evolve a new species that walks upright on two feet when a primate has to shuffle on its feet to access food from trees and at the same time it can be the reason for riots in 16 countries as happened in 2008 due to the rising prices of food.

The policy of divide and rule used by the British in India to control the masses included the use of the English language as a tool. This tool has also resulted in providing jobs to the 11 million English speaking graduates, that come out of Indian universities every year , through the new industry of global outsourced contact centers. Alternatively, the power of the" Big Bang", the ultimate conflict, is creating and expanding the Universe while the power of the "Human Small Bangs" are destroying millions of species to extinction. A criminal and a policeman both carry fire arms. The criminals fire arm is a weapon i.e. a gun while the policemen is armed with the fire arm. The criminal uses his gun for oppression while the policeman uses his "arm" for protection. The motivation of the criminal is mired in the adversarial process of unworked for gain while the policeman's motivation is the benefit of society and a compliance with the moral laws. One is a net destroyer of communal wealth while the other is a net generator of benefits. The transformation of a criminal to a policeman or a "civilian" to a "guardian of the Law" is a process that requires extensive training, knowledge, humility, faith and trust. The process is derailed when the "guardian of the Law" becomes the criminal and an oppressor by choice. He is worse than the other criminals because he has the knowledge and resource to provide, the, "Right Response" but chooses not to.

This then is the essence of the Leadership of Governance that we will analyze in the next chapter in an attempt to understand its interdependent relationship with the crucial evo-devo skill of the Leadership of Conflict.

"The enemy will attack you not at your strongest point but at your weakest and if you do not know your weakest point be sure, your enemy WILL"
SUNTZU

CHAPTER 14

LEADERSHIP OF GOVERNANCE- Political and Apolitical

LIFE, LIBERTY and the Pursuit of Happiness. FOR the people, BY the people and OF the people. "SATYAMEV JAYATE." - Believe in the Truth and the Truth will always prevail. These are the foundations on which the two of the largest democracies were built. The United States of America and the Republic of India were both born out of the adversity of revolt against the British Empire and its imperialistic policies with the altruistic intent to transfer power to the people from the hands of the monarchy and its representatives. An evolved leadership that set the rules for this progressive mode of political governance was entrenched in a belief system that propagated the altruism of "SERVICE before SELF." The execution of the democratic concept over the last 300 years has left much to be desired and now stands at the crossroads of its own evolution.

The net result of this experiment in the political evolution of governance is the loss of altruism with the gain of prosperity and the diminishing of adversity. The problem of "Self before Service" is not limited only to the democratic form of government but applies equally to other existing political structures such as Monarchy, Oligarchy, Communism, Dictatorship or in some cases Familial. The Ecclesiastical "nations" have also been affected by the "greed" gene to some extent. The value system in this crucial area of leadership is still mired in the Master --Slave mentality although appearances are deceptive. On the other hand the growth in science and technology is pushing the boundaries of information and communication into the hands of the masses who are now equipped to provide inputs into the process of governance but are being held at bay by the existing leadership. It is not by chance that the divide between the "governed" and the "governors" is widening at a pace that is accelerating the lack of faith in the entire system of political governance.

Aristotle defined three basic forms of government - MONARCHY government by a single individual by birth or acquisition, ARISTOCRACY, government by a select few by birth, and DEMOCRACY- government by many by choice. The current state of these three governing processes is as under:

188

a) TYRANNY- Rule of a single individual for his self-interest.

b) OLIGARCHY- Rule of a select few for their own self-interest.

c) OCHLOCRACY- "MOB RULE" of the strongest for the self-interest of the strongest.

The difference is apparent in that the advantage of self-interest has replaced the benefits of altruism. Altruism in terms of political governance is behavior that benefits another to your own self-detriment. Self-Interest is the behavior that benefits you at the disadvantage of others. If we were able to corner all the rewards without any of the risks we would consider ourselves to be winners in the race of political leadership. This violates the basic principle of governance and society itself. **When risks are involved the best way to survive is to pool the risks**. This basic need of survival is the foundation of society and politics. Where we fail is in the equitable distribution of rewards. **The paradox is that if we corner all the rewards we are responsible for all the risk as well.**

The Pursuit of Happiness is an inalienable right as predicated in the Declaration of Independence and the governance of the United States in its domestic and international policies. The greatest happiness for the greatest number is the foundation of Morality. Happiness though is an elusive feeling that is symptomatic to being "Healthy, Wealthy and Wise," The pursuit of Happiness and its governance is then the need to be "Healthy, Wealthy and Wise". Maslow's Hierarchy of Needs describe the attributes to this state of happiness that we are all pursuing as a right. In the pictorial representation of these needs that govern happiness we have also mapped the evo and the devo that you need to add in order to attain the Leadership of Governance and understand its role in the Hierarchy of Needs:

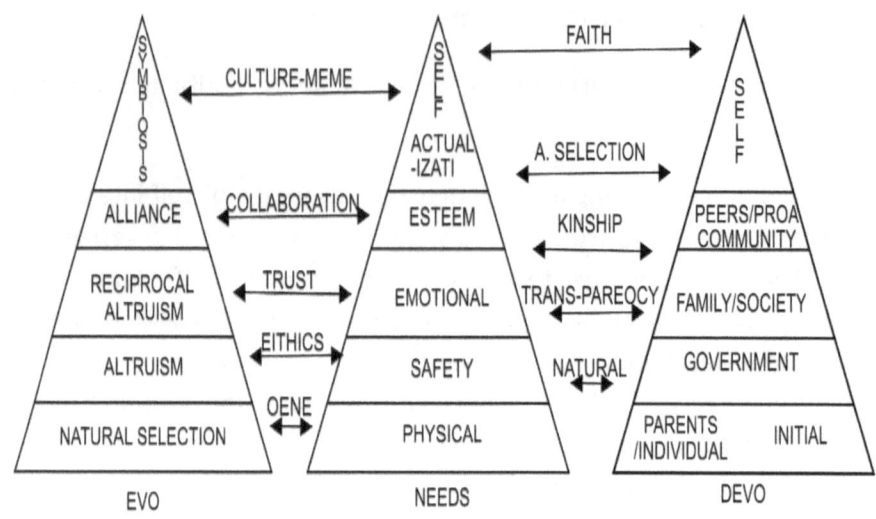

THE EVO-DEVO OF THE HIERARCHY OF NEEDS (Fig 38)

In the cycle of needs and their attainment , the role of government is primarily that of Risk Mitigation. The ultimate goal as you climb to the top of the pyramid is to attain self-actualization that should also lead to the Leadership of SELF-GOVERNANCE that will be symbiotic in nature and be culturally transferable. **The Leadership of Governance is therefore a process of Artificial Selection that can create an environment of self-actualization for its constituents to collaborate in a symbiotic manner for sustainable growth.** The process of self-actualization works best if we can equate the pursuit of happiness to the realization of contentment. Contentment is the state that allows you to pursue your goals through the application of your honest effort within the parameter of your given circumstances. The evo-devo of Leadership of Governance is the incremental improvement of your circumstances by extending your grasp by enhancing your reach for the achievement of reasonable gains. The gain of actualization wherein you understand your circumstances, adapt and innovate to govern the factors in your reach for the selection advantage is the basis for the leadership of both political and a political governance.

In a survey, published in the USA TODAY, 23 of the 24 nations surveyed on the subject of President Barack Obama vs. President George W. Bush for

"Doing the Right Thing", Selected Obama by a thumping margin. The results of the survey are illustrated above.

BUSH			OBAMA	
17%	▭	BRAZIL	▭	76%
30%	▭	CHINA	▭	60%
11%	▭	EGYPT	▭	42%
15%	▭	FRANCE	▭	91%
14%	▭	GERMANY	▭	93%
23%	▭	INDONESIA	▭	71%
57%	▭	ISRAEL	▭	56%
25%	▭	JAPAN	▭	88%
22%	▭	RUSSIA	▭	37%
2%	▯	TURKEY	▭	33%

"The Right Thing" Obama vs. Bush – Pew Research (Fig 39)

The huge margin of approval for President Obama gave him a near "Rock Star" status and assisted in repairing some of the damage and battering that was received by the USA over the eight years of Bush rule. The survey also brought out another interesting fact that for the first time in eight years there was more confidence in the new American President than in the late Al-Qaeda Leader Osama Bin Laden (who came a close second to Mr. Obama) One of the root causes of the success and failure of governance as well as the rise and fall of empires is the "kinship" value. As a visual illustration of the phenomenon of "kinship" value is illustrated in the diagram below:

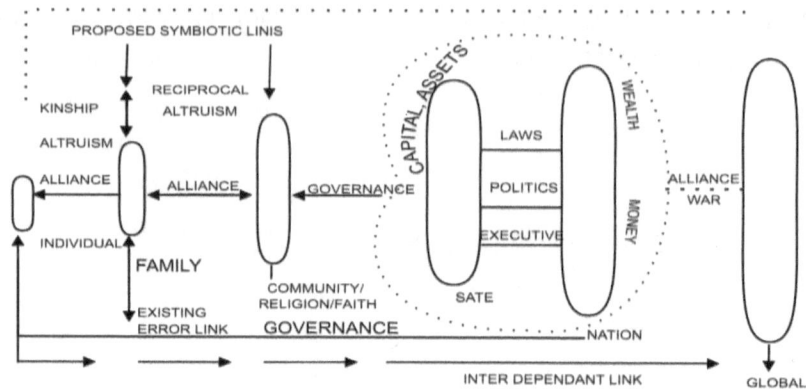

KINSHIP VALUE and it ALLIANCE with GOVERNANCE (Fig 40)

In this diagram you observe that the battle of the minds is between the altruistic natures of family ties versus the forced culture of the existing governance structures. Some forms of government like communism, nationalism, fascism and even ecclesiasticism have tried to become a substitute for the familial nature but have not succeed in their attempts since these fell much lower on the "kinship" scale of altruism.

Let us try to understand this powerful force that can destroy empires and create dynasties. "Kinship Value" is the result of four key tautologies:

a) You cannot be a "Half Pregnant" kin - The TRUE-FALSE nature of Kinship does not allow any room for doubt. You are a kin or you are not.

b) You cannot be an "individual" self-kin: The relative nature of Kinship does not allow you to be a kin of yourself. You need be a kin of someone else.

c) You cannot be an "unnetworked" kin: The family tree structure of kinship ensures that you are part of a defined network with membership rights.

d) You cannot be an "not in the Box" kin: The self-contained nature of Kinship ensures that the altruistic culture and the values are defined within the family structure so that the "value of the whole is greater than the parts."

The "kinship value" automatically creates measures of solidarity, trust, tolerance, empathy, sympathy and support to a family member or an extended kin. As an example an alliance formed between a husband and wife is also an alliance of families of the two individuals genetically, politically and commercially, The Leadership of Governance requires that the family and the government coexist in harmony. The fundamental paradox is that governance needs to be "free, fair and equal" in its nature while the "kinship value" is inherently biased in favor of the family.

In an attempt to obfuscate the issue, the political governance has formed an unholy alliance between government and money. This direct influence on the individual by the governing leaders is in contradiction to the role of governance which is to assist the nurturers (the mother), the provider (the fathers) and the peers (the community) to develop the potential of their wards and create a culture of evolutionary growth in peace. In lieu of the money, mostly in the form of debt, the family and the community have relinquished their role and handed over the reins of their kins to the political machinery.

Mayer Rothschild once said "Let me issue and own a nation's money and I care not who writes the Laws." The alliance of political and corporate governance through money wherein employment, salaries, perks, taxes, incentives, consumption, globalization and stock markets all work together to govern individual behavior in order to develop a level of "kinship" with him or her. This compensation based relationship is non-sustainable and unfriendly. If you follow the money you can gauge the dependence of one entity on another. Independent decision making and thinking comes out of having your freely owned or acquired tools for survival. In today's scenario the freedom of individual that was available as a kin is now indebted to the government or corporatism. The government uses the consumer debts and its ability to print money to buy the loyalty from the private and public corporations which in turn use it to influence the individual in favor of the government that is most benevolent to the leaders. Various examples of the subjugation of the family and the individual exist that clearly prove the effects of this "capital based' governance strategy.

You can observe the alliance between the defense industry and the government from the 1800's to the 2000's as the extensive periods of growth and depression and boom have preceded the wars. The France-British wars, American Revolution, WW-I, WW-II, Cold War, and the War on Terrorism are all indicators of the way money and fear are used to control the individual, familial and communal will. The alliance between the Pharmaceutical companies and the government that has been in existence from the 1970's is controlling the freedom of individuals through the fear of disease and "disease" care (mostly referred to as Health care.). The bond amongst the knowledge providers and the government through grants and endowments ensures that the "wisdom" provided to the individual supports the governance policies in existence. If "Health, Wealth and Wisdom" are all under the direct control of the government through the aegis of money then so is our happiness. Herein lies a recipe for disaster as the government cannot be free, fair and equal to all the constituents all the time and needs to select one or the other of these ideals while the individuals are never content with their share. A further erosion of trust and "kinship" value takes place at this point.

If governance cannot be All Free, All Fair and All Equal at all times the question is How do we attain leadership of governance alongside a symbiotic relationship with the family and the community to allocate the Natural Capital equitably ?

Firstly let's look at the three options that are available in politics while framing the nature of governance:

A) THE "FREE" OPTION: When the need of investing in A exceeds the benefit of investing in B then the investment should be moved to A. In this A gets a free option to reach and develop his or her potential.

B) THE "FAIR" OPTION: If the merits of B and its performance exceed the benefit and performance of A then invest in B. Now B gets a fair option as it receives more investment based on merits alone.

C) THE "EQUAL" OPTION: Share the investment equally amongst A and B. Use the performance benefits produced by each to reinvest in A and B respectively. At the same time share some of the benefits of A and B with C within the "kinship" domain as well as the community to generate ongoing sustainable growth.

The Free option is altruistic, the Fair option is a reciprocally altruistic in its nature and the equal option is symbiotic. Thus the Leadership of

Governance boils down to two simple parameters i.e. Ethics and Transparency. The more transparent and ethical the leadership the higher its "kinship" value with the constituents due to the alliance of objectives and a symbiosis of mutual growth.

The ETHICAL nature of the Leadership of Governance can be observed if we evaluate an unique and extremely powerful form of governance that exists in society today known as the "ECCELESIASTICAL STATE." The ecclesiastical state is unique in the sense that it is formed to overcome prior adversity and is founded in virtue. In its culture this form of governance allows "perpetuity" of existence and growth on faith independent of the nature of the leaders themselves. The Ecclesiastical State has certain distinct characteristics that are close to the evo-devo required in the Leadership of Governance:

a) This form of governance has states and a sense of nationalism and does not need to defend these states of nationalism.

b) These states have "citizens" but the state does not need to govern them.

c) The "citizens" follow the suggested "way of life" faithfully but ungoverned.

d) The "citizens" do not feel the necessity of being governed and continue to follow the principles happily without force or fear.

e) The states though undefended cannot be taken away from the citizens.

The virtues of freedom, wisdom, faith, relationships, trust, altruism, moral hope and moral laws that lead the Ecclesiastical Nations act as temporal a force that eliminates confusion of contingent political goals. Ecclesiastical states achieve greatness through goodness and empathy while the other forms of governance attempt greatness through force, fear and conflict. Ecclesiastical Leadership becomes revered and esteemed as it combines the forces of the individual, the family and the community to foster faith and trust in governance. The unique advantage offered in the culture of the ecclesiastical nation is that it is not an "agent" of change but is the change itself and the leadership becomes the trigger that lights the fire of developmental and cultural transformation through a temporal process that provides guidance, knowledge and wisdom to the citizens irrespective of boundaries or other alliances. Visualize the leader as a lit candle and the flame being the "process and knowledge" of ecclesiastical faith. As the leaders candle lights other candles which pass on the flame to the next till the process of transference becomes natural and ongoing both mimetically (through memes)and genetically (through genes). The beauty of this process is beholden in the fact that even if the First candle that started the enlightenment against adversity and chaos is extinguished, the growth of the ecclesiastical state does not stop. The flame is passed on from one to another and from generation to generation. You do have to take into account that the ecclesiastical state though temporal in nature is based on faith in a higher power THE BIG "G". The infallible nature of that faith is to some extent responsible for the success of this form of governance.

The idea though is to understand the process of ecclesiastical governance in order to get the values of transparency and ethics for the elusive goal of self-governance in the evo-devo of the Leadership of Governance.

The ecclesiastical nation that we will observe as a model for the ethical form of governance is in tune with the non-religious definition of the word that qualifies it as "a member of an assembly." The same can apply to Christian, Jewish, Hindu, Sikh, Muslim, Buddhist or any Atheistic order to understand the process of sustainable growth of the flame to create a sense of belonging and nationalism that result in the formation of an esteemed governing relationship.

As an example we will take the growth of "Punjabi" nationalism that came into existence 500 years ago. This assembly has its own language and code of conduct defined by a "way of life" that encourages the principles of self-governance. The citizens of this global nation have built large stores of "communal wealth" and are known for its helping, sharing, lively, and entrepreneurial nature. Protection of minorities against oppression and a "fair" dealing attitude is also its forte. The members of this group are held in esteem with the title "Sardarji" or "Respected Leader" all over the world. Punjabi nationalism has survived multiple attempts against dissolution, created a social and political structure for governance and has continued to evolve against all odds based on the principle of "Sikhi" or a "disciple of knowledge". The flame of Sikhi and Punjabi nationalism was ignited by Guru Nanak Dev in the   16th century in response to the discrimination of the Hindus and the oppression of the Mughals. The flame was passed on through the Ten Gurus and given its final shape in the 18th century by Guru Gobind Singh who entrusted the community with the "Guru Granth Sahib", the Living Guru, in the form of the teachings of the ten gurus for a universal form of self-governance. The way of life as learned by the Sikhs, with a common surname of "Singh" for males and "Kaur" for females, is to attain contentment and symbiosis with all beings while performing their duties honestly and having a propensity to play with their lives to protect the virtues of the downtrodden across the world.

The ideals of Guru Nanak were entrenched in truth, equality and ethics with a renaissance of literacy, culture, poetry, knowledge and sharing. Nanak traveled all over the world to have a dialogue with other ecclesiastical leaders to learn and teach the basic tenet of Sikhism based on the ethos of equality. In his words he said there is no "Hindu or Muslim" in order to innovate a life-style that was non-ritualistic with equal rights for all and the freedom to develop individual potential without the boundaries of caste. Nanak himself lived the way of life he promoted and performed his civil and familial duties as a farmer and a father. The Sikhism of Nanak was not to run away from temptation but be able to face temptation ("MAYA") with contentment and ethics. Nanak also set up centers of learning across Asia and used the local languages with local beliefs in an attempt to disseminate the knowledge to people from all walks of life in a simple and straight forward manner. Nanak's ability to explain the principles of humanity, monotheism, and ethical behavior can be seen in the simple quotes below:

"WHEN I AM QUIET THEY SAY I HAVE NO KNOWLEDGE,

WHEN I SPEAK I TALK TOO MUCH THEY SAY,

WHEN I SIT THEYSAY AN UNWELCOME GUEST HAS COME TO STAY,

WHEN I DEPART I HAVE DESERTED AND RUN AWAY,

WHEN I BOW THEY SAY IT IS OUT OF FEAR THAT I PRAY,

NOTHING CAN I DO THAT IN PEACE I MAY SPEND MY TIME,

PRESERVE THY SERVANTS HONOR NOW AND HEREAFTER,

O LORD SUBLIME."

(HISTORY OF THE SIKHS-Kushwant Singh)

Sikhism and Punjabi Nationalism under Nanak also become the political force of change with its own consciousness and culture. Nanak passed on his flame to Bhai Lehna, a diligent disciple, rather than his own sons.

Bhai Lena, now called Guru Angad Dev ("part of my body") by Nanak, took over the reins of the Punjabi consciousness. Nanak in his humility, bowed before Angad as the next guru and then went to tend his fields.

Angad took the flame and added his knowledge and process to it. He developed the concept of LANGAR i.e. "The Common Kitchen" which was a communal kitchen open to all to eat with no bar on caste or social status. The simplicity and beauty of this principle is carried on till today in all Sikh places of faith. Three meals plus refreshments and a place to stay are integral part of any Sikh Temple or Gurudwara and are fully funded by the community. Angad also created the script of thirty-five letters from the writings of Nanak and named it "GURMUKHI" or "From the Guru's mouth." Gurmukhi became the language of governance of the community as well and was taught to all the members unlike the elitist Sanskrit of the Hindus or Urdu of the Muslims. Angad believed in physical fitness and he started various arenas for wrestling and exercise to keep the community healthy and prepared to play the role of the protectors of the oppressed. Angad passed on the flame with all the cumulative knowledge and processes to the next Guru i.e. Amar Das.

Guru Amar Das made the "LANGAR" an institution of the governance process itself. He made sure that anyone who came to see him first sat down and enjoyed the meal with the community. One of the most famous and prolific Mughal Emperors in India, Akbar, visited Amar Das and ate in the "Langar" with the community. Akbar became one of the strongest supporters of the Punjabi culture and added both revenue and prestige to the community. Amar Das's teachings were simple" Do good to others by giving good advice, by setting a good example, and by always having the welfare of mankind in your heart". Amar Das passed on at the ripe old age of ninety-five and handed over the flame of governance of the ecclesiastical Punjabi nation to his disciple Ram Das.

Guru Ram Das, an established administrator, built a huge lake and commenced building a town around it. This town became the virtual capital of the Punjabi nationalism and its governance. Amar Das invited tradesman from all over the continent to come and work for the town as well as establish their businesses in the town. This generated employment and new revenues which helped in spreading the flame of Sikhism all over India and abroad. He passed on the mantle to the next Guru Arjun Dev.

Arjun completed the central pillar of the community called the "Harminder Sahib" (The Temple of the GOD) which was built on the lake and town both called "AMRITSAR" or the "pool of nectar" Amritsar is now the central place for both commerce and pilgrimage for the entire Punjabi community. It has one of the highest per capita incomes in India and is a teeming metropolis. Guru Arjun Dev also wrote and completed the "Granth Sahib" (the scriptures for the Sikh way of Life). The design of Golden Temple (Harmandir Sahib) , as it is known all over the world, is unique as it is open on all four sides and is built lower than the land around it. The significance of this design is to expand on the theme of equality and humility. Guru Arjun Dev succumbed to the torture of Mughal Emperor Jehangir who felt threatened by the growing force of Punjabi nationalism. He offered to convert Arjun to Islam in exchange for his life but to no avail. In Guru Arjun Dev's words in the "Guru Granth Sahib"- the Living Guru-- he says:

I DO NOT KEEP THE HINDU FAST NOR THE MUSLIM RAMADAN

I SERVE HIM ALONE WHO IS MY REFUGE

I SERVE THE ONE MASTER,

WHO IS ALSO ALLAH,

I HAVE BROKEN WITH THE HINDU AND THE MUSLIM,

I WILL NOT WORSHIP WITH THE HINDU,

NOR LIKE THE MUSLIM GO TO MECCA,

I SHALL SERVE HIM AND NO OTHER

The Evo-Devo of Leadership

I WILL NOT PRAY TO IDOLS,

NOR SAY THE MUSLIM PRAYER,

I SHALL PUT MY HEAD AT THE

FEET OF THE ONE SUPREME BEING

FOR WE ARE NEITHER HINDU NOR MUSLIMS.

With these words the flame of Punjabi nationalism and the Sikhi "way of life" was transformed to a fire that spread rapidly across the globe.

After the death of Guru Arjun Dev, his son,(eleven year old Hargobind took the fire and created an army of citizens to stop the oppression of the Mughal Emperor. Guru Hargobind also built the "Akal Takht" (The Eternal Throne of GOD) in Amritsar which became the seat of the Punjabi and Sikh political leadership and governance and still stands strong 350 years later. The Punjabis' who are natural fighters now transformed the pacifism of Nanak to the positive aggression of conflict to defeat the Mughal and Afghan armies time and again to protect both the Hindu and Sikh communities. The raging fire of Sikhism and its might was now handed over to Har Rai by Hargobind.

Guru Har Rai, a man of peace, who said " You can rebuild a temple or a mosque but not a broken heart" and brought back the era of Nanak by preaching peaceful co-existence. He recaptured the essence of faith by aligning the power of pacifism with the strength of aggression to eliminate the conflict of discrimination. This controlled fire with all its in-built energy was handed over to the next Guru - Harkishan.

Harkishan was a man who wanted to help the sick and poor. He used the power of the fire to set up hospitals and medical camps to fight the epidemic of smallpox that was raging in the Indian Subcontinent. He himself was stricken by smallpox while helping the community and handed over the distinguished flame to Guru Teg Bahadur, the ninth guru.

Teg Bahadur traveled across the Indian sub-continent and abroad to spread the fire of Sikhism. He also set up systems that would help the Hindus from the tyranny of the Mughals and their officials. Guru Tegh Bahadur gave his life to protect the Hindu faith and was martyred in the court of the emperor at New Delhi by beheading. The now mature fire of Punjabi nationalism and Sikhi faith was taken over by Guru Gobind Singh, the tenth guru.

Guru Gobind Singh was only ten years old when the decapitated head of Tegh Bahadur was brought home to be cremated. The young Gobind Singh in this time of adversity took the lead to create what Sikhism is today in the shape of the "KHALSA" or the Pure. As a leader he understood the vision of Nanak, the strength of Angad, the calm of Amar Das, the patience of Ram Das, the martyrdom of Arjun, the discipline of Hargobind, the peace of Har Rai, the mercy of Harkishan and the sacrifice of Teg Bahadur. He saw the face of the Punjabi nationalism combined both the virtue of forgiveness and the discipline to fight against the powers of destruction that threatened the survival of the community. He told each Sikh to learn to fight and carry an arm for mercy and protection. He told each Sikh to learn the Gurmukhi script and teach it to others. In his words he said "Not one of my Sikhs should remain illiterate". He gave the community a code of conduct which included abstaining from tobacco, smoking, and drugs. Respect for women required a Sikh to treat them as his own mother, sister or daughter and be faithful to their spouse. This army of disciplined Soldier-Saints then went ahead to carry the flame of the Punjabi nationalism under the aegis of the teachings of the gurus as written in the Guru Granth Sahib or The living Guru. The ethics of self-governance under the "Aakal Takht" was now established. Guru Gobind Singh lost his life and the lives of all his four sons in the fight for ethics and became the "father" of millions of SIKHS around the world. The Punjabi "gene" and "meme" both flourished across the world and is a model our evo-devo of the Leadership of Self-governance. The ecclesiastical nature of the model of governance does not guarantee that corrupt or unethical elements will be completely eliminated. What it does ensure is that the principles of ethical self-governance are adhered to by the vast majority of the citizens of the community so that they can face adversity and come back stronger each time.

The concept of transparency that can help achieve the goals of an evolving leadership alongside ethics, to meet the needs of governance, is the other primary area of focus that we will now analyze. The emphasis of transparency on governance and its leaders is directly linked to its propensity to achieve the "Right Solution" for the "Right Reason" at the "Right Time" with the "Right Action". This "RIGHT CUBE" is illustrated as under:

REASON		TIME		EVENT	FACTS	SOLUTION		ACTION	
R	IMPACT 1	R	> HRS	CRITICAL	F	OPT 1	R	KPI ROWNGR / 1 RESULT	R
I		I	> DAYS	HIGH	A	OPT 2	I	KPI / 2 RESULT	I
C	IMPACT 2	C					C		C
H	IMPACT 3	H	> WEEK	MEDIUM	C	OPT 3	H	KPI / 3 RESULT	H
T		T			T		T		T
R	IMPACT 4	T	> MONTH	LOW	T	OPT 4	S O L U T I O N	KPI / 4 RESULT	A C T I O N
E		I							
A		M	LONG TERM TIME 2012	TEST	S	ASSUM-PTIONS		KPI / TEST RESULTS	
S O N	TEST	E	SHORT TERM						
					TEST DATA				

THE RIGHT CUBE (Fig. 41)

The "Right Cube" can only work if the relevant facts linked to each event are available at the appropriate moment of decision making and are evaluated for the impact on the constituents of those decisions by collecting their inputs before the decision is made and auctioned.

The RIGHT CUBE of the Leadership of Governance for transparency is founded upon two major factors:

1) e-Governance, and

2) Facts for Events with Impacts and Risk Mitigation.

The system of "e-Governance" is an excellent tool that can be implemented across the government and the citizens to create an information bridge for enhancing the efficiency of the system to select the RIGHT SOLUTION within the RIGHT CUBE. The capability of e-governance to capture, disseminate and receive instant feedback is an extremely powerful methodology for achieving the dual objectives of Transparency and Risk Mitigation through facts. The convergence of telecommunication, media and electronic information through global networks can ensure near 100% representation of the citizens in governance at the same time allow the government to interact with the constituents on a one-on-one basis. If you, as evo-devo leaders, establish a transparent "e-governance" process that any geographically dispersed fact, decision impact, idea or complaint reaches its correct source within a specified time frame and the required response is triggered as planned the results will be apparent immediately. The system of e-governance has to have an automated "escalation process" built into the solution that ensures compliance. The escalation process will mandate a response within a certain time-frame from a responsibility matrix and in case of delay in execution it will escalate the event through the chain of command to guarantee a successful resolution. The event classification as Critical, High, Medium and Low is necessary alongside a responsibility KPI (Key Performance Indicator) and a defined chain for decisions in order to implement the e-governance process for a transparent ethical and participative governing process.

The existing capabilities of global human intelligence, knowledge and process connected in a seamless e-governance methodology that can assess and analyze the facts will provide a huge boost to the current governance processes. Fortunately, there is enough "black fiber" that can be lit instantly to solve most of the "critical" and "high" level issues facing us today. The evo-devo Leadership of Governance can implement the RIGHT CUBE utilizing the existing capacity available to eliminate the barriers to sustainable growth within their domains. The advantage of e-governance is also beneficial in increasing the "kinship value" as it fosters communication and inputs from the constituents into the governance process.

The introduction of ethics and transparency into any governance methodology creates a framework for the individual, families and communities to achieve their maximum potential unhindered. This form of governance that exists without the forced limitations of duties and rights or the confusion of temporal and contingent political goals, however laudable, linked to the absolute conviction of facts for synergy is our goal. The self-governance paradigm will lead to the essential characteristic of ESTEEM for the leaders.

Esteem is one of the critical success factors needed for the Leadership of Governance. The esteem of a leader is built by creating great enterprise alongside a "way of life" that provides the community with an extraordinary example of his own image. The reverence of Esteem and the rare personal goals of the leader will result in the faith and trust of the community in his leadership. The esteemed leader can accomplish great tasks since the entire Natural Capital of the community is behind him. This necessarily means that the leader should be above reproach at all times and uses the natural capital judiciously to continue build great enterprises successfully and consistently.

However, within all this esteem thinking that temptation and failure will not exist or will always be surmountable is false and delusional; that the system will be able to adapt successfully in spite of its weaknesses and temptations to follow the basic factual principles is possible. In order to achieve the competitive advantage of esteem the Leadership of Governance requires that the esteemed leader passes on the values of personal esteem to the entire enterprise and the community for virtual kinship.

The Esteemed leader has to govern fairly and extraordinarily both internally and externally. This entails the sharing of both risk and reward in a just manner. At the same time nothing works more to enhance the esteem of a leader when he is viewed as a True Friend or a True Enemy. A leader who does not make compromises at the expense of the people and alliances of convenience or makes enemies or remains neutral to please a convenient ally. An esteemed leader will make enemies and friends based on synergy for the accrual of communal benefits rather than just situational alliances for personal advantage. The alliance formed in esteem should also be given enough time to fall into the right category of friend or foe.

Leadership esteem is not enhanced if a leader makes associations with others more powerful than him in order to control or eliminate competition.

An old saying that comes to mind is "When elephants fight the grass gets trampled", Esteem cannot come out of just association with a more powerful ally who will only look after their own interests in time of adversity.

Esteemed leadership will build their own resources of cash and KASH to cover the "critical" level contingencies while "high" level issue responses are prepared and "medium" or "low" level are planned with a system of triage in place based on facts and KASH.

An Esteemed leader also recognizes esteem in others and encourages them by creating an environment of growth, innovation and self-confidence. The nature of esteemed leadership is to encourage diversity and sharing without prejudice. This would include providing an equal opportunity to the constituents in terms of access to infrastructure, health, education, arts, sciences, utilities etc. that allows them to attain their potential.

The synergy of esteem in the Leadership of Governance is the first crucial step to the ultimate goal of a global interdependent and symbiotic relationships and alliances that lead to self- governance. Alliance, in your evo-devo world, is the union of Virtue and Esteem. The peer to peer alliances amongst esteemed leaders who have the desired characteristics and diverse qualities that can create a "value-added" competitive advantage for the alliance is an excellent process to attain SUCCESS.

These alliances are FOR synergy and diversity but not AGAINST other esteemed leaders. In their culture these alliances are a low risk and high value strategy to gain sustainable growth. In the process of natural and artificial selection alliances and collaborations have consistently contributed to incremental enhancement of both evolutionary and cultural development. The alliances can be STRATEGIC and TACTICAL in their nature. The commonality of interests in terms of low risk and high value have also to be supported by the equivalency of Leadership Core Values and an equitable sharing of both risk and reward in order to achieve the symbiosis of alliances. For example the DNA of one organism makes up the genome. The DNA from all the organisms in a system constitutes the metagenome. The alliances of symbiosis found in the metagenome suggest that the entire community or system is governed in unity within the diversity of the genome. This provides us a powerful lesson in the Leadership of Governance as we search for the points of convergence to attain symbiosis and self-actualization by pushing the envelope of Esteem, Alliances and Diversity further.

In the natural ecology process evolution is an emergent process of governance with no conscious "selector". In the governance of Human Ecology we have a defined "selector" i.e. The Leader. This crucial difference moves us away from the process of natural selection alone to the modified process of artificial selection. If this modification of artificial selection deviates too far from the natural process the "Implosion Effect" is triggered.

The "selector" or the leader is responsible for the standards of governance that are implemented. The selector also acts the catalyst for cultural and evolutionary transformation of governance from both a political and an apolitical standpoint. The values of Esteem through ethics and transparency alongside the virtues of honesty, humility, tolerance, patience and justice are required in any selector to ensure that the gap between the natural processes and the artificial transformations does not exceed the "stretching" point but takes place incrementally and symmetrically both at the genome and the metagenome levels.

In an attempt to understand this complex linkage and the symbiotic nature of this alliance let's look at a recent study conducted on a mysterious ailment called COLONY COLLAPSE DISORDER (CCD) that has wiped out large numbers of bees and other pollinators who are essential to our survival. Nearly 100 crops require pollination by honeybees. The annual value of the bee's work is $215 Billion worldwide as per the Scientific American article by Ms. Cox-Foster and Dennis Van Engels. Bees are communal and have similarities to our governance processes. After extensive research the reasons for the CCD epidemic boiled down to the study of the bee's genome in relation to the metagenome of the environment. It was discovered that the cause of the CCD was due to the compromised immune system of the bees and other pollinators due to poor nutrition and food diversity. Honeybees and wild pollinators no longer have the same number or variety of flowers available to them because we have tried to "neaten" our environments. We maintain large green lawns free of any "weeds" such as clover or dandelions" says the article. The fact is that to the bees our green lawns and "weed" free parks and roadsides are akin to a barren desert. In 2008 the U.S. Congress for the first time modified its agricultural policy to include pollination protection measures such as setting aside conservation land where wild-flowers can grow to create multiple "nectar corridors". Without the bees many foods included in our daily breakfast such as an array of fruits, jams, jellies, almonds, milk etc. would disappear from our tables. The ancient alliance between the pollinators and nature is being violated by our selectors and their governance resulting in a diet without fruit and vegetables we now take for granted.

The evo-devo of Leadership of Governance has the crucial responsibility of the UNIVERSAL SERVICE OBLIGATION (USO) that all great leaders have to be aware of and perform effectively for the sake of the metagenome and your role as the "selectors" of beneficial traits. The USO trait of governance is the essential component of any form of self-governance whether altruism, reciprocal altruism, alliance or symbiosis. The alliance of esteem between the family, the community, the government and the leaders has to begin now in order to meet the RIGHT CUBE parameters of RIGHT Solution at the RIGHT TIME for the RIGHT REASONS for attaining the evo-devo needed in the Leadership of Governance. The question of how we will balance these critical elements of SUCCESS against the economic advantages is the next step in our evo-devo journey as we analyze the Leadership of Economics in the subsequent chapter.

"BEYOND GOVERNANCE TO SELF-ACTUALIZATION"

"Evo-Devo Statement"

CHAPTER 15

THE LEADERSHIP OF ECONOMICS

Wealth has become synonymous with economic leadership. Wealth is defined as an abundance of valuable possessions or money and the state of possessing this is economic prosperity. Communal Wealth can be defined as the condition in which the individual prosperity is directly proportional to the number of people with whom we share the rewards of our increased specialization and prosperity. This then is the Leadership of Economics in its evo-devo avatar based on the single and unique focus of creating a shared, sustainable and synergistic environment for all the constituents. The "ECONOMIC MAN" of the 20th century and the "PSYCHOLOGICAL MAN" of the 21st century have to merge together to achieve the above mentioned goal of the evo-devo economics.

The word "Economic" itself is derived from the Greek word "Ockonomia" which literally means "managing a household". This then is the fundamental principle of economics. How we as leaders managed to confuse and twist this simple fact into a system that occupies whole sections of huge libraries is a mystery. IF each household is sustainable and synergistic in its "Ockonomia". THEN the entire community is automatically prosperous when the rewards are shared. The mystery of supply side economics, demand projections, market research, valuations, mergers and acquisitions, inflation, deflation, GDP growth or greed is unveiled in the "ockonomia" principle of fact based economics at all levels of leadership.

The current scenario wherein the "corporate nations" have all the rights of an individual with none of the responsibility is the primary cause of the mystery surrounding the economic environment of today. The leadership of these corporate nations who are making the laws but remain above the laws and have a continued unhealthy alliance with the government of the people need this mystery of economics to achieve their personal goals of wealth acquisition at the detriment of other weaker nations. For example the fact of globalization is that Third World surplus was $ 1 trillion in the 70's and currently stands at a deficit of $11 Trillion. 1% of the households in most countries control 90% of the wealth. Most of the world's population has an income of less than $2 per day. The Corporate Emperors and their supporting governments are as autocratic and controlling in their Economic Imperialism as those of the past. The factors that defined the empires of old are similar to the economic empires of today as you will observe below:

a) RESOURCE HOARDING from Occupied Territories or Subsidiaries, Patents etc.

b) RESOURCE EXPLOITATION from Occupied Territories or Sweat shops etc.

c) FORCED SUBJUGATION by armies in the Occupied Territories or "SHOCK and AWE" of Iraq, World Wars, Nuclear threats, WMD's and UN Peacekeeping Force to implement economic strategies beneficial to the emperor.

d) CULTURAL DOMINATION of the Occupied Territories or language, arts, food, music, movies, social networking sites and education is used to destroy diversity.

e) SINGLE CURRENCY in the Occupied territories or Controlling the trade through the oil cartel and the Dollar as well as debt control via currency through institutions like IMF/World Bank.

f) INFORMATION CONTROL in the Occupied Territories or media ownership, technology ownership and telecommunication ownership.

g) JUDICIAL CONTROL of Occupied Territories or undermining laws through force and creating judicial non-independence through economic power.

The 7 factors of commonality as demonstrated clearly define the nature of economic leadership and the culture of unfair advantage promoted in the world today. Economic considerations governing leadership behavior are currently mired in the attempt to predict the opponent's response. The tendency of the economic considerations to exist in the domain of conflict rather than the synergy of mutual pooling of risks to gain an alliance of benefits is apparent in all the economic trends we observe around us. In order to understand the principles of unification for the leadership of economics we will assess ten diverse areas of economic growth in the following domains: a) Collaboration b) Beauty c) Happiness d) Negotiation e) Risk f) Trade g) Technology h) Threat i) Sharing and last but not least k) Cheating. We will also look at the key "Quotients" that define economic value and the economic drivers that create the shared success and sustainable and synergistic benefits for all constituents.

The above objective can only be achieved if you take a moment to define the two common principles of evo-devo economics that will enable you to understand the commonality of goals and the unification of strategies that will transform the economic leadership of today to the Leadership of Economics that is desired for tomorrow. The commonality principles of evo-devo of economics are stated as under:

1) "SERDUCT" Principle

2) "BAR STOOL" Principle

The SERDUCT principle is the merging of the concepts of products and services at all economic levels including processes with a view to retain synergy across the enterprise. The goal of SERDUCTS is to deliver enhanced benefits to users and providers in a healthy symbiosis. The idea is simple but as all simple solutions it is marred in execution due to the complexity syndrome i.e. "We tried this before but it did not work" or the eternal favorites of all management gurus "It does not match our core competencies". The fact is that these complexities to the SERDUCT concept are self-created not mandated. The principle of SERDUCTS is derived from the combination of Tangible and Intangible benefits for all solutions that promote ethical consumption .The idea of effectively minimizing risk, through shared responsibility and quantifying the metrics of benefits including the plugging of any gaps in knowledge and process that existed due to the inflexible nature of stand-alone products and services or a non-synergistic marriage of convenience of the two, is our goal in the Leadership of Economics.

In the existing products and services world of demand scarcity, cash shortages and market share focus the solutions are measured in three distinct domains i.e. FEATURES, ADVANTAGES and BENEFITS or FAB. In an attempt at success both the users and the providers are trying to gain competitive advantage with FAB. The problem is that the restrictive nature of FAB allows competitive advantage for a few but averages out the benefits to the many. The features are common but multiple while the advantages are many but not personalized and the benefits are similar for all. The FAB process tries to fulfill the quantity gap which is finite while the abundant area of sustainable growth is left untouched. In order to play the FAB game technological obsolescence and feature based selling continuously consumes more energy than required. The SERDUCT principle is based on the factor of abundant demand and Natural Capital that is supported by FACT based economics. The four pillars of SERDUCTS and FACT based economics are:

a) FULFILLMENT of NEEDS and WANTS of THE CONSUMER

b) ADVANTAGE of WISE CHOICE

c) CUSTOMIZATION for PERSONALIZED BENEFITS

d) TIMELY and TECHNOLOGICALLY STABLE

The primary advantage of the SERDUCT principle in the FACT paradigm is the synergy of process and knowledge to deliver individual benefits with minimum wastage' on time for stable and sustainable growth. The movement from FAB to FACT and scarcity to abundance is the "MIDAS TOUCH" of a leader who can turn the existing solutions to gold by streamlining the benefits to meet the needs and wants as well as execute the solutions flawlessly for the timely delivery of these benefits. The negative effects of the "MIDAS TOUCH" are also eliminated by the SERDUCTS shared nature of the benefits since there is no greed in sharing.

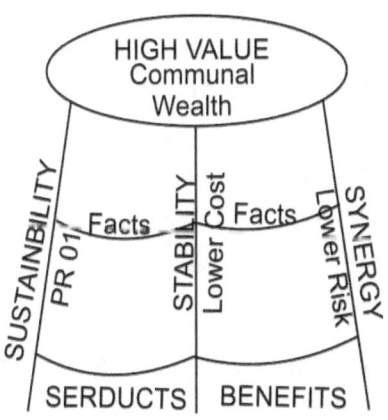

THE BAR STOOL of ECONOMIC VALUE (Fig. 42)

The second principle of evo-devo economics is the "BAR STOOL" analogy. The FACT is that "Benefits are the reason for all economic activity". You also saw in the previous process that the consumption of benefits has to ethical, personalized, and shared equitably. The BAR STOOL analogy is illustrated above.

If the unification principle of evo-devo economics is based on stability, sustainability and synergy then a BAR STOOL standing on just one leg of LOW COST or CASH as a indicator of wealth is inherently unstable. On the other hand the BAR STOOL of economic value that is sitting on a tri-pod of communal wealth that has the stability of LOWER COST, the sustainability of RAPID RETURN ON INVESTMENT and the synergy of LOWER RISK thus creating High ECONOMIC VALUE is the desired solution. The effect of the HIGH ECONOMIC VALUE that is shared by the provider of SERDUCT with the users who then share it with their consumers creates a cycle of competitive advantage across the entire domain of ethical consumption of lower cost, lower risk and rapid ROI.

The commonality of objectives of both the SERDUCT Principle and the BAR STOOL is to combine tangible and intangible benefits in a timely manner to achieve significantly high ECONOMIC VALUE. Let us know delve into the realm of ten key segments of economic value to understand the unification of goals across the entire spectrum of economic growth:

1) ECONOMICS of COLLABORATION: The economics of collaboration is the advantage of symbiotic adaptation. The symbiotic adaptation of collaboration increases the economic "kinship" value by allowing the SERDUCTS and the BARSTOOL to work in tandem. Collaboration requires faith, trust and a sharing of mutual benefits. Any economic collaboration is successful if it promotes precision, efficiency, effectiveness and specialization and also lowers complexity. Collaboration evolves as you interact repeatedly and memorize the advantage of reciprocally beneficial behavior.

2) ECONOMICS of BEAUTY: 36-26-36 or 0.70 or less Hip to waist ratio are the economic values of the current economics of beauty. The evo-devo economics of beauty are mired in the concept of symmetry. The beauty of symmetry and its evolutionary capabilities are a key driver of economic value. The idea of

DNA based personalized medicine to an anti-aging "fountain of youth" are all part of this fascinating area of economic growth. The beauty of symmetry and its economic value can become a source for sustainability and stability if you can move away from the fear of loss to the advantage of economic gain of synergy. The current race is for status and pride where "We love to win but we really hate to lose". If we can look for Esteem in the beauty of symmetry the economic value of the beauty of symmetry will be substantial.

3) Economics of HAPPINESS: Today America consumes more than 25% of the world's services with only 6% of the population. In order to be "happy" we have added twice the number of cars per person plus microwaves, color TV'S , DVD's, mobile phones, laptops, computers, and $15 Billion worth of shoes to our personal inventory over the last 40 years. Happiness is a powerful economic force. The current perception that wealth is directly proportional to happiness is unfortunately proving to be a myth. The pursuit of happiness that drives consumption without need is a recipe for unhappiness. The evo-devo of economics that transforms the elusive goal of happiness to the economics of contentment meets the advantages of the BAR STOOL principle and is sustainable. The economics of contentment is not measured by the wealth of the few but the freedom of choice and the contentment of the many. The economic engine of contentment will be measured in terms of the purchasing power "parity" of the masses for ethical consumption of SERDUCTS that are beneficial for the community.

4) ECONOMICS OF TRADE: The economics of trade works on the simple paradigm that favors are traded for profit of both parties as long as the economic gain of what they acquire is more than what they lost. This of economic gain is the current value of trade. There is no issue if both parties receive the transaction gain at the same time. The problems start when reciprocity of gain does not occur simultaneously. The delayed exchange of benefits where one party accrues the gain before the other party is the cause of disruption in the economics of trade. The existing solutions money, debt, letters of credit, collateral, Insurance etc. are temporary in nature and increase the risk of the trade. The evo-devo of economics of benefit exchange that trades KASH (Knowledge, Attitude, Skills and Honest Effort), in an-atmosphere that shares "risk and distributes rewards equitably, the reciprocity of delayed exchange of gain happens successfully. The reason is that the party which

receives the benefits early also carries the larger risk initially and as the ethical consumption of benefits progresses the risk is gradually transferred to the other party. In the evo-devo economics of exchange of benefits industries such as Information, Knowledge, Process improvement and SERDUCT are the best trades as a small investment of time and effort at the individual level can translate into a huge advantage for the user community and vice-versa.

5) ECONOMICS of NEGOTIATION: In the successful exchange of benefits, negotiation is a crucial catalyst that allows the timely delivery of the benefits. The time lost in negotiation due to the lack of facts and relevant decision criteria is currently a huge waste of economic wealth in the guise of "Opportunity Cost". The existing economics of negotiation suffers acutely from this malady of "Opportunity Cost" because each party in the trade is trying to minimize profit to the other. The winner is the one who eliminates the freedom of choice for the other either by monopolistic behavior or setting a limit to concessions. The Power of NO in negotiations sets the boundaries of the exchange and usually ends up sacrificing key needs and trust. Is this economics of Negotiation sustainable and stable? The answer is NO. The evo-devo economics of negotiation works is at when there are no limits in sharing risk and, high value other than continuity of the relationship. This can only happen when both the parties in the negotiation are in a peer-to-peer environment that ensures equal leverage on both sides. It is a fact that negotiations really begin when both the parties walk off the table and say NO. The evo-devo economics of negotiation is focused on the advantages of customer retention and trust rather than a constant push for customer acquisition.

6) ECONOMICS of RISK: The economics of risk are hidden in the promise of benefits. The minimization of risk is currently based on the principle where the beneficiary of the promise carries the risk in direct proportion to the amount of faith he has on the provider of the promise of benefit accrual. As a substitute for faith and trust we have created debt instruments that minimize this risk. These instruments of exchange while reducing the risk also lower the benefits of the promise to both parties. The worst risk is predicated when one of parties in the exchange has nothing of value to lose. Unfortunately, the worst risk is being practiced extensively in the current economic structure because we continue to deal with strangers in matters of trade and

consumption without building a relationship for the alignment of values. The evo-devo of economics of risk works best when used with the BAR STOOL principle that allows you pool the risk. Risk Mitigation is automatically achieved in any exchange or negotiation as soon as risk is shared. The most efficient process to pool the risk and share it equitably is to minimize the **Variance Levels** in the exchange process. The lower the Variance levels of a transaction the higher the probability of success and lowers the risk of unplanned failure. The elimination of variance also ensures flawless execution to guarantee the delivery of the negotiated promise. The other key factor for lowering the risk and enhancing economic gain is to make yourself irreplaceable as part of the promise of benefits by providing unmatched value. The two factors of lower variance and unmatched value are crucial to the evo-devo economics of risk and need to be included in any trading process for sustainability, stability and synergy.

7) ECONOMICS of THREAT: In the economics of threat "Size Matters". The current focus on size and its leverage as a threat is a primary cause of the elimination of communication. The problem is that the economics of threat only delivers results if you can carry out the threat. The ability to carry out the threat is negated if the other party makes it impossible for you to carry out the threat or "force" a showdown knowing that the threat will not be carried out. The strategy is fraught with danger for both sides if no ethical motive or gain exists. Threat is a promise and the economics of threat is the foundation of some of the most profitable economic drivers of today's world. Unfortunately, the current economics of threat is a "zero-sum" game as it also destroys trust and culture to create an unmanaged "Implosion Effect". The solution to this threat option is to create leverage of "shame" or dishonor against the use of threats as leverage for economic gain. The offender needs to lose the moral advantage and be required to follow a rehabilitation methodology for correcting the behavioral flaw. This peer-to-peer methodology of rehabilitation should also remove the fear of revenge as well as the causes that promoted the use of the economics of threat in the first place. The economics of rehabilitation are a strong growth area for the generation of economic value and far exceed the gain accrued from the economics of threat. Also abundant growth can be achieved if the economics of threat is focused on the threats that are common to all and are global destroyers of economic gain. The

elimination of threats such as poverty, hunger, pollution, energy shortage, global warming, lack of bio-diversity etc. are all areas that can push the economics of threat as the ultimate economic driver. The Wise Choice of fact based economics is the evo-devo mandated in the nature of the economics of threat to attain the "survival of the wisest" paradigm, instead of the "survival of the fittest", for positive transformation.

8) ECONOMICS of TECHNOLOGY: Technology is a well-known multiplier of wealth. In our current trends the economics of technology are used to gain an unfair advantage over the exchange process. The reason is the massive amounts of investment in research and development that is poured into the technological enhancement that the investor needs the unfair advantage of Intellectual Property protection to receive economic gain. The evo-devo in the economics is to share the investment and the rewards of the initial advancement of technology amongst all the constituents or beneficiaries. At the same time allow innovation to improve the process and share the competitive advantages by enhancing the economics of technology across the entire spectrum of the consumers. The same technology will be innovated multiple times with economic gains for the innovators and the community. Unique technologies and innovation can also help lower risk while making the community that owns the technology irreplaceable as the gains are shared in a sustainable environment. The economics of technology in the evo-devo form supports sharing and sustainability of the solutions created. This also creates new areas of growth and abundant demand that will be in the used in the future. As an example, areas such as Teleportation, Genetics, Gravity Energy, Quantum Mechanics, Bio-Technology, Simulators, Telemedicine, Distance education etc are highly profitable technology plays as economic drivers since they transform scarcity into abundance through technology. The key is the Wise Choice of using technology for the benefit of all rather than just a few.

9) ECONOMICS of SHARING: You have observed that in our journey we have used the advantages of sharing as a catalyst to promote sustainable growth as well as economic advantage. Sharing is an evolutionary form of humanity. The economics of sharing can be an excellent growth driver as human Sciences and humanity are areas of abundant demand. Even the supply side of economics in its FIND, OBTAIN, CREATE, STORE and DISTRIBUTE process can do with a huge dose of sharing as the supply points become geographically dispersed and

interdependent. The current economics of sharing are mired in the problems of self-interest. We share only if can get something extra in return. Even the sharing in religion comes with an expectation of salvation and guilt elimination. Sharing is a cultural development and the need for sharing without expectation requires a higher level of maturity and trust. The economics of sharing work best if you give first and then consume. Unfortunately, we prefer to share with those who will share with us. Sharing, currently, is equivalent to a line of credit and is therefore a commodity for trading in the economics of sharing. Bankers will only share a line of credit with you when you have the least need for it and will take away this "favor" when you need it the most. **The evo-devo of the economics of sharing is based on the SERDUCT and BAR STOOL principles of utilizing sharing as a multiplier of benefit exchange**. IF we share our prosperity with the community THEN it expands relating more demand for ethical consumption. The "Double Dip" of economic gain of sharing is felt as you get the initial uptake of demand of the SERDUCTS and as you share the benefits of the uptake through the transfer of wealth, knowledge, and process the second and third waves of demand are triggered. The higher the number of people involved in the sharing process higher the economic gain accrued for all. The multiplier effect of sharing is also enhanced since the cost of one party becomes the revenue of the other as the **"zero marginal cost" phenomenon kicks in for creating stable and sustainable growth.** The ability to defer the reward of gratification is a sign of culture and humanity. Great Nations and enterprises have been built on the deferment of rewards. The current growth and prosperity that we are so proud of is due to the investment made by earlier generations in building infrastructure, knowledge, and processes that we are using today. The question is ARE WE DOING THE SAME FOR OUR FUTURE GENERATIONS?? The Answer is NO.

The economics of sharing as part of the evo-devo of Leadership is mandated for the future as expertise in all societies is becoming more unevenly distributed and the only way to create a bridge between the "centers of excellence" and the users is through the "TECH SHARE" strategy. In the economics of sharing you have to stop discounting future gain because of mistrust and "cheaters" but continue to share the rewards in order to keep the economic cycle running smoothly.

10) ECONOMICS of CHEATING: Cheating is a highly profitable enterprise and the temptation of "unworked for gain" its key motivation. At the same time cheating is also one of the key factors of lowering the economic value for the "non-cheaters". The entire legal system, governance and laws are designed for cheaters. The entropy that exists in the economic system can solely be attributed to the cheaters. A cheater can be local, national or international and even a combination of all three. A cheater can be a net-cheater i.e. one who does not reciprocate fully or a gross cheater i.e. one who does not reciprocate at all.

The flaw in our current thinking, that accounts for the consumption of a large amount of resources in the economics of cheating and its prevention, is that we can solve the problem of cheating through the use of laws and logic alone. Logic can teach you rational thought but not about the nature of man. The domain of cheating is entrenched in our nature. Rationality and logic fail in the economics of cheating since it exists in our nature and is governed by possibilities and probabilities. The possibility factor is the foundation on which resides the economics of cheating. This factor is governed by two principles: a) the quantity and quality of cheating and b) the circumstances and the chances of getting caught. In a recent survey it was found that 50% of men and women would cheat by going on a date with a stranger in spite of being in a relationship. It was also observed that only 6% of the women went to the stranger's apartment after the date. 69% of the men though went willingly to the women's apartment. 25% of the men who refused to go cited the reason that their fiancée was in town. This experiment was repeated across the nation with similar results. The economics of cheating still seems to be a bastion of the males of the human species.

Another example of the economics of cheating can be found in the world of Ants. Ant colonies have a social structure similar to human communities. Ants are altruistic towards their own but will go to war and take slaves from rival colonies. All Ant colonies have a certain percentage of "cheater" ants. These cheaters do not perform their duties but steal food from the communal stocks. The Ants in the colony set up various strategies to control the cheaters including social ostracism. In a recent controlled experiment the scientists eliminated all the cheater ants from the colony. The result was unexpected. The ants became complacent and ill-prepared. In the end they were taken over by a rival colony of ants. In an alternative experiment the percentage of cheater ants was increased to over 40% of the colony. As the cheaters prospered the whole colony collapsed in a matter of days. The moral of the story: You may not want them but we do need the cheaters for survival but in small numbers. There are multiple examples of this phenomenon today if we look   at the Russian black market economy or the Colombian drug cartels and their impact on the community. The time and energy we spend on negotiating contracts and a pact to prevent cheating is another example of the counterproductive nature of the current solutions. In fact we currently spend more time finalizing the divorce than on the marriage.

The evo-devo required in the economics of cheating is two-fold. Firstly we need to evolve an excellent "cheater detector". ESP or a "mind reader" might be a good tool, if available. Firstly, the cheater detector has to be ethical, moral, transparent and public. It should log all the parameters of the exchange of benefits and the promise of their delivery. The responsibility matrix would identify the cause of cheating. Secondly, public disclosure of the cheaters and their modus operandi is necessary to lower the economics of cheating. Rehabilitation, forgiveness and behavior transformation should be in-built into the system. The unlocked energy from the reduction of the current processes to monitor and control cheating will create fresh Natural Capital and eliminate the "zero-sum" nature of the economics of cheating.

As you must have observed from all the above economic values, the key to success is to enhance the economic values through sustainability, synergy and sharing and for the entire community in order to attain the Leadership of Economics. The Question: What are these evo-devo factors that connect the core economic values of sharing, sustainability and synergy??

The Answer: Economic management as it is practiced today is a function of "Who is Right". The evo-devo leadership of Economics is based on the function of "What is Right". William of Occam, in his famous principle of the Occam's razor, said "Frustra fit Plura, quod fieri potest per pauciora" which means that "it is unwise to do with more what can be done with less". He further added "Entia non silent multiplicand praeter neccessitatem" which translates into "It is wise not to multiply entities unnecessarily" The wisdom of Occam's Razor allows us to handle ambiguity while the principles of the BARSTOOL and

SERDUCTS are practiced in the evo-devo paradigm. These principles that promote lower cost, lower risk, high value and a rapid return on Investment through the judicious use of available Natural capital are in line with the wisdom of Occam.

The secret of stable, sustainable and synergistic growth is therefore hidden in the economic value of the enterprise. The measure of this Economic Value is derived from three key quotients as illustrated below:

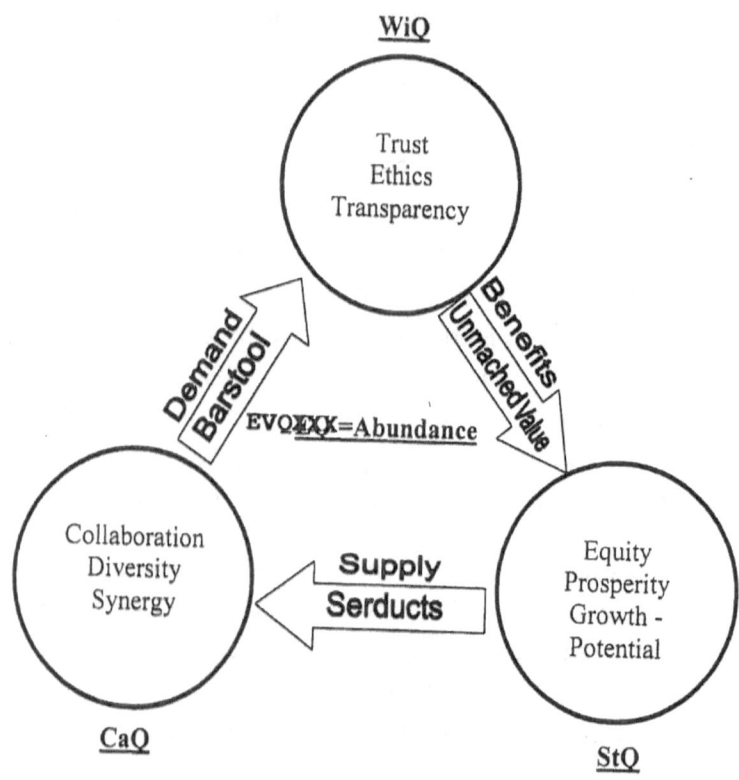

ECONOMIC VALUE QUOTIENTS – EVO's (Fig 43)

The Economic Value Quotients or the EVQ's i.e. StQ, CaQ, and WiQ, are the key measures of the Economic Value (EV) of any enterprise. The Economic Value or EV of the system is the true indicator of its success. These three quotients affect every sphere of economic activity by imparting competitive advantage. The higher the EVQ's the higher the efficiency, THE effectiveness and productivity of the enterprise.

The Evo-Devo of Leadership

As the community becomes more mobile, more virtual and more informed the Leadership of Economics is transformed from being purely monetary to a more diverse combination of the EVQ's. The ideas of the technology multiplier as an enhancer of Digital iQ and Technical Civilization are mandated today when the entire global environment is shedding economic value with no end in sight. The current leaders are at a loss to explain this economic slide into oblivion. Traditional models of demand and supply, increased productivity, and understanding customer needs are not robust enough to stand the chaos of this GREAT DEPRESSION of the 21st Century. Therefore the EVQ's and its attached EV is the only solution to retain sanity and achieve the evo-devo of economics. The Leadership of Economics that will re-create the EV for the great "STARS" is supported by the three EVQ's as under:

a) THE STAKEHOLDER QUOTIENT- StQ

b) THE COMPETITIVE ADVANTAGE QUOTIENT- CaQ

c) THE WISDOM QUOTIENT- WiQ

The correlation of these quotients with the true economic value of any enterprise will be apparent as you analyze the strength of the EVQ's as economic drivers of sustainable growth.

a) **The StQ** is a pure derivative of the diverse needs and wants of the various stakeholders within the leader's sphere of influence. This includes the shareholders, the employees, clients, the collaborators and the competitors.

b) **The CaQ** is derived from the needs and wants of the benefits of stable, sustainable and synergistic solutions. This CaQ will result in combining KASH with Technology to create "centers of excellence" and domain expertise for flawless execution.

c) **The WiQ** is the derivative of the needs and wants of the community for an innovative, evolutionary and globally beneficial Leadership. WiQ is the measure of UNMATCHED VALUE of an ethical, principled, and transparent leadership that is founded on the evo-devo of "best practices".

The EVQ's are directly proportional to the Economic Value Drivers that exist for each of the quotients respectively. The economic value drivers can be broken down into nine key areas of greatness resting on the pillars of StQ, CaQ and WiQ.

The StQ Drivers:

1) Equity: Equity as an economic value driver of the StQ is the **quantative** measure of the intrinsic value of the entity. This would include the net worth, earnings, retained earnings, debt ratios, market value, brand value, P/E ratios (Price to Earning) and EBITDA (Earnings Before Interest, Taxes, Depreciation and Amortization). Equity is a strong indicator of corporate greatness and can be modified for use in governance and communities as well.

2) Prosperity: The prosperity driver of StQ is the measure of the contentment value of all the constituents in the sphere of influence. It includes the practices that share risk and rewards, the sum of the value of the parts, individually, and the valuation of the whole, collectively. It also measures the economic reserves and entropy of the entity for the resilience to withstand failure.

3) Growth Potential: The growth potential driver is a quantitative measure of the market scenario in relation to the SERDUCTS offered by the entity as well as any innovative advantages that create unique and "inflation proof" solutions. The growth potential would look at horizontal, vertical and cyclic projections that cover the capacity, capability and vision gaps in the target markets. The advantages of "zero marginal cost" growth through alliances, technology, and sourcing, shoreing and process improvement practices are all part of the measure of growth potential.

The CaQ Drivers:

4) Collaboration: The CaQ driver of collaboration is the measure of the quantitative and qualitative values of cooperation that exist in the entity both internally and externally. This would include processes that assist in flawless execution while promoting equitable sharing of risk and rewards. It also measures the kinship values of the Leaders with the community and vice-versa. Collaboration drivers exist in owned, acquired, merged and shared Natural Capital of the entire system.

5) Diversity: Diversity is a strong indicator of the CaQ with respect to the economic value drivers. Diversity is a combination of the intrinsic and extrinsic values to withstand evolutionary and developmental transformation in order to adapt to stimuli in an effective manner.

6) Synergy: The CaQ of synergy is the measure of the number of existing beneficial processes that are "open" sourced and provide a seamless integration across the enterprise by reducing "bottlenecks" and "internal back flux". The use of "Tech Share" strategies, user groups, escalation processes, "Right" Cube response rimes and MTBF (Mean Time Between Failures) are indicators of the CaQ of synergy. Synergy is also directly proportional to the number of efficient implementations of planned processes within the system to achieve the desired results.

The WiQ Drivers:

7) Trust: Trust is the key measure of the economic value of leadership as well its WiQ. Trust bridges the talents and the potential of the community with the innovation of the leaders in a strategically focused, flawlessly executed, performance oriented, and fast "Right Response" culture that is practiced consistently. The trust that empowers the leaders to deliver the results that are desired while allowing the community to develop its potential to the maximum, both individually and collectively, defines this core value driver. Trust is the economic driver that creates symbiotic relationships that are mutually beneficial and will stand the test of time. Trust is also the measure of the trustworthiness of the entity in an interdependent role. Unfortunately, "IN GOD WE TRUST" is the only economic value of the U.S. Dollar today.

8) Ethics: Ethics is the economic value driver that combines the sum total of our values, beliefs and faith systems. Ethics is the value driver that increases trust through the provision of strength to resist the temptation of greed and individual unfair advantage. Ethics as an economic value driver promotes synergy of goals that encourages loyalty and communication amongst all the constituents.

9) Transparency: The WiQ of transparency as an economic value driver is a measure of the inclusive nature of the leaderships' Wise Choices that allows the participation of the constituents to achieve shared SUCCESS.

Transparency is directly related to the number of beneficial decisions made by leadership that enhance the sustainability and synergy of the entire community in a shared mode for the Leadership of Economics.

These Three Quotients and their accompanying value drivers are in essence the real economic values of the entity under consideration not just money. These EVs are also the key to "unlimited communal wealth" without the scarcity of cash which is currently a limiting factor to growth. The EVQ's alongside the SERDUCTs and BAR STOOL PRINCIPLES are all sources of free energy that generate new Natural capital based on the mutual exchange of benefits and risks. This "free capital" reduces our constant dependence on external sources of funding allowing you the luxury of abundant growth with independence under the Interdependence paradigm. The Evo-devo leadership of economics under the economic values as defined in our system can make the myth of "perpetual" growth, unmatched value and unlimited wealth a reality through the "S" curve of shared, sustainable and synergistic growth.

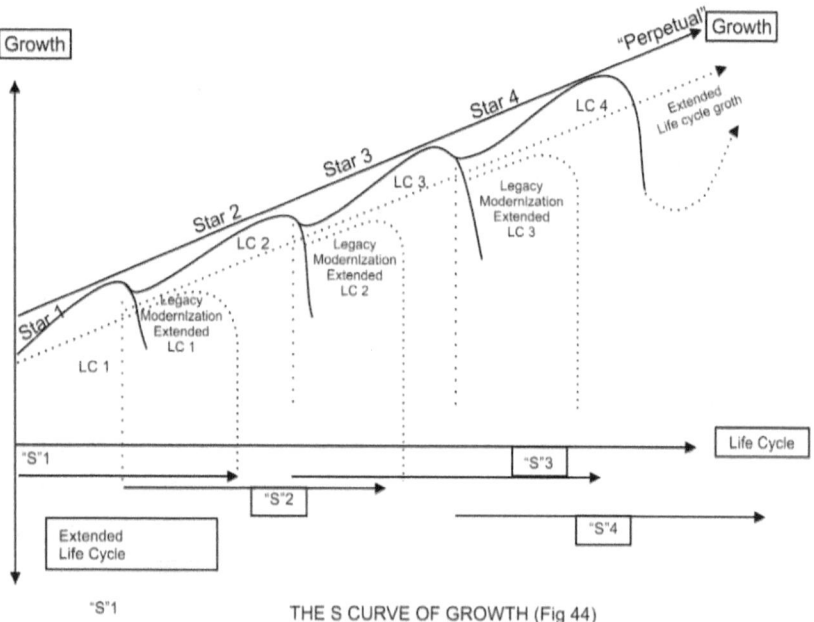

THE S CURVE OF GROWTH (Fig 44)

The "S" curve of EV is an excellent measure of the degree of SUCCESS and greatness of the entity. The "S" Curve combines the evo-devo principles alongside the associated economic value drivers (EVD) and the economic value

(EV) in an economic model that is founded on FACTS. A study undertaken of the greatness and success of key corporations, leaders and nations from an economic perspective has clearly shown that the EVD's are a common characteristic of all the entities and have lead to the "S" curve of Economic Value that is unified by the shared, sustainable and synergistic growth paradigm as shown above.

The concept of the "S" curve is to assemble the known FACTS of the StQ, CaQ and the WiQ and the EVD's in their logical structure and according to their degree of Probability (1-10) and Practice within the structure. You also need to ascertain the degree of Verifiability (1-5) of these FACTS. You also need to collect all the rational facts that contradict the first set of FACTS and weight each of them according to their verifiability. The set of ramifying possibilities and their degree on the "S" curve will find the one path that is consistent and real.

The assembly of this logical structure is like peeling an onion layer by layer. Each layer will annihilate branches one pair at a time and create new branches one pair at a time. In this entire process the orbit or "structural stability" of the onion is not destroyed and hence can grow perpetually while the orbits are rearranged to adapt. Similarly, the "S" curve of any system in its perpetuity allows the system to alternate between order and chaos of sustainable growth and time to create new avenues of growth as the existing ones lose their energy for growth. The "S" curve of growth, based on the EVQs and the EVDs of the entity, is a prime indicator of their degree of SUCCESS and the RIGHT SOLUTION for enhanced Economic Value. The mathematical representation of the "S" curve paradigm would be as under:

RIGHT SOLUTION DEGREE-"S" CURVE = (No. of FACTS in a LOGICAL STRUCTURE (1-9) X (DEGREE of PROBABILITY (1-10) X VERIFIABILITY INDEX (1-5) ÷ (Contradictions to Known Facts (1-5).

RANGE:

FACTS = 1-9 (No. of facts)

(EVD's)

Probability Degree (1-10)= Low-1

High-l0

Verifiability (1-5) = Low-1

High-5

The Higher the Degree of the Right solution on the "S" Curve the higher the probability of SUCCESS for a shared, sustainable and synergistic environment for becoming a "STAR". The Economic Value of the entity in its ability to use the chaos process to fund new branches of growth of the system symmetrically is the true measure of the "S" curve.

The "S" curve of "perpetual" economic value growth and greatness in its varying degrees is entrenched in the principles of renewable energy that can create managed "implosions" under chaos to release the free energy of entropy in the system to fuel explosive growth and move the entity towards perfection in a symmetrical manner that balances both time and distance. The "S" curve principle can be practiced in our day to day lives as leaders to reach the Right Solution for enhanced Economic Value consistently.

One of the key economic indicators of any corporation or nation or leadership in its ability to generate sustainable growth through the aegis of the "S" curve is known as **the PEG° ratio**. The PEG° ratio is a combination of the existing Price to Earnings ratio divided by the expected sustainable growth over the next 3, 15 and 10 years with the °(degree) of the probability of achieving the projected growth.

EV (Economic Value) = $P/E \div G°$

The growth potential on the EVQ's, the EVD's and the FACT based degrees of the solution hinges on the known probabilities and verified facts alongside the contradictory facts as seen in the earlier formula for the Right Solution Degrees of the "S" curve. The PEG° ratio is the measure of the entity to attain shared and sustainable growth with synergy. The worst case, best case and middle case scenarios can be run to quantify the ratio by using the different degrees of the indexes such as the industry P/E average, Industry growth rates, unique/inflation °proof" solutions, entropy, EVQ's and EVD's that are existing within the entity and externally. **The higher the PEG° ratio the lower the sustainability of the structure.** The lower the PEG° ratio compared to 1 i.e. PEG° ratio is equal to or lower than 1, the higher the Economic Value of the entity.

For example if the current P/E of the company is 15 and its projected Growth (G) is 20% over the next 3 years and the degree of probability based on the EVQ's, EVD's and Facts is 1 then the Economic Value is enumerated below:

EV= 15 ÷ (20 x 1) = 0.7° i.e. PEG° ratio of 0.7° which is lower than 1.

If we lower the growth rate in 5 years to 10% and the Degree of the Right Solution is still maintained at 1, then the structure becomes unsustainable as below:

EV = 15 ÷ (10 x1) = 1. 5° i.e. PEG° ratio of 1.5° which is higher than 1.

The further the PEG° ratio increases over 1 the higher the probability that the enterprise will not be able to sustain its Economic Value over time. This in turn implies that a fresh infusion of energy through Cash will be required to retain the edge of competitive advantage. The PEG° ratio within the "S" curve paradigm is a better approach to valuations in evo-devo economics rather than the current cash based methods such as multiples of EBITDA, EBIT or even cash flow. The PEG° ratio is a risk mitigation and high value strategy that provides the true measure of the economic energy of the entity. The PEG° measures the ability of the enterprise to survive in chaos and adversity where new sources of capital are not freely available. The mining of the existing legacy business logic to extend the life cycles through modernization are another benefit of the PEG° ratio.

The different processes that you have observed as part of the evo-devo of economics are all based on the principle that the leader is the custodian of the Natural Capital and the Communal Wealth. The Key Performance Indicator (KPI) of "STAR" Leaders is to use their vision to enhance the economic value for the entire community. The unique connection of the Leadership of Economics is a product of SPACE (Leadership Sphere of Influence), its MASS (the Economic Value) and the TIME (Sustainability and Sharing) to generate the ENERGY (Synergy and Symbiosis) for the benefit of all the constituents. This is the epitome of the evo-devo of Leadership of Economics.

The unmatched value of this formula i.e. SPACE x MASS x TIME= ENERGY for economic growth that is synergistic, shared and sustainable is further illustrated below:

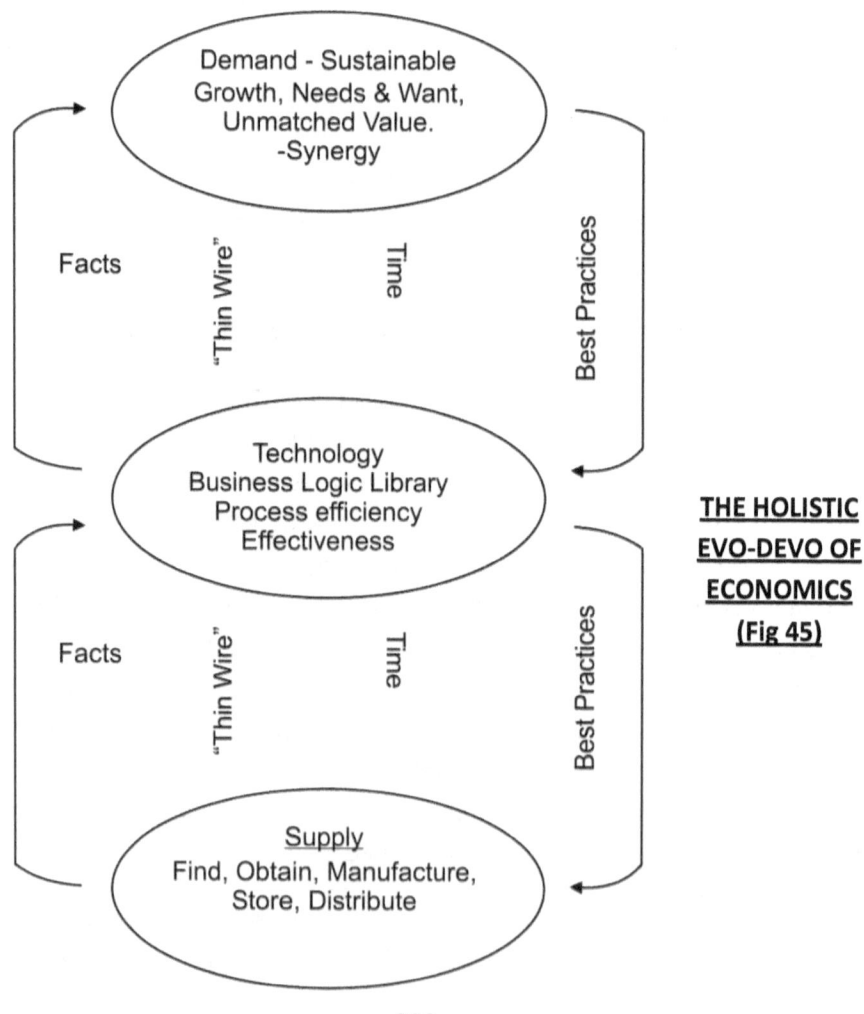

THE HOLISTIC EVO-DEVO OF ECONOMICS (Fig 45)

The holistic nature of the evo-devo of the Leadership of Economics is based on the process that links Facts, EVQ's, EVD's and Wise Choices with the Cycle of DEMAND and SUPPLY. The advantages of innovation and technology act as a constant source of modernization that is self-sustaining and minimizes the use of Natural Capital but maximizes ECONOMIC GAIN. The Leadership of Energy is a consequence of the above mentioned principles as you will find in the next part of our quest.

"A Foundation Eaten From Within Cannot Stand"- An Evo-Devo Statement

CHAPTER 16

<u>THE LEADERSHIP OF ENERGY with THOUGHT</u>

The evo-devo of leadership consciousness entails the ability to foresee facts that may not exist in the present. This transcendental power to understand events that are not observed by the five senses is not the domain of a few blessed humans. This facility will be given to those who seek it and practice the evo-devo principles of leadership. The five senses demand instant gratification which destroys energy and convolutes the thought process. This occurs because the five senses work with the five enemies of the Leadership of Energy with Thought i.e. **G**reed, **L**ust for unworked for gain, **A**nger, **S**elf-Interest and **S**elf ego in our evo-devo acronym of GLASS. The greatness of the Wise Choice that is based on Wise Laws and Moral Hope is the measure of the Leadership of Energy. The energy that has intellect, knowledge, and processes in place to move you away from the crisis management focus created by "internal back flux" to create innovations that enhance the communal wealth and Natural Capital.

The power of consciousness is about self-awareness. Every one of us aspires for greatness and recognition. Peter Ducker, one of the most advanced management thinkers of our times, said "In a few hundred years, when the history of our times is written from a long-term perspective, it is likely that the most important event these historians will see is not technology, not the Internet, not e-commerce. It is an unprecedented change in the human condition. For the first time literally substantial and rapidly growing number of people have choices. For the first time they will have to manage themselves." and SOCIETY IS TOTALLY UNPREPARED FOR THIS TRANSITION. The ability to make choices is leadership. The capability to make Wise Choices is the evo-devo of leadership that will be mandated for a large portion of your populace. The ability to make wise choices consistently can only be achieved through evo-devo.

The wise choices help in increasing the ENERGY QUOTIENT (EQ) of the community. The EQ of the community and the leadership sphere of Influence is enhanced as new thought processes are inducted into the system and bad traits are eliminated. Your leadership SUCCESS is your self-determinism to create the thought leadership of the Right Solutions and generating free energy for sustainable growth for the community. As Albert Einstein once said- "The significant challenges we face cannot be solved at the same level of thinking we were at when we created them". In order to jump to the next dimension of leadership thinking we need the fresh energy of Wise Choices. This energy is the EQ of evo-devo leadership. Fortunately, for you as leaders, the WISE CHOICE is hidden amid the Good and Bad Choices. The key is to have the vision and practice to find it consistently. Let us look at three examples to demonstrate this evo-devo process:

A) The Leadership of Energy with Thought that leads to the generation of large amounts of energy is one of the most famous discoveries of the 20th century i.e. the equation $E=MC^2$. This equation actually provided us with an answer to the How, What, When, Where and Why of the "Implosion Effect" for the explosive growth of energy. The equation also explains the seamless relationship of symbiosis between mass and energy in the universe. The idea of energy and mass as two unrelated domains was inbuilt into the entire scientific consciousness. It was also what our 5 senses and GLASS told us - Energy is the lightning, battery, electricity in electric wires while Mass is the rock, the tree, the grass which exist in the physical domain hence the two are distinct and separate entities. There was no common point of transpose or bridges between the two till a evolved Leadership of Energy with thought presented light as a wave and a particle and correlated it with speed with light.

When Einstein concluded that a light wave can only exist if it is continuously and actively moving forward, the inference was clear that "light", which is a form of energy, is in "perpetual motion" in order to exist. It also proved that light needs a constant source of energy that is freely available for it to achieve its forward motion. The fact is that a light wave keeps moving by virtue of one part moving forward and in that process releasing free energy for the movement of the next part. This true process of interdependence or the "exchange of free energy" and sharing is the being of all matter and the underlying truth of the equation $E=MC^2$. This brilliant equation does not end here. Like the stars this equation also created the linkage between Energy-Mass-Space and Time as well as attempted to relate the electrical, electromagnetic and gravitational forms of energy in a general theory. The fact that the nature of all these forces and dimensions are interconnected at the

Quantum Level in spite of their existence as individual domains proves our paradigm of unity amongst diversity. This can only occur if we can raise our level of thinking to transcend the 5 senses and the "internal back flux" of GLASS to connect the dots at the highest echelon of leadership.

B) The Leadership of Energy with thought can also be found in the area of bio-fuels and renewable energy. Rising energy costs and concerns over climate change from carbon-dioxide emissions have reignited interest in moving "Beyond Oil". Unlike oil, Biofuels are renewable and potentially carbon neutral. Burning a plant releases no more carbon than it absorbed while growing. Currently, the predominant fuel from organic sources is ethanol which is derived from corn in the USA and sugarcane in Brazil. Using the same crop as a source of both food and energy causes the demand to skyrocket which has caused rapid price hikes in the food prices. The graphs and illustrations below represent the current and future trends in Bio-fuels: (Ref: SEED's CRIBSHEET and US DOE-'REPORT)- Fig 46

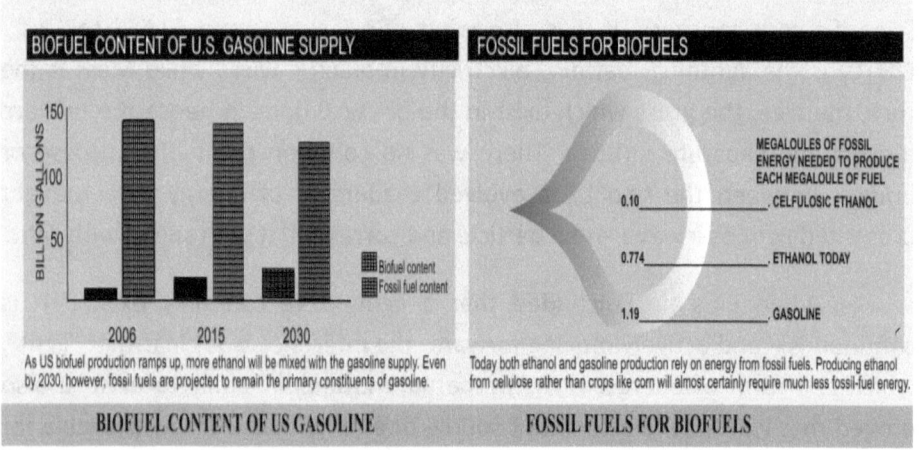

BIOFUEL CONTENT OF US GASOLINE   **FOSSIL FUELS FOR BIOFUELS**

Fig 46

Fortunately, a process under investigation can create ethanol from cellulose. This process, though complex, uses the plant stem and leaves and is less disruptive to the food supply as it uses the plant waste to generate energy. Also as we see in the illustration cellulosic ethanol uses only a fraction of energy from fossil foil compared to other processes of creation energy sources. While corn is easier than cellulose to convert to ethanol it requires more resources to grow than many other cellulose sources. The advantage of converting a waste product to fresh source of new energy is the Wise Choice. The same would apply to algae oil and other viable biofuels that await us in the third generation or beyond when highly efficient energy production from genetically modified sources become a reality.

C) A simple phenomenon of 4 (four) pure Hydrogen molecules, each having its own mass of 1 unit of wt., joining together in an implosion under "chaos" and "stress" of extreme pressure and heat (nearly 20 Million degrees Centigrade') to create a new element known as Helium. In this process of fusion the mass of Helium ends up 3.993 units of wt. and the free energy" of 0.7% is converted to energy that sustains the entire solar system. This energy was available 1 Billion years ago and will be able for at least 5 Billion years more. The 4 pure hydrogen atoms imploding to fuse together to form Helium with no regards for their individual identity is a process that occurs in the Sun consistently to convert nearly 4 million tons of hydrogen to pure energy every second. This extraordinary process does not end here. The multiple implosions that occur in the Sun in a coordinated manner to generate "free energy" across multiple system in an environment of sharing and "free exchange" allows the localized process to spread globally across the Sun. The "Helium Ash" created now forms Carbon. As the "S" curve of the process reaches its zenith in other stars similar to our Sun the carbon is utilized to generate life forms such as us. As the process of combining carbon atoms now occurs in the stars, new ash is produced at temperatures 2 Billion degrees centigrade, elements such as oxygen, silicon, sulfur are produced which all add up to create a sustainable environment for growth.

As the star itself finally explodes it sends out all these 200-250 different elements across the universe in a journey that landed around 100 of these elements on earth that currently sustain our growth. The exploding star ends up as a "Black Hole" or a concentrated mass of energy in the form of gravity that has the ability curve time and space. This curvature of time and space creates a primordial soup of anti-matter or "dark energy" that allows the Universe to expand further. A true evo-devo process in the Leadership of Energy.

As seen in the above examples, The Leadership of Energy with Thought is thus a combination of the leaders' choices and the community potential to adapt against any challenge. **This is achieved through the aegis of using the overall strengths and eliminating the individual weaknesses by complementing strengths through collaboration. The necessary organizational evo-devo required for implementing these processes successfully within yourselves and the community will require a higher level of thought and energy to achieve this goal.**

The question: "HOW DO YOU ACQUIRE THIS QUANTUM LEAP?

The initial step is to understand what this "Quantum Leap" entails. The nuts and bolts of this extraordinary process provide fresh impetus to growth in adversity as well acts as a source of Natural Capital for leadership. The Wise Choice or the Third Alternative, as you saw in the above processes that are pure and untainted is an integral part of the equation to attain Leadership of Energy with thought. An equation is the reason for transcending consciousness and taking thought leadership. Equality will prove the relationship between two or more disparate thoughts that were previously not related or maybe not even in existence to create or innovate an interdependence that will benefit the creator and the community simultaneously.

The ability to connect the dots that may seem random in nature to generate the energy of cohesiveness is the route to achieving the "quantum leap" and acquiring the Leadership of SUCCESS with your energy and thought process. The practice of the evo-devo principles and the constant search for knowledge while enhancing your skills within the framework of a positive attitude while motivating yourself to use a pure and honest methodology is the **Quasimodo for Self-Awareness and Energy.**

The Quasimodo "X" factor that enhances the EQ (energy quotient) of some leaders to achieve greatness while others are left in the black and white domain of good and bad is not a mystery anymore. The secret of the "X" factor of leadership greatness of thought and energy that allows you to make the quantum leap is shown in the pictorial representation below:

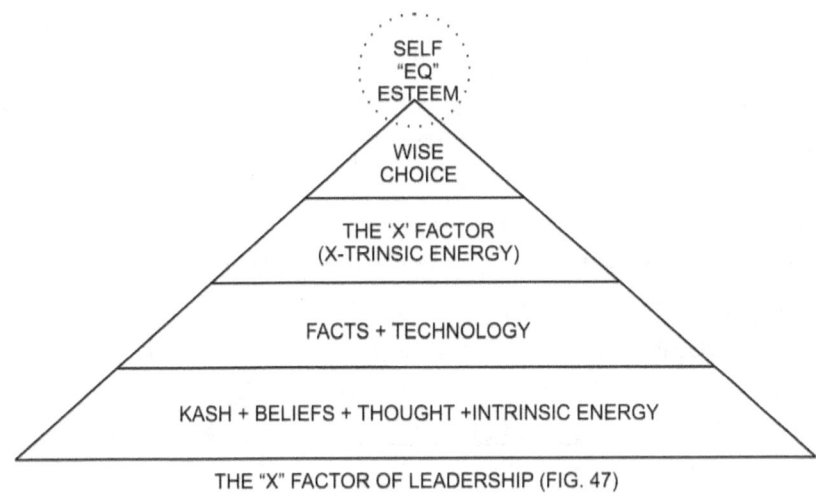

THE "X" FACTOR OF LEADERSHIP (FIG. 47)

The attributes of the leadership "X" factor are a combination of pure thinking and the elimination of GLASS in a evo-devo belief system based on FACTs built on an environment of Trust to generate leadership energy for the Wise Choice. These attributes are:

- X-CITER

- X-CEEDER

- X-CELLER

- X-PANDER   (Multiplier)

- X-ECUTOR

- X-OTHERMAL

-X-TRAORDINARY

The "X" factor is revealed and the mystery is no more but you might have more questions on the attributes running through your mind to create new connections amongst these qualities. Let's take a step back and make an assumption for a leap of faith. Let's assume that a huge reservoir of energy that is timeless and pure exists that created perfection.

The perfection is marred in the adversity of GLASS and the chaos of human nature. The "Uncertainty Principle" dictates that this chaos will occur in any perfect state. This Perfect-Chaos-Perfect cycle is as true as the Energy-Mass-Energy cycle or the holistic circle of Space-Time-Mass-Motion-Energy in theory. The "X" factor of Leadership of Energy with Thought provides energy to the leaders to maintain the equilibrium within these disparate yet interconnected elements. The Leadership Energy Quotient (EQ) for "X' factor leaders will act as the catalyst for growth by finding, obtaining, creating, storing and distributing communal wealth to deal with chaos and lead to the ultimate goal of perfection and more chaos. **The "X" factor of WOW leadership that we aspire and admire in a Gandhi or a Mother Teresa or an Einstein is their extraordinary ability to be competent, capable, compassionate and creative at the same time while communicating their success with humility.**

A simple demonstration in the visionary art of "X" factor Leadership may be in order here. Please read the lines given below and try to remember them:

B A C K	N O T E
E H T N	V E R Y
O T A P	O N E W
D O O G	I L L G
A F L E	E T I T
S R U O	(2)
Y E V I	
G W O N	
(1)	

(Assume there is a perfect message in (I) and (2))

In the first example other than the first line "BACK" the rest appears to be gibberish. You have assumed that there is a perfect message and an answer is there but our 5 senses and our GLASS takes over and we reject this message as a piece of trash. The first line is the clue and if you read it backwards from the bottom you get "NOW GIVE YOURSELF A GOOD PAT ON THE BACK". GO AHEAD DO IT- PAT YOURSELF. The answer to the second figure is given in the final chapter "THE LAST WORD".

The thought process behind these examples is to understand that you, as leaders, are constantly getting confused messages at work, in business, at home, from the media, from the Government and even from GOD in the church or temple or mosque. The problem is not in the message but the fact that you have not developed the "X" factor of energy and thought that will allow you to perceive and receive these messages correctly. The ability to "SEE" and "Profess" rather than "Preach" is the foundation of the evo-devo of leadership that will be able to prophesize the outcomes of choices. If we delve deeper into this leadership phenomenon of vision and growth lets look at three different scenarios that are based on the supply side economics of Find, Obtain, Manufacture, Store and Distribute as well the demand side economics of satisfaction of needs and wants at the right time and price.

The Three scenarios are as under:

a) IF WE BUILD IT THEY WILL COME.

b) BUILD WHAT IS HEEDED.

c) FIND and CREATE WHAT COULD BE NEEDED.

The first two options need a fresh infusion of energy with (a) needing more energy than (b). The Third option will generate free energy for long term sustainable growth. The reason is simple as the third alternative will transcend the present to prophesize and profess the future. The "iPhone" or Windows OS or non-violence as a strategy of war or biofuels or $E=mc2$ or Social Networking are all examples where leadership with the "X" factor focused on the existing processes to "see" the future by eliminating the bottlenecks and uncovering the entropy to create a solution that generated a new "S" curve for stable growth.

Good Leaders developed Telegraph, Telephone, Mobile and Entertainment systems to progress technologically but only a few asked the Question " WHY is Communication stationary and Entertainment Mobile??". Only one saw the convergence and joined entertainment with telecommunication i.e. SONY. Steve Jobs, of Apple Inc. took it further and made both communication and entertainment mobile by converging voice, data and image. The iPhone. In this process Apple also transformed itself from a technology company to a music company. The iPOD and iTune.

Bad Leadership took the equation of $E=mc^2$ to create the chaos of Hiroshima and Nagasaki or Chernobyl rather than creating mini-nuclear reactors that are safe and would meet all our energy needs for the future. Bad leadership took the power of Magnets to create an EMP (electro- Magnetic Pulse) weapon without thinking of building a transport system using the electromagnetic forces for propulsion and using the earth's gravitational field for electricity.

The "X" factor of Leadership Energy with Thought is the key to survival of the wisest. The faster you can eliminate the disadvantages of GLASS and transform yourself from MICE to WISE the faster you can make the quantum leap to greatness. The common factor amongst all GREAT LEADERS who have achieved the Leadership of Energy with thought to leave their mark on society is the fact that they did it for others not for themselves. This evolutionary transformation is the subject of our next chapter.

"GOD DOES NOT PLAY DICE WITH THE UNIVERSE"

ALBERT EINSTEIN

CHAPTER 17

THE LEADERSHIP OF EVO-DEVO TRANSFORMATION

The tautology that change will, happen and if it happens it is change is the principle that guides leadership currently. Today's leadership is engrossed in trying to manage change which in most cases is the result of self-inflicted chaos. Evo-Devo Transformation on the other hand is the outcome of rational, logical and planned effort to incrementally enhance the "quality of Life" of the constituents through the energy of Leadership Core Values (LCV) founded on the predispositions of the community. These incremental improvements of both knowledge and process have to be transferred from the leaders to the community to enhance its competitive advantage. Advantage is a Leadership Core Value and is one of the characteristics of the WOW!! Leader. Competitive Advantage is the evo-devo of transformation that leads chaos for change that improves the nature and culture of the community. Evo-Devo Transformation is not a "knee-jerk" response to stimuli or a reactive fluctuation to circumstances rather it is a systemic transformation of the LCV's to attain a more beneficial state for leadership and its sphere of influence. The sphere of Influence for the LCVs are all the elements within the metagenome of the leadership that can benefit from the process of "fixation" and replication of these traits amongst the constituents.

The fact based evo-devo of Leadership Transformation may be profound but the steps are logical and incremental. The process of "key" adaptations in sync with the predispositions of the community will gradually shift leadership behavior and actions towards a new mode of culture which in turn will create further systemic changes in a cyclic manifestation. Ten Thousand Years ago, there were less than 10 Million people on earth. That figure soared to 200 Million by the time of the Roman Empire. After the 15th century onwards the population of the Homo-Sapiens has grown exponentially to reach nearly 6.4 Billion today. These facts point to the evolutionary competitive advantage of the human gene pool. The unfortunate part is that exponential growth of the human population and its culture should have also resulted in a parallel evolution of LCV's to support the system for a long-term and sustainable growth phase which has not occurred. The leadership of this vastly diverse community is still in the hands of "medieval" Leaders.

The cultural shifts that are sparking the seeds of human evolution and its explosion have not ignited the spark of an evolutionary transformation of leadership. The leadership has to go through this cultural metamorphosis to evolve and acquire the LCV's for sustainable success. Individuals are definable but Groups are abstract. As population density builds , you as leaders, need to lead the Group Dynamics governing the culture that develops as the knowledge and intellect of the individuals within the group and hence the group itself evolves to a transformed state. Leadership culture now becomes the competitive advantage of the diverse community as it creates the environment that motivates the individuals to achieve their potential even under adverse circumstances. The Leadership culture and its LCV's thus becomes the harbinger of transformation that will allow the community to architect its success.

The Question is simple HOW DO WE ATTAIN THE PARTICLES of EVOLUTION THAT WILL LEAD TO THE EVO-DEVO of LEADERSHIP OF TRANSFORMATION?

The answer is derived from the complexity of the culture of leadership. Knowledge, Intelligence and Technical Civilization create a positive feedback loop within the culture. Increasing Intelligence increases the complexity of culture which creates new avenues of knowledge and process to expand our Intelligence which forces a further cultural shift in complexity. Culture alone becomes the environmental trigger for the evo-devo of leadership transformation.

The LCV's play a major part in the preparedness of leadership to transform its vision and gain the wisdom that will enable the leaders to survive this cultural metamorphosis. The LCV's are potentially available to all of you within the leadership domain. The trigger of wisdom that allows you to adopt the cultural shift is hidden in the adversity of chaos and the entropy of the system. Once unleashed the cultural shift of the leaders will manifest in a cultural explosion for the community. **Leadership today stands at this crucial juncture wherein the existing and attainable technological thresholds can create systemic macro mutations for a cultural explosion that may even take us beyond the hurdle of "Natural Selection".** All we need is an evo-devo leadership with the right LCV's. The LCV's that are required for the Leadership role that will create the "quantum leap" of the cultural explosion for the community are enumerated as below:

l) The first LCV of evo-devo leadership is to encourage and **enhance the diversity** of the sphere of influence to widen the cultural landscape. Leadership has to escape from the pressures of holding on to a culture of sameness and evolve to a culture of divergence. The global paradigm of the culture of divergence has to be applied across all the critical areas such as knowledge, process, economics, finance, language, governance, politics and consumption. Local communities alongside the leader have to adapt to the nature and culture of global interdependence using their local predispositions for competitive advantage. The domain knowledge and expertise has to be preserved while being transformed for efficiency and effectiveness. The alternative is not a mere loss of cosmetic and ethical values but as local "centers of excellence" are sacrificed at the altar of sameness vast stores of accumulated "BUSINESS LOGIC" and knowledge disappear.. The LCV that understands the advantage of diversity in a complex interdependent global world will be able to survive the adversity of chaos and gain the competitive advantage of using the entropy of their existing business logic.

In effect you can now acknowledge that nature and culture are both symbiotic relationships. As you evolve the LCV of diversity of culture you are simultaneously transforming the nature of leadership which in turn is the image of the community. The ultimate value of diversity is to create redundancy against critical failures. **It is estimated that the current economic value of the LCV of diversity is around $ 33 Trillion.**

2) The second LCV for the Leadership of Evolutionary Transformation is to understand that **leadership behavior** shapes the nature of the community in every instance and in turn the community shapes leadership behavior. The same paradigm applies to the fact that Leadership image shapes the communities who then create the image of the leader. Thus Nature shapes the behavior of communities and the communities shape the culture with the leaders acting as the bridge and the catalyst amongst the two. Leadership Behavior therefore is the variable quantity in this constant of nature and culture of the communities.

The Evo-Devo of Leadership

The LCVs of Leadership Behavior are defined in the following 7 C's and their benefits:

7 C's	Benefits
Competence	Productivity
Commitment	Effectiveness
Communication	Efficiency
Creativity	Vision
Character	Trust
Chaos	High Value
Culture	Wisdom

The 7-C's and their benefits are self-explanatory and simple. The natural form of leadership behavior is akin to a musical symphony where each individual member is playing "his own tune" to the its potential and the leaders listen and distinguish each tone to conduct the symphony in a coordinated manner for the common goal of achieving a communal epiphany that evolves into an orchestra of global interdependence through convergence. The common goal that is shared resolves the ambiguity of divergence and convergence by ensuring the unity within diversity. The LCV of leadership behavior, as the foundation of the nature and culture of sustainable growth, is understood that each individual sound is integral to the symphony and each transformation should lead to a better harmony. Leadership Behavior whether willing or unwilling; courage or cowardice; productivity or waste; just or unjust; fact or falsified; KASH or Cash; shared or GLASS; and WISE or MICE will impact the nature of the community. The Culture of leadership that fights GLASS rather than institutionalizing it is the evo-devo transformation of the LCV's.

3) The third LCV of desirable traits is that the real power of leadership lies in the **service of the community and its constituents.** This ATTITUDE should MOTIVATE the leaders for acquiring more power. Power without wisdom and

mercy is just another form of the Leadership of Force. The ATTITUDE of Leadership to use the power of intellect, knowledge, process and technology in the service of the community to create beneficial solutions for the constituents is the most important trait for SUCCESS.

ATTITUDE

V

MOTIVATE

V

SERVICES

The use of knowledge and information as a source of power through falsification, hoarding and politics is one of the key barriers to stable growth and loss of leadership control on transformation.

4) The fourth LCV for the evolution of leadership is to be able to understand and use the power of **"Synchronicity"**. Synchronicity is the phenomenon of leadership coincidences (some call it luck or fortune) that happen when you are at the right place at the right time. These coincidences seem random but their propensity in proportion to rational, logical and shared risk leadership strategies proves otherwise. The LCV of Synchronicity is an important trait that brings order to chaos in an acasual synchronous manner. The higher the rationality and fairness of leadership, higher the synchronicity of the system. The reverse is also true. If leadership behavior is irrational and illogical even good systems will become chaotic and unmanageable.

5) The fifth LCV that is crucial for the nature and culture of an evolved leadership is the ability to **transcend the ambiguity** of seemingly diverse processes and understand the reality of convergence within the synergy of differences. Leadership transformation can happen within moments if you train yourself in the evo-devo principles but for reaching maturity and fixation it requires that the LCV's be honed at all times through practice. The practice of the LCV's reconciles the ambiguity of short term goals and long term

SUCCESS. While you practice synergy, you still have to handle conflict and corruption. As you practice "service before self" you have to lead the community and the constituents through incentives and rewards. The ambiguity of handling diversity while promoting the concept of objectives and goals is another chaotic situation. This dichotomy of thought for handling ambiguity in day to day decision making vis-à-vis the overall SUCCESS of the entity is a key trait for evo-devo transformations. The issue of ambiguity is complex and simple at the same time. The basis of the simplicity lies in the dichotomy that is founded on the principle that requires the **LCV that leadership is not only about doing good but doing good with the awareness of bad.** The maturity to consistently achieve the Right Solution at the Right Time and for the Right Reason while retaining the reality of the process is the economic value of the LCV's that will in their totality affect the nature and culture of the transformation of leadership.

The transformation of the nature and culture of leadership through the acquisition of LCV's is mandated as the LCV's have a direct bearing on the economic value of the system and hence its sustainability. A little math here should go a long way in clarifying the co-relation between the evo-devo of Leadership of Transformation and the abundant value creation of LCV's and their self-funding nature and culture.

FACTS: The GDP (Gross Domestic Product) of the world in 2012 on a cumulative basis was approx. $70 Trillion. The Global Interdependence in terms of exports worldwide was $15 Trillion. The spending on "back flux" of Conflict, Health Care, Defense, Terrorism, Justice and Environmental issues was pegged at an average of 15% of GDP i.e. approx $ 11 Trillion. Process Improvement strategies that promote synergy and symbiosis while reducing ambiguity through technology and innovation can on an average enhance the value of the process by over 35-40%.This would add approx $21 Trillion to the economic value at a conservative estimate of 30% of GDP. Diversity is currently valued at nearly $33 Trillion. Attitude and Motivation of shared risk and reward with 7 C's of evo-devo leadership can contribute around 80% to ultimate SUCCESS of the individual. In these terms keeping the GDP constant the leadership factor of ATTITUDE would be $56 Trillion as a % of GDP. The current "Debt Virus" and deficit financing is valued at around 20% of GDP which would peg this at nearly $14 Trillion. The loss of value at the Financial

The Evo-Devo of Leadership

Markets and Asset Devaluation of the housing sector that dropped nearly 44% in value from 2007-2011 (Oct 9 2007 to Oct 29 2011). This lack of vision of leadership and a consequence of the malady of GLASS if extrapolated globally would account for a total loss of over $ 12 Trillion on an asset valuation criterion.

THE EQUATION: ANNUAL RETURN = $\frac{LG- F (100\%-L)}{TP}$ = Economic Quotient (EQ)

where L is the Likelihood of Success or Failure as a %.

G is the expected GAIN

F is the expected Loss of FAILURE

T is the TIME for the ROI

P is the current value of the assets (GDP)

THE NUMBERS: (Trillion Dollars)*

The Expected GAIN: Diversity + 30% improvement = $33 + $10 = 43

Process Improvement (30% of GDP) = $21

ATTITUDE, 7C's, Leadership EV= $56

Convergence Advantage = 50% decrease in debt+ 50% increase in trade= $14

Conflict Resolution=60% decrease in "back-flux"= $7

TOTAL GAIN = $141

The Loss of FAILURE:

Diversity Loss = 20%   = $7

Debt/Deficit up 50%   = $10

Defense/"Back Flux" up 50%= $6

Leadership Failure (ASSET-Devaluation)= $12

245

Loss of Trust-50% of Trade=$7

TOTAL LOSS = $42

The Likelihood: 80% SUCCESS, 20% Failure

The Time: Two Years

ANNUAL RETURNs on LCV's = $\underline{141x80- 42 (100-80)}$ = $\underline{11280-840}$ = $\underline{10440}$ = 75%

$$2 \times 70 \qquad\qquad 140 \qquad\qquad 140$$

Economic Quotient=LCV= 75%

The Annual Return on LCV's is an Unmatched and WOW!! value of 75%. No current IRR or hurdle rate can match this increase of the Economic Quotient (EQ) and its economic value. The Rapid ROI of the evo-devo Leadership of Transformation that can enhance the nature and culture of leaders and communities alike is thus a source of sustainable energy for ongoing growth.

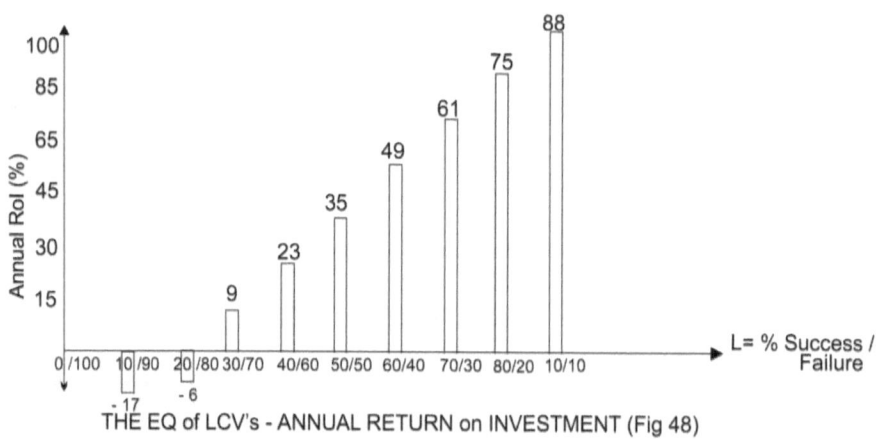

THE EQ of LCV's - ANNUAL RETURN on INVESTMENT (Fig 48)

WHAT is the CULTURE OF LEADERSHIP that can create such UNMATCHED VALUE and play an integral part in the evo-devo Leadership of Transformation?

In the context of evo-devo, culture is the amalgamation of habits, some inherited and others acquired, that reflect the personal traits of the leaders and their sphere of influence. The habits can be "good" traits, "bad" traits or even 'indifferent" traits. The exact definition of the three traits is founded on the leadership belief system but the truth is that some habits have a positive effect and some have a negative effect on leadership behavior. Also some habits can be present without causing benefit or chaos unless faced with adversity. Every leader has a culture of leadership that is the sum of all his traits.

The critical factor for the Leadership of Transformation from an evo-devo perspective is to consistently hone the "good" traits while Imploding the "bad" traits and utilizing the entropy to replace the "bad" traits with "good" traits that cover the capability gap at the same time modifying the "indifferent' traits to "good" traits for use under adversity and chaos. This transformation of LCV's has to be transferred throughout the system to evolve the culture of the community. The community will in turn absorb these traits and regurgitate the traits for their daily use and provide the feed-back to the leaders to modify and enhance the culture of the community. This cyclic process is constantly in motion in great societies and communities.

The confusion though lies in the concept of Time and Fear of Loss that creates a temptation for the leaders to change for the sake of change as a response to external stimuli. The fact is that the current leadership views time from a short-term perspective only: Quarterly for a CEO, 1-3 years for technology, 4-8 years for a political leader, 10-20 years for science or medicine and 20-30 years for a good leader. The temptation of Time and the fear of Loss essentially tends to force leaders to conform to established processes and stick to their individual "safety" nets. In the protective mode leadership failure is compounded as each leader ignores the benefit, injury or waste to leadership Economic Quotient (EQ) as the traits remain unmodified thus reducing the competitive advantage of the community.

In lieu of the fear of loss the leaders are further tempted to "falsify" results to justify their habits in order to meet the self-imposed barriers of time. The "falsification" of results is the worst form of leadership "failure blindness" as these-traits get "fixated" into the metagenome of the leaders. The solution is to ensure that leaders identify the particles of transformation hidden in the potential of the community and create a new culture through new habits that will guarantee SUCCESS.

The key is that you, as evo-devo leaders, cannot find these fault lines and growth areas by looking down from the top but you will need to stand at the bottom and look up to find the particles of transformation that are in line with the pre-dispositions of the community. These particles of Transformation are also the seeds of evolutionary development and the cause of the evo-devo of leadership.

The particles of evolution, that are the cause of beneficial transformation, and their true value needs to be extracted through the medium of leadership intelligence and communal wisdom. The critical areas that can completely transform the enterprise and also have the most potential to enhance the synergy of **Leadership Wisdom** are as under:

a) The first crucial area of evo-devo transformation in the dynamics of leadership wisdom is the function of **PREDICTIVE FORESIGHT (PF)**. The PF function will extend the evo-devo capability of leadership by providing greater insight into the "predict and act" strategies that are essential for the fast-paced technological environment around us. The current and future economic and cultural situation mandates the ability to adapt quickly as the environment transforms around us in profound evolutionary shifts. The "predict to act" capability, as is portended in the evolution of the PF function of Leadership Wisdom, takes us beyond the current focus of **intuitive response** to an **illative response** that guarantees results and the desired transformations. The PF function can only be attained by enhancing the domain expertise while fine tuning the incremental processes around Leadership Wisdom. Simply put **PF= Subject Matter Knowledge + Effective Process + Illative Response founded on factual information.**

b) The second evolutionary transformation of Leadership Wisdom that will create a collaborative and synergistic environment for growth is the function of **AGILE RESPONSE (AR)**. The key to the AR function is that it executes beneficial transformations in an incremental format that is adapted to respond to external and internal changes both adverse and positive in near "REAL TIME periods. The collaborative nature of this function eliminates falsification and functional overkill while delivering the required benefits in time for efficient deployment. The idea is to build the test schedules and quality assurance of the AR within the function itself in a TOLLGATE METHODOLOGY that checks the facts, functionality and delivery of benefits while the AR is under development.

c) The third key dimension of Leadership Wisdom that is desired for the sustainable yet unmatched growth of the enterprise is **PERSONALIZED TOOLING (PT)**. The PT function personalizes the information and the "decision objects" by adapting them to the user's FRAME of REFERENCE. The higher the alignment of the objects to the users **FOR (FRAME of REFERENCE)** the higher the relevance and the Intelligence imparted. This FOR based user functionality of the tooling allows the extraction of the true value of the information and the decision objects for better collaboration.

d) The fourth step in the transformation of Leadership Wisdom is the **ENABLED VIRTUALIZATION (EZ)** function. The EZ function is based on the principles of flexibility and "on-demand" capabilities. The EZ capability enhances the elasticity factor of the enterprise to respond to enormous fluctuations in a planned and effective manner. The virtually enabled nature of this function allows the "dashboard" controls to be available to the leaders and the community in a lower cost and lower risk environment for an "on-demand" utilization scenario that creates ethical consumption. The benefit of conservation of Natural Capital also assists in balancing the stability of the enterprise.

e) The fifth corner of this Leadership Wisdom Pentagon is the function of **EMPOWERED KNOWLEDGE (EK).** The advantage of EK is to allow innovation and beneficial transformation to happen at all levels of the enterprise or the community. The entire leadership sphere of Influence would be pervaded with leadership LCV's and combined Intelligence, at the same time, providing the constituents the leverage of using the EK to create innovation in a symbiotic manner for the benefit of the community. The EK function also helps in narrowing the gaps between the users and the intelligence which automatically leads to better ways to make informed decisions as well as monitor the results of these decisions on a real-time basis.

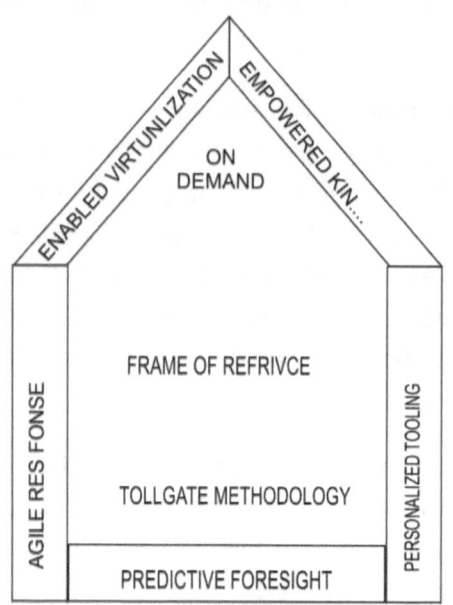

THE PENTAGON OF LEADERSHIP INTELLIGENCE (Fig 49)

LEADERSHIPWISDOM

The combination of Predictive Foresight (PF), AGILE RESPONSE (AR), PERSONALIZED TOOLING (PT), ENABLED VIRTUALIZATION (EZ), and EMPOWERED RNOWLEDGE (ER) enables the entire enterprise to evolve in a coordinated manner and "THINR BIG" in small cohesive increments. This fosters sustainable growth while planning for adversity and chaos. It also permits Leadership Intelligence **to transform itself from the "I am" thought process to the "We Become" thought consciousness of Leadership Wisdom; a highly valuable trait for growth.** In essence the opposition and conflict situations actually become the "points of inflexion" for evo-devo transformations. These "points of inflexion" under the collaborative effects of the PF,AR,PT,EZ and ER functions of Leadership Wisdom are the empirical tests of an evolved community and its culture.

The culture of transformation that is desired for the evo-devo leadership is to choreograph the collaboration between the two domains of the physical and the digital to enhance the **Technical Civilization of the**

enterprise. The combination of Leadership Wisdom and Technology is the next breakthroughs that is required for the evolutionary transformation of the enterprise and increase its **DIGITAL IQ**.

The potential for the transformation of Technical Civilization and Digital IQ is identified in the exploration of the concept of the Motion of Change in both its derivative and integral forms. The idea of analyzing our entire sphere of influence including technology in the pantheon of its culture will expose the basic rational workings of the community and is the best method to identify the derivative and integral potential of each system. The rational, analytical and unbiased approach will unveil the fact that the Leadership of Transformation is not an impenetrable, unknowable and unpredictable entity. The man-made obfuscation is self-created but the combination of the energy of Leadership Wisdom with enhanced Digital IQ is an intriguing gold mine that is available for use provided you have the desired Technical Civilization to take advantage of this potential source of unlimited wealth.

The innovative approach to combining the energies of the two worlds i.e. Wisdom and Technology, will immediately start delivering the benefits needed so that the transformation of "the way it works" to "the way it should work" can evolve and develop. The evolutionary shift of FACTS and DATA merging together in a technically civilized and wise culture, that includes both the integral and derivative strengths, can be applied to diverse issues such as population engineering, economics, resource, consumption, habits, "way of Life' or even golf.

The game of golf is a great example to demonstrate this cultural shift that will combine Leadership Wisdom and Technology to create a profound impact on the motion of change for the competitive advantage of the community. Let us assume you need to hit a golf ball a certain distance to win but your integral potential can only reach part of the distance. The derivative potential of technology could provide you an exact solution. The derivative potential could be to hit the ball at a certain trajectory and height so that you can gain the additional distance to achieve your goal. Calculus would provide you the exact force with which you can hit the ball to the right height to achieve the time and distance you need.

The simplicity of the advantage of the Leadership of Transformation that multiplies the integral and derivative potential of Digital IQ and Wisdom can be seen in various examples such as designing a new bridge or putting the VOYAGER on Mars or a gravitational lens that can measure the effect of gravity on Light in relation to Time and Space across the universe. The power of rational thought combined with the energy of technology can also assist in bringing order to the chaos of approximation. We saw that groups are abstract objects and are ambiguous in nature. The effect of enjoining the strength of the two worlds i.e. the physical and the digital, can predict change to attain the evo-devo of transformation within a group. This is a great strategy to achieve shared, sustainable, and synergistic success.

HOLD ON, IT IS NOT ALL GOOD NEWS!!! The bad news is that the leader i.e. you, who is at the helm of this leadership of evolutionary transformation is facing the fight of his life to flawlessly execute the desired change. The fact is that nothing is more complex to handle, or more questionable (think a "live grenade" or a "hot potato") to manage than to be the one introducing the transformation. Your detractors are looking for both proof and guarantees. Your enemies are waiting for you to fail since your zealous enemies are the ones who currently benefit from the existing processes and see a threat in the motion of change. Your supporters are "fence-sitters" or passive since they fear the enemies who might control the existing laws plus they do not know the advantages of the transformation or have adequate experience of its proposed benefits.

The solution for leadership in the introduction of beneficial evolution and developmental transformation is two-fold:

1) Create a culture of change and dialogue within the system, and

2) Introduce the change by initially implementing it on your-self and incrementally enhancing the motion of change across the enterprise. The innovator has to be firm in his preparedness to execute the transformation flawlessly. There is no better "empirical test" for the LCV's, the integral and derivative strengths of technology and wisdom as well as the functions (PF,AR,PT,EZ,EK) to create and implement evo-devo transformation to reach fixation within the community. Leaders who pass this test will be held in

esteem in a manner that will belay time. **The "can-do" leaders will leave a mark on the metagenome of the enterprise that will remain in their image even after they "pass away".**

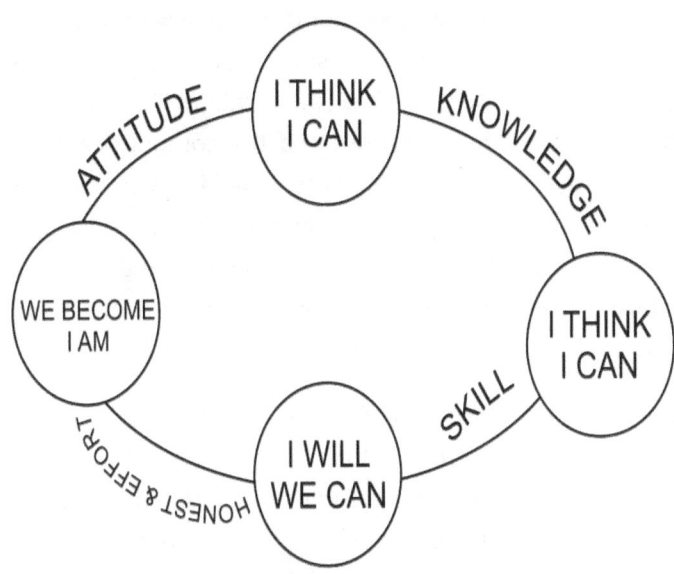

THE CAN CYCLE OF LEADERSHIP TRANSFORMATION (Fig 50)

The Greek word "Mataneno" means "change your mind". This is the cause of change as well as the first step of transformation. The effects of "Mataneno" are meaningful and beneficial if succeeded by analysis of the facts and concluded with the conviction of change. The benefits and the subsequent acausal synchronicity evolve further "Mataneno". The cyclic interpretation of the Leadership of Transformation which habitually predicts beneficial change and executes the change to near perfection with the minimum use of Natural Capital, to release the "free energy" locked up in the system, for growth is the foundation of great communities.

The above is only possible if the essence of leadership is never to predict change based on truths that are geared towards a pre-agreed or foregone conclusion that reacts to the immediate stimuli based on pre-existing biases. Rather the Leadership of Transformation mandates change that is an "open conclusion" **that meets the criteria of sustainable growth and carries a**

real risk of failure and substantial loss if the transformation does not happen. If this criterion is not met then the prediction is false.

A question that has bothered leaders over time: **Why is the Leadership of Transformation so crucial to the overall success of Leadership?** The answer lies in the concept that stagnation is equivalent to Death and change equates to Life. Therefore the Leadership of Transformation in its evo-devo form gives life to the enterprise and the competitive edge for a "Wise Selection Advantage" to survive adversity. A leader with the LCV's, trained in the Leadership Wisdom Pentagon and having a high Digital IQ is the trigger and the catalyst for transformation. In order to understand this process let us look at an evolutionary biological example that demonstrates the abstraction of the Wise Selection Advantage.

When the DNA of a group of   5000 year old skeletons from Europe was analyzed it was discovered that it did not contain any sign of the Lactase allele that allows for the digestion of milk in adults. This despite the fact that the same gene was present in other populations nearly 8000 years ago. The cultural transformation that triggered the gene in Europeans nearly 3000 years ago was mired in one or two leaders either through migration or change in habits. In the modern population of Europe the frequency of this gene is around 90% and the tests show an incremental increase in the nature of this transformation over 3000 years. The transformation started at a slow pace and accelerated rapidly across the community once the beneficial nature was accrued. There are many such evolutionary examples that predict the frequency of transformation once leadership adopts it and the beneficial effects then spread it across the enterprise rapidly towards "fixation" i.e. when all the members of the community have the beneficial gene, and it now becomes an integral part of the culture of the community.

The advantage we have today that can spread the altruistic effects of the Wise Selection Advantage of "Mataneno" rapidly through Technical Civilization is by using the power of the existing networks such as the Blogosphere, Cloud Computing, Personalized Social Sites and Virtualization of resources. The answer to the seemingly arbitrary values of the fundamental constant of change in the 21st century and beyond can be found in the evo-devo of the Leadership of Transformation that can incrementally increase the selection advantage of the enterprise by using the predisposed traits and molding these for the overall SUCCESS of the individual and the community. The Wise Selection Advantage paradigm of this evo-devo leadership through incremental adaptations can generate tremendous success even in inanimate systems such as stock markets, commodities, currencies, consumption, governance and economics. The animate systems such as interdependence, diversity conflicts, relationships, faith, trust and cultural shifts can be successfully transformed through both macro and micro mutations that will be part of the "survival of the wisest"" paradigm.

The process can be better explained if we look at another coherent model developed by Nobel Laureate Gerald Edelman to explain the phenomenon of how the immune system rapidly creates antibodies targeted at pathogens it has never encountered. The human body already has a unique population of antibody molecules created on a variety of cell types. When the environmental challenge of infection occurs the system searches through its population for a match and then selects and multiplies only those cells that can deal with the change in the most effective manner. The above process clearly demonstrates the Wise Selection Advantage, especially in times of the "Implosion Effect" of chaos and adversity, wherein our "library of decision and knowledge objects" can be evolved in advance to tackle multiple challenges. This library would be stored in a plethora of beneficial traits across the Interdependent constituents to respond efficiently and effectively. The right challenge would be met with the right trait adapted to deploy rapidly to evolve globally. The "library of decision and knowledge objects" and the "good traits" would be shaped based on the inclusive population dynamics of collaboration and altruism that can override the exclusivity of self-interest in the evo-devo of leadership. **The transformation of collaborative behavior of leadership through "group selection" for adaptations of traits that may not be beneficial to the leaders but still bestows the advantage to the community becomes the Wise Choice for transformation. This here is the key to solving the global challenges that face us today and will pervade us in the future.**

The issue here is that the self-interest of leadership and communal benefits are the "tension of opposites" stretching the boundaries of wise decisions and rational choices. Leadership of evo-devo Transformation requires the skill to lead the "tension of opposites" within the tensile strength of both the integral and derivative potential of the leaders, the technologies and the community.

The interplay between individual survival and group selection is the ambiguity of leadership transformation that is governed by the "rational choice" that blends them cohesively in a strategy of symbiosis that ensures the sustainable growth of the enterprise. The Wise Selection Advantage offered by the leadership of evo-devo transformation which selects beneficial individual traits and organizes collaborative behavior for the success of the community by pooling the risks and sharing the rewards is essential for the leadership of SUCCESS.

"The stretch of Time as we know it today is that the longest period of time is 13.7 Billion years ago with the "BIG BANG" and the shortest period of time that can exist according to the Quantum Theory is known as Planck Time or 1×10^{-43} seconds or----

0. 00000000000000000000000000000000000000000001 sec." An evo-devo fact.

CHAPTER 18

THE LAST WORD

You started this journey with a question-"Do Leaders make History or does History make Leaders?" The question, as we have seen in our journey across the vast universe of Leadership and its evo-devo is a false dichotomy of flawed reasoning. Great Leaders are not born or made but are evolved by the Wise Choices they make consistently under chaos and adversity. This "history" of the Right Responses is then transferred to the community through the aegis of efficient and effective execution. The practice of these responses leads to the historical transformation of the enterprise for shared, sustainable and synergistic success. Leadership is thus a function of choices and history is the representation of these choices as traits in the leaders sphere of Influence.

The spear of leadership behavior that is inherent in all of you is nurtured by the environmental factors that prevail around you to create a belief system that is personalized. The flames of adversity harden the "Tip of the Spear" and fortune provides the opportunity of synchronicity that allows you to use this spear for the service of the community effectively to generate the competitive advantage of Moral Hope, Wise Laws and SUCCESS. The rest, as we say, is "HISTORY".

The evo-devo of Leadership is waiting to happen. Our adventure through the multiple dimensions of leadership has left no doubt that in the existing universe of communities the fundamentals are uncannily suited for leadership SUCCESS and "STAR" if you practice the evo-devo principles as dictated. The three dimensions of the Physical, Emotional and Faith world's are all exuding the opportunity FOR (Frame of Reference) an evo-devo leadership that we cannot dismiss them as mere accidents. These needs can be fine-tuned and satiated if the leadership can achieve their "breakthrough" and enhance their peak performance through "calm commotion" to meet these challenges using the existing Natural Capital wisely and the predisposition of the community judiciously.

The Leaders among you who grasp the direction of the evo-devo process that is contained and emerges from the contradictions and collaborations of the chaos around you will not only be able to shape the process beneficially but more importantly be shaped by the process to ensure SUCCESS and eliminate the PAINS of the community. When this leadership potential combines with environmental opportunities you can use the free energy of the Implosion Effect to create sustainable explosive growth. This habitat of "STARs" will be fully equipped to handle the variegated and diversified nature of communities that need to interdependent in their culture.

Unfortunately, we are not evolving towards this habitat of synergy that is available to us rather we are contaminating it further through the lethal combination of bad leadership habits, the influence of GLASS and the "falsification" of truths. The great news, that is the tangible and intangible benefit of the evo-devo journey that we took together, is that all it takes is ONE (1) to start the transformation of culture to one of the "RIGHT CUBE" i.e. the Right Solution at the Right Time for the Right Reasons with the Right Action to deliver the Right Results and to then fixate this trait within the metagenome. These new traits will also trigger the "survival of the wisest" paradigm that will guarantee a "selection advantage" for the community.

It is your duty as leaders to impart this "selection advantage" to the community and to satisfy the need for a microcosm of a rational choice that understands the dynamics of the cyclic nature of the perfect-chaos-perfect syndrome as well as the want of a "feed-back loop" with an inherent escalation process that provides the communication platform between the leaders and their communities. This is the fundamental cause and effect of human nature and its success. Leadership has to be aware of "What Right is" and "What the practice of Leadership Ought to be". The constant failure on the part of leadership to deliberately avoid the "Right Cube" by falsifying facts will lead to the extinction of the communities and hence leadership itself as the planet and our environment becomes smarter than us.

The Altruism paradigm that points to the "way of life" that needs to be adopted by the leadership given the constraints of a smart planet is simple "If everyone in a group shares knowledge and process, everyone is better off". Yet as more work selflessly for the common good cheating becomes tempting as the ones who do not chip in feel they have attained an advantage over the others. **This exploitation in turn actually reduces the altruism pay-off for everybody. As punishment becomes cheap a lot of people are punished and**

the cycle of the cause and effect of "selfish punishment" and "smarter cheating" replaces the principles of communalism. Communalism under the principles of evo-devo leadership is a form of group advantage under the umbrella of interdependent communities. The idea of communalism is based on the highest principles of sharing and wisdom while creating competitive advantage for groups for the benefit of all by pooling the global risk and the equitable distribution of the global rewards. The local execution of the communalism paradigm is equally matched by the adherence to global wise laws.

Is evo-devo Leadership only a cause and effect or is there an ambiguous element of an "X" factor that defies pure logic as we know it? The conclusion you must have reached, as we progressed through the dimensions of faith, the BIG "G", relationship, free energy, thought consciousness, chaos and perfection, is that there is an abundant source of energy and synchronicity available to all of us. The conduit to this source of Natural Capital is the leader who grasps the direction of rational choices of actions with the preparedness to emerge victorious from the chaos of contradictions using the competitive advantages of communalism. To deny the existence of this source and not plan to share the knowledge is to plan to fail.

You have to believe that leadership is not the domain of a selected few. It is available in all its glory and esteem to those who want to create unmatched value for their sphere of influence using the local potential around them for the benefits of the community and therefore themselves. You can be a great father or mother or teacher or prime minister or president or priest or monarch or gardner or ceo or a shepherd or any ordinary person provided you have the "X" factor to do extraordinary things. The core-value of the evo-devo of leadership is to give you the tools that will make you a "practitioner" of excellence in order to achieve the breakthrough for SUCCESS.

The "domain expertise" for leadership Is the value of the evo-devo principles as enumerated in the book. We are all classmates in this human community studying in different schools of culture that are founded on the principles of training us to do extraordinary acts of leadership. This entails you, as leaders, to create an environment where all your classmates can do amazing things based on their predispositions for the benefit of all the constituents.

A community in the evo-devo concept consists of all the constituents that inhabit a particular leadership domain. This metagenome is an assemblage of populations of many diverse cultures. The evolution and development of both inherent individual traits and environmental traits in tandem to create a great community through the process of assimilation and sharing is the evo-devo paradigm. The kinship value of this metagenome can be better explained if you imagine a doctor who treats every women patient as he would his mother, sister or daughter and every male patient as if he were his father, brother or son. This then is nature of the evo-devo leaders, their communities and the culture of each individual inhabitant that is desired to face reality and resist temptations.

The facts of "Reality" vs. the "Illusions of "Temptations" are the cultural conflicts that are the pinnacle of evo-devo leadership. Reality is chaos and Temptation gives the illusion of order, Reality is complex while Temptation gives the perception of simplicity. The Reality is in the strength of "We become" while the Temptation lies in the falsehood of "I am" and its weaknesses. Reality is about eliminating oppression and discrimination while Temptation is the Illusion of war. Reality is "and" Temptation is "but". Reality is therefore being aware of Temptation and Temptation is the Illusion that excludes reality. This is not a philosophical treatise of abstraction but a clear path to evo-devo transformation. **An ability to see the consistencies within the inconsistencies**.

The Tools of evo-devo leadership are Wisdom, Trust, Empathy, Patience, Humility and Contentment. The transformation of Leadership Behavior and its Core Values is through a series of 'key" adaptations that will be based on individual pre-dispositions and the environmental factors.

The evo-devo paradigm of Leadership Behavior that you have observed as we undertook this journey is not a hypothesis but a "connecting of dots" in a logical, rational and professional manner to understand the entire universe of leadership and its inherent anomalies. It is an attempt to connect the ambiguous, the seemingly inconsistent and the different in a cohesive set of processes that will help you in failing successfully. Anomalies do not falsify the evo-devo paradigm but actually strengthen it by evolving the paradigm itself. This "Open Loop" architecture of evo-devo is the secret of your SUCCESS as you follow the RIGHT CUBE methodology.

In any "open" system energy   (and often matter) can be transferred between the system and its surroundings and vice-versa. The "open" system in its nature is not closed or exclusive. The "open" architecture of evo-devo Leadership takes advantage of the randomness and uncertainty around us to transfer the energy of entropy that is abundant in the "implosion" to generate sustainable growth. Evo-Devo principles understand the Wisdom of the natural laws that state that the quantity of energy is a constant at the same time the quality of energy is a variable and defined by the leader. The leaders who can learn and practice the "breakthrough force" of utilizing the right quality of energy will create a lasting effect on the energy of the community to utilize its available free energy effectively.

Free energy is the portion of a systems' energy that can perform work spontaneously without consuming any additional resources. The "Implosion Effect" of adversity, chaos and randomness is a critical source of free energy and is currently available in abundance to provide a rich source of Natural Capital for the evo-devo of leadership. The next illustration demonstrates the competitive advantage of the quantity and quality of energy that can be generated using the evo-devo principles.

THE STAGES OF FREE ENERGY GENERATIONS:

Stage 1 : The system is not stable and has a higher entropy value but a low productivity value. The system has stored energy that can be extracted through chaos or through spontaneous transformation.

Stage 2: The release of "free energy" makes the system less chaotic but more productive.

Stage   3: The system becomes stable as the entropy is lowered and "free energy" is utilized for growth.

Stage   4: System nearing Equilibrium and slowing down needs new energy to grow or it implodes.

As you will observe the quality of energy is always better when the system is not in the state of equilibrium or stagnation but when it is trying to achieve equilibrium. The evo-devo process of creating an "Implosion Effect" to release "free energy" by utilizing the entropy of the system that is built up during the energy generation process itself is the key. The "Open Source" nature of this process allows the evo-devo leaders to plan and prepare for chaos and order both. It also identifies the "points of inflexion" at which the "Implosion Effect" can be triggered so that the system remains energy efficient. The entire gamut of the energy spectrum is used in the evo-devo process of virtualization and visualization. In the evo-devo paradigm the Natural Capital is shared so there is no Apartheid of class i.e. Third World, Lesser Developed,G-7,G-20 etc or the Ism's of Capitalism, Consumerism or Casteism. Each shared resource has its own quality of energy which is harnessed for removing the gaps of capacity, capability and vision.

The "classless" classification of energy and its EV (Economic Value) is once again substantiated by the Laws of the Universe. The table below

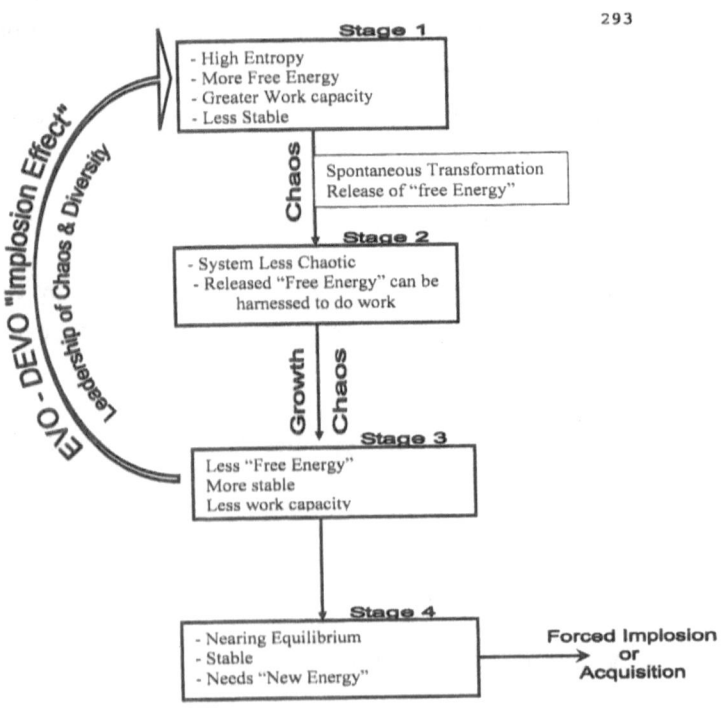

293

THE "FREE ENERGY" GENERATION PROCESS FOR EVO-DEVO. (Fig 51)

provides the Genome sizes and the number of genes across multiple organisms:

ORGANISM	GENOME SIZE	Est.No. of Genes	Genes per Mb*
H. Influenza	1.8 Mb	1,700	940
Yeast	12 Mb	6,000	500
Plant	100 Mb	26,000	260
Nematode	97 Mb	19,000	200
Fruit Fly	180 Mb	13,000	72
H.Sapiens	3,200 Mb	30,000-40,000	)10A

*Million base pairs

The above data is a clear indication of the fact that the energy is not in the number of genes as it does not explain the vast functional differences. The energy is hidden in the truth that the human genes are 10 times longer than any other species. Our DNA is designed to give us more "bang for the buck". We can perform multiple functions at the same time by multitasking at the genetic level that would actually give us the equivalent of nearly 100,000 genes. These principles of collaboration, symbiosis and synergy are the secrets of the success of the human gene pool and hence its leadership as well.

The synergy of the Leadership Core Values and the StQ, CaQ and WiQ's enhance the Energy Quotient (EQ) of evo-devo leadership to create a "higher than normal" peak performance state. The practitioners of the evo-devo principles as enumerated also allows them to be intuitive, illative and intelligent in the use of this higher quality of energy to increase the limits of integration for the benefit of the Summation advantage of traits. The Sigma process of summation that combines all the beneficial traits in the leaders sphere of influence across multiple COE's (centers of excellence) is the source of leadership greatness. This network of beneficial traits and the relationships create their own gravitational pull that brings other evo-devo communities into its fold to generate a global Sigma effect. The same applies to the process of relationship retention (which as you saw in the formula R= N + (n-1)) is far more beneficial than the process of acquiring new relationships for growth. The energy of relationships can be further explained in the fact that it takes nearly $10 to replace every $1 of economic value lost when a beneficial relationship is terminated.

In the evo-devo of leadership Economic Value = Size X 1OR. The EV is directly proportional to ten times the number of beneficial relationships that are owned by the leader. It also demonstrates the fact that if a larger entity is losing its beneficial relationships its EV is dropping drastically. Relationships are a great evo-devo tool to pool the risk and motivate the right attitude through equitable rewards for the innovator. Infosys, a global IT company, shared their ownership equitably with their employees to create huge economic value that surpassed the expectations of the community because of summation. The founder, Narayan Moorthy, transformed the global information industry. Dirubhai Ambani and Sons distributed the risk amongst 30 million shareholders of Reliance to create a global force for growth. Bill Gates and Warren Buffet shared their wealth with the whole of mankind to promote the altruistic principles of giving without expectation. The Tata group, an Indian conglomerate, has always allowed professional control of the Tata companies to promote the ideation of Intrapreneurs that have created a culture of trust and sustainable growth. Bhai Puran Singh, a simple farmer, gave his entire life and all his energy to help people less fortunate than himself by opening hospitals and medical facilities for the poor. His esteem and brand value is far greater than some of the other leaders that have size but few trustworthy relationships.

The secret formula for SUCCESS is hidden in the leaders and the miracle of shared communal wealth that is hidden within the KASH in the communities. The secret of synchronous, sustainable and synergistic growth is hidden in the evo-devo principles. The formulae for SUCCESS

$$\sum_{\substack{\text{COMMUNITY} \\ 1}}^{\substack{\text{GLOBAL} \\ \alpha}} \int f(x) \cdot d(x) = F(\alpha) - F(x)$$

THE FORMULA FOR SUCCESS. (Fig.52)

(Answer to Riddle: NOT EVERYONE WILL GET IT)

If f is a continuous function of leadership and the EQ (economic quotient) of leadership in its Limits of Integration moves from the chaos of One to the perfection of Infinity and d is its derivative of negative "back flux" then F is the function of SUCCESS that moves between the variable leadership value of infinity and the effect of the back flux on the execution of leadership decisions. The F of SUCCESS is an infinite source of EV (economic value) and communal wealth for the global community to evolve rapidly and overcome the current disadvantages of "natural selection". The Sigma Effect of summation will transform the leaders and the communities as part of the evo-devo process.

In the future as we nudge the tensile strengths of Leadership Core Values beyond its limits through both evolutionary and developmental means the process will mandate the use of technology and wisdom to artificially enhance the leadership gene pool to meet the growing pace of needs of the community. The evo-devo of leadership will also require the taking on the responsibility of "Deliberate Selection" for the survival of the wisest. The symbiosis of the metagenome and its culture with the nature of the leaders assisted by the process of empathetic Technical Civilization will be the path to the future. It is hard to feel empathy for all humans and diverse populations since there are physical, emotional and cultural barriers built into our belief systems. Unfortunately, as dictated by wisdom, there is no other solution except to feel empathy with all the constituents of your metagenome. This can be achieved through the aegis of faith and virtual kinship. The fact that these feelings are part of our cultural evo-devo defines us as leaders and community members in the process of evolutionary development. The fact that these feelings, emotions and faith have been retained in our executive memory and decision processes over aeons is because these are essential skills in the evo-devo of leadership. These traits are also procreated and fixated as they are in line with the Laws of Nature and Science.

The persistence or the continual existence of these traits in our memory processes is a desired and highly valued commodity. The ability to be "Human" is an essential leadership trait and is associated with key neuronal changes as we learn and memorize behavior that will lead to SUCCESS. This

The Evo-Devo of Leadership

"Plasticity" of memory that can guide us to use the evo-devo processes and knowledge, through constant practice, to attain our personal goals of self-actualization while achieving long-term success for the community is the secret of evo-devo. The diagram below will assist you in understanding this crucial character of the evo-devo of Leadership:

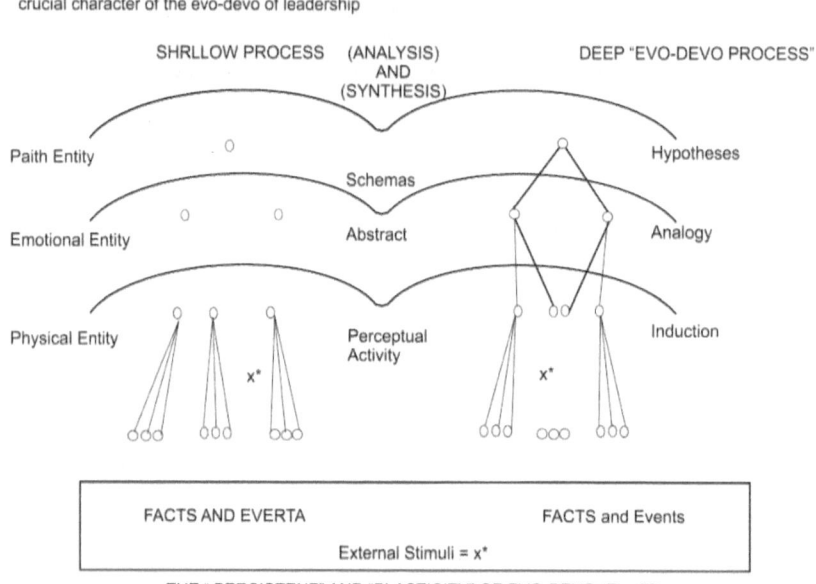

crucial character of the evo-devo of leadership

THE " PERSISTENE" AND "PLASTICITY" OF EVO-DEVO (Fig. 53)

As soon as you "connect the dots" that link the "STAR" leaders and their processes with the community you will be able to visualize the transformation required. The Links are:

a) FAITH – SCHEMAS - HYPOTHESES

b) EMOTIONS   - ABSTRACT - ANALOGY

c) PHYSICAL - PERCEPTUAL ACTIVITY - INDUCTION

The stimuli of facts and events that guide all the executive processes in the evo-devo of leadership will stem from these links. **The Three Entities of Faith, Emotions and Physical in balance with the ethical SCHEMAS of The "RIGHT CUBE" HYPOTHESES; The correct ABSTRACT thought processes that are based**

on the 7A's of ANALOGY; and finally the PERCEPTUAL ACTIONS that are INDUCTED into our culture and nature as evo-devo traits is the only way to achieve the goal of a shared, sustainable and synergistic SUCCESS.

The Leadership of the "Implosion Effect" of adversity created through our own bad traits and self-created "back-flux" has to be transformed into the "Explosion Effect" through the evo-devo traits that you have acquired as a part of this quest in order to lead you to the ultimate objective of self-sustained growth for the enterprise and your metagenome. This is the GIFT of the EVO-DEVO OF LEADERSHIP. The LAST QUESTION you need to ask yourself at the end of our journey is:

"What will Leadership look like 10, 000 years from now?"

The Answer:

YOU DECIDE.

"ONLY THE ONE WHO SERVES IS QUALIFIED TO LEAD."

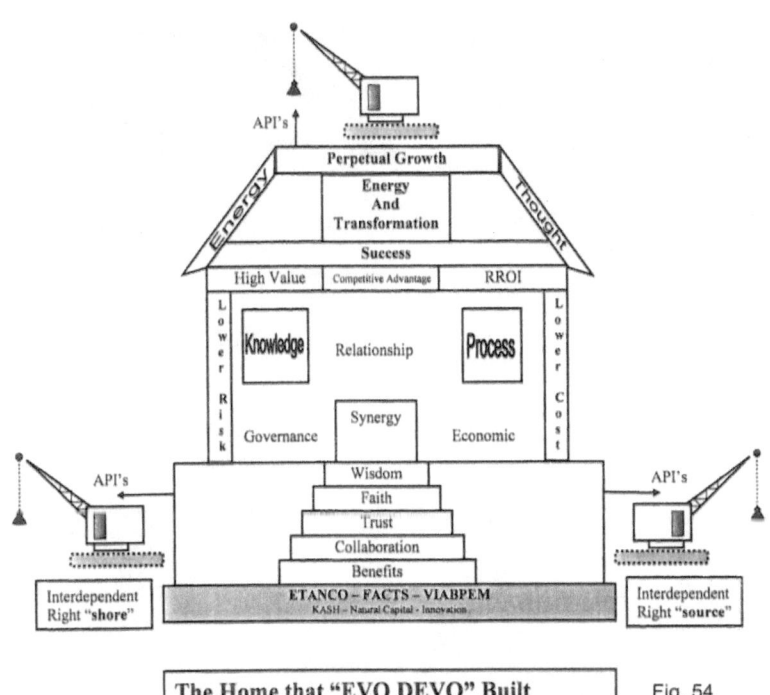

The Home that "EVO DEVO" Built   Fig. 54

POWERED BY

CHAPTER 19

<u>EVO-DEVO KEY's.</u>

As the limits of growth are defined by the evo-devo leaders and their communities instead of the "barriers" of the enterprise, it becomes prudent to reiterate the KEY's that you have acquired as a part of our quest. These KEY's are listed for the specific purpose of practicing the art and science of the evo-devo principles in your personal and professional domains. An extra insight into some of the KEY's and the various Illustrations present the journey has been added for your convenience.

 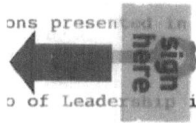

KEY's (SCAN AND TAKE THE KEY - Download scanner at www.indo-solutions.in

1. Evo-Devo of Leadership is not a domain of the rich, the mighty or the powerful. It is not acquired by birth but can still be owned, inherited or acquired by "STAR" leadership values.

2. Values are a function of observations, inductions, deductions and intuition to create unmatched value for the attainment of evo-devo.

3. The evo-devo of Unmatched Value happens in incremental steps based on the predispositions of the Leaders and his community.

4. Leadership Image is the Image of the community. The communities' actions are the Image of the Leader.

5. Evo-Devo is not just an individual achievement. The SIGMA effect of Summation through "fixation" is the global synergy driver.

6. Questioning is an evo-devo process. Questioning should unearth beneficial FACTs and should be devoid of falsification.

7. Modernizing the Business Logic already stored within the Leaders and their relationship is an excellent process to enhance the competitive advantage of the enterprise.

8. The consistency of the "Right Choice" as the "Preferred Choice" that benefit the enterprise is a measure of "STAR" leadership.

9. The Leadership Parabola (fig   1) is   a   combinations   of   the characteristics of Great "STAR" Leaders and the Point of Inflexion at which the evo-devo traits influence the community to achieve their maximum potential with the minimum loss of resources. The Who, When, Where, and What define the physical entity; while the Why and How define the entities of emotion and faith.

10. Fig 2 (i) illustrates the incurable zone where we continue to expend resource without any gain or opportunity; Legacy Modernization processes can assist at this point but you have to learn to "let go" when the results are not in line with the efforts being utilized. This can only occur through " Prestroika". Fig 2 (ii) demonstrates the points of "Prestroika" that can utilize the "free energy" available within the system to incrementally enhance the competitive advantage of the community by using quantitatively small changes and Symmetry.

11. SYMMETRY is an essential evo-devo function to manage chaos and adversity. SYMMETRY ensures that the BEAUTY or the STRUCTURAL STABILITY of the system is not comprised during transformation.

12. The combination of VISION, PROCESS and KNOWLEDGE with WISDOM is the basis of Leadership Faith and Esteem. (Fig 3)

13. The idea of Winning BIG in small increments with flawless execution and focus on benefits is the only way to gain sustainable competitive advantage.

14. The altar of Success is mired in the sharing , sustainability and synergy of benefits. The sacrifice of individual ego's vs. the loss to the community is the preferred choice.

15. Chaos and Order are both part of any evo-devo strategy. The harmony attained by being able to balance the two in a controlled manner is the focus of "STAR" leaders. (Fig. 5)

16. The Relationship Curve (Fig. 6) confirms that transformation occurs at the individual evo-devo level but the benefits accrue to the Leaders "sphere of Influence" which ensures its spread. The transformation of the evo-devo trait to progress from the state of "desired behavior" to the state of "accepted behavior" or Fixation is a function of benefits and the constant feedback from the community.

17. The Cultural Evolution (Fig. 7) is an excellent example of the Relationship Curve as the periods of excessive violence are also observed as the eras of low cultural growth. The fact that the violence did not benefit the masses ensured that the culture did not evolve.

18. Resilience is an evo-devo characteristic. It is the measure of the ability of the enterprise to achieve the evo-devo goals of sustainable growth. The Resilience Quotient (RQ) is a function of the Survival and the Diversity of the system to handle change.

19. The HUMAN LIFE CYCLE (Fig. 8) demonstrates the fact that at both the highest level of Wisdom and the Lowest DNA level Nature, the leader, and the community are interlinked. The potential of linking the genome and the metagenome to unleash "free energy" for growth is available to evo-devo leaders as a third alternative as observed in Figs. 9,10 and 10 (i).

20. The evo-devo strategies of Modernization of Infrastructure and "Inflation" proofing the deliverables has to be focused on the NEED to Have segment instead of the NICE to have sector in order to gain long term growth and a Rapid Return on Investment.

21. The BIG "G" is the creator of the small "g". The small "g" has to follow the natural laws laid down by the BIG "G". The small "g" needs to be in harmony with the BIG "G" at all times in order to get the evo-devo BONUS of SUCCESS.

22. The small "g" cannot replace the BIG "G". The small 'g" cannot fully comprehend the BIG "G" but can follow the principles of evo-devo to attain the desired goals for the benefit of the community and oneself as desired by the BIG "G".

23. The constant emphasis of the evo-devo on the community is not about a political structure that uses the community to replace the BIG "G". The process of communalism in its evo-devo avatar is to enhance the Faith and linkage of the community directly with the BIG "G" without any intermediation requirement. The small "g" plays an active role in sharing the benefits across the entire metagenome to achieve the common objective of communal wealth and communal growth.

24. Adversity, Chaos and Implosion are all Great Opportunities for Great "STAR" leaders. The practice of transforming the negative energy of chaos into the positive energy of Symmetry through the Beauty of the evo-devo principles is the desired trait.

25. The Yin and Yang of values and virtues alongside the symbols of knowledge and process that ensures a stable "center of gravity" for the entire system is the measure of the greatness of Leadership. (Fig. 27). Internal Back Flux within the system is one of the key reasons for failure. Identification, reduction and if possible elimination of the processes that promotes back flux is a mandated evo-devo trait.

26. Communal Wealth is an exponential enhancer of Capital. The measure of Back flux is also a function of the entropy and the "free energy" within the system. As you reduce back flux "free energy" is released which automatically translates into communal wealth. Technology, Digital IQ and Modernization through Technical Civilization is a constant feature of evo-devo growth. As the Capital increases the benefits of Communal Wealth vs. Individual Wealth grow up to 10 times their economic value. (Fig. 12)

27. SUCCESS is in abundance not scarcity. Evo-Devo is the transformation of scarcity into abundance.

28. Fig. 13 denotes the concept of Time in relation to evolution and its abundance. The scarcity of time as you observe as leaders is another cause of back--flux and falsification.

29. Evo Devo of SUCCESS is to learn to fail successfully. As we fail and recover quickly without losing competitive advantage we attain evo devo.

30. Planning and Preparing for Failure is a direct route to SUCCESS. The Role of the Champion and the Challenger are both part of the strategy to avoid failure blindness.

31. Identifying and Observing Consistent Inconsistencies is an evo-devo trait that needs to be practiced at all times. The Eureka Point is the clear measure of advantage. (Fig. 15)

32. The FedEx Arrow is an example of the process of Visualization for Success within the evo-devo paradigm. Many such processes exist within your leadership domain that are not seen by you as hidden capital. (Fig. 16/17)

33. The Virtual Solution Models and the Real World Problems are only solvable through communication and factual information. As you interpret results and abstract Data across the two you end up bringing the VSM's closer to the RWP's to achieve the breakthrough of SUCCESS. (Fig. 18)

34. The Breakthrough Force that can allow you to perform at peak levels that are higher than normal is a function of the evo-devo principles. The Higher than normal peak performances of "STAR" leaders is a competitive advantage that creates SUCCESS. (Fig. 19/20).

35. The process of calm commotion that frees you from anxiety and stress even under chaos is an essential component of the Breakthrough Force. Faith and Practice are the paths to achieving the trait of calm commotion.

36. The interdependence of multiple domains, communities leaders, Big "G" small "g", knowledge, process and wisdom are all sources of "free

energy" for growth. The greater the number of dots you can connect across the Leadership evo-devo domain the higher the chances of success through the lowering of risk. (Fig. 21).

37. Cash is a source of scarcity and diminishing returns. Natural Capital is a source of abundance and exponential returns. The Virtualization of Resource is the path to Natural Capital in abundance.

38. Knowledge, Attitude, Skills, Honest Effort, Community Potential, Chaos, Adversity, Implosion, and Technology etc are all sources of Natural Capital. The need for Ethical Consumption is an integral part of the evo-devo of abundance. The concept of "Zero Marginal Cost" linked to the Professional Skills of both the user and the provider to follow the "Need to Have" curve is the practice of KASH. CASH is always under pressure while the cyclic nature of KASH linked to the Mapping of both supply and demand is free from a resource scarcity mentality. (Fig. 24)

39. The only way to migrate from scarcity to abundance is to implement process improvements that are self-sustaining and self- replicating. The current trend of forced process improvement (Fig. 25) is not working since it is not sustainable nor is it replicating.

40. Questioning to handle Objections and Indifference through facts is an element of ethical consumption. The Pichichis and the Polychromes have to be handled in order to fulfill the ethical needs of the enterprise. The process of Penetrate to Radiate is essential to ethical consumption through the aegis of relationships that stand the test of time.(Fig. 26)

41. Relationships are a huge source of Natural Capital. The addition of a new relationship or a deletion of an existing one has a large impact on the Relationship Index as you will observe in The Exponential Nature of Relationships (Fig. 27.)

42. Ethical Communication and a Feed-Back loop strategy alongside an escalation process are essential to evo-devo.

43. The difference between Shallow beliefs and Deep Beliefs are highlighted in the Thought-action Cycle (Fig. 28) that governs our relationships. The Schemas are built in the first five years of our lives. These schemas are strengthened throughout our existence through Faith and Values. The Abstract is a consequence of learning and emotions. The Perception activities based on facts, events and experience designs the Perceptual base. The Deep Beliefs connect all three with wisdom. The shallow beliefs are only concerned with the five senses that create perception without substance.

44. Evo-Devo cannot be delegated to Agents. It has to practiced as a Way of Life by the Leader within the community. Desired Traits once acquired by the "STAR" can be "fixated" within the community through ethical communication and congregation.

45. Wise Laws, Moral Hope and Just actions are essential to an evo-devo Way of Life. These are not conveniences to be used only in "good times".

46. You need to prepare for the "Implosion Effect " of chaos and adversity in times of growth.

47. The "STRING of Entanglement" connects us all together. The "free energy" of entanglement is an excellent source of growth. You have to locate the Strings to understand the entanglement.

48. Laws of Force associated with Size are no guarantee of Success in the evo-devo world.

49. The entanglement of the three Entities of Faith, Emotions and the Physical is a fact. You need to ensure that as a part of the evo-devo a harmony is retained amongst the three. This harmony will be translated from the leader to the community and from the community to other communities across the globe. (Fig. 29)

50. The Rock and the Seaweed example in Fig. 30 expand on the above concept of entanglement and its derivative strengths.

51. The Maturity of interdependence (Fig. 31) explains the fact that as we mature and observe the strings connecting multiple domains through BEST EVO-DEVO PRACTICES we gain the competitive advantage of both efficiency and effectiveness. (Fig. 31)

52. The centers of excellence based on domain expertise are determined by their integral and derivative advantages of lower Cost, lower risk, Rapid Return on Equity/Investment/Natural capital and Unmatched High Value. Right Shore and Right Source are a consequence of mapping needs and wants as well as demand and supply chains across the gamut of the enterprise.

53. The advantages of intellectual capital retention, legacy Modernization, Sunk Cost Recovery and abundance are linked to the "Barstool" and "Serduct" principles of evo-devo. The combination of products, services, benefits, demand and supply are crucial to the evo-devo of interdependent sustainable growth.

54. The Evo-Devo of Conflict and aggression should deliver the advantage of Synergy through the reduction of waste.

55. Conflict and aggression should be utilized as powerful and ethical tools of communication only against oppression, discrimination and waste.

56. False Alarms and Misses are essential to evo-devo decision making. The evo-devo leaders have to gauge the impact of both the false alarm and the miss from a quantitative and qualitative perspective. The Right Response lies within the boundaries of these principles. The equilibrium point should be identified as the point of go-no go for the Right Response. The Likelihood of Success in adversity, chaos and implosion can be virtually guaranteed if you follow the Right Cube and the Right Response strategies shown in Fig. 36, 37 and 41.

57. The event Response Cycle when linked to the Right Response that reduces and eliminates the "error links" ensures the advantages of sharing, synergy and sustainability: the three goals of evo-devo leadership.

58. The And-But evo-devo strategies associated with the IF-THEN Right Response processes are mandated for SUCCESS.

59. Contentment is evo-devo. It is a higher plane of self-governance than the pursuit of happiness alone.

60. The Hierarchy of Needs under the evo-devo paradigm is the linkage of the genetic factors to the cultural "memetic" processes that lead to symbiosis, Self-actualization and Self-Governance. (Fig. 38).

61. The Kinship values that link individuals, families, communities and the apolitical environment have to be maintained in accordance with the flow in Fig. 40. The "error link" is established when government tries to replace the links of the family and the community to control individual behavior. If the government can form an alliance with the family and the community through meeting the hierarchy of needs in the safety and potential development areas such as education then the leadership of Governance can be achieved. Altruism, Reciprocal Altruism and governance need to work together to create the symbiotic links between the individual's potential and the global community in an interdependent strategy.

62. Trust, Faith and Esteem of Leadership is essential for governance. The example of an ecclesiastical form of governance from the evo-devo principles is only to demonstrate the strengths of Trust, Faith and Esteem in order to retain long-term success.

63. The advantage of Self-governance and the acceptance of an Universal Service Obligation to the metagenome is a desired evo-devo trait.

64. The "S" curve of growth is the only solution for ensuring sustainable, stable and synergistic growth by creating new LIFE CYCLES (LC) as old ones become inefficient. At the same time by extracting the business logic stored in the current or past offerings you can use legacy modernization techniques to extend the LC of the offerings. The retention of Business logic and the extension of the LIFE CYCLE are evo-devo strategies that enhance the economic value of the enterprise.

65. The FACT's mandated in the Right Solution Degree of the "S" Curve are the EVD's (economic value drivers) of the StQ and the CaQ and the WiQ. Each enterprise or community or Leaders will have a certain arsenal of these EVD's which will decide the Degree of the Right Solution using the EVQ (economic value quotient).

66. The PEG ratio and the Degree of the Right Solution combined can predict the intrinsic and extrinsic strengths of any system as well as the Likelihood of SUCCESS.

67. GLASS is the acronym for Greed, Lust for Unworked for Gain, Anger, Self-interest at the cost of others and SELF-EGO. GLASS is one of the largest contributors to the loss due to "internal back-flux".

68. The evo-devo "X" factors are the largest contributors to the "STAR" leadership. The goal of SELF-ESTEEM replaces the negative effects of the GLASS-internal back-flux. [Fig. 47]

69. The LCV's required for the evo-devo of Transformation can only be attained through practice. The Economic Quotient (EVQ) is equivalent to the Economic Value (EV) and the Energy Quotient (EQ) when calculating the Annual Return on Investment or the annual return on energy. In both these cases i.e. ROI and ROE you, as evo-devo leaders, are looking for Rapid Returns as demonstrated in the illustration. [Fig. 48]

70. The tools of Predictive Foresight (PF), Agile Response (AR), Personalized Tooling (PT), Empowered Knowledge (EK) and Enabled Virtualization (EZ) are essential to extract the maximum competitive advantage from the LCV's.

71. The "free energy" generation process as illustrated in Fig. 51 indicates that the point of inflexion for the Implosion Effect is at the stage at which the system is nearing equilibrium. This point is also the stage as which the next "S" curve needs to begin.

72. The Persistence and Plasticity of EVO-DEVO as shown in Fig. 52 predicts that the stronger the links between the three stages of the

Leader, the higher the chances of SUCCESS. The only way to strengthen these links is to practices the evo-devo principles as a way of life.

73. The current and future threshold of Technology linked with the ability to make wise choices through the Evo-Devo of Leadership can allow us to jump the Hurdle Rate of Natural Selection to attain the Competitive advantage of Artificial Solution.

FORMULAE

74. The Resilience Quotient (RQ) is based on the days of Liquidity (L) multiplied with the square of Diversity (D) Value, expressed as a percentage, divided by the product of the Rate of Change (rc) expressed as a percentage, and the frequency of change (fc). For e.g. IBM and Microsoft are both diverse product companies but IBM more so. If we award IBM a Diversity Value of 80% and Microsoft a value of 60% then we also see the IBM has only 45 days of Liquidity while Microsoft carries liquidity of approximately 450 days. In terms of the RQ: Microsoft can absorb a faster rate of change and a higher frequency of change. But if IBM increases their liquidity to around 225 days, then would exceed The RQ of Microsoft because of IBM's higher diversity value.

75. The Prestroika or Point of Inflexion is equal to the product of the opportunity of chaos and the resource of the community, divided by the Inefficiencies in the system measured by the number of small perturbations or ineffective changes due to the Back-flux of the entity. These changes are wasteful and the higher the system inefficiency more the resource that will be required to reach the Prestroika or POI. Similarly small effective changes applied at the POI will result in capitalizing on the opportunity of Chaos and the Resources of the community by using minimal Natural Capital and achieving maximum results.

76. The Potential Energy (PE) of wind is equal to half the product of the Atmospheric Pressure (p) multiplied by the Air Density (A) and the cube of the Velocity of the Air (V). The Velocity of the wind thus

becomes a key factor in the harnessing of wind energy. Similar parallel can be drawn to the evo-devo of Leadership as well.

77. Individual wealth (W) of any entity is equal to its Resource multiplied by the square of its Technology (T). $W = PT^2$. The Communal Wealth (C.W.) of any entity is equal to the product of the available Natural Capital (including knowledge, Attitude, Skills and Effort), the square of the Technology (T) (both owned and shared) and 10 times the "free energy" (ΔG) of the entire system. The ΔG is the difference between the existing Enthalpy or strength of the entity (ΔH) and the product of the Entropy or Chaos (ΔS) of the system and the internal back-flux or resistance (t). $C.W. = NT^2 10 \Delta G$. C. W. will always exceed W.

78. USER + VIABPEM = SUCCESS + PROVIDER + ETANCO = SUCCESS. In order to achieve SUCCESS both the USER and Provider have to follow the evo-devo principles of VIABPEM and ETANCO respectively.

79. $R = N + (n-1)$. Relationship Value ® is a direct function of the number of existing relationships and the total number of entities in the relationship minus 1 i.e. the self.

80. The Likelihood of Success and the Right Response are dependent on the Expected Risk (E) which is a function of the False Alarm (EA) divided by the Miss (M). if the FA impact is higher that the impact of M then the expected risk (E) may exceed the Likelihood of SUCCESS (L) value and the Right Response will be not to go ahead with the decision.

81. The Degree of the Right Solution in relation to the "S" curve is linked to the EVD's and their probability and verifiability within the system. Depending on the existence or non-existence of the EVD's the number of contradictions to known facts will become available. For e.g. if a system has 5 observable and verifiable EVDs the Degree of the Right Solution will be = $(5 \times 10 \times 5) \div 4 = 62.5$ degrees. To calculate the PEG ° Index the following table is used:

EVD No.	Degree	PEG$^{\circ}$ Index
9	450	3
8	400	2.7
7	175	1.5
6	100	1.25
5	62.5	1.00
4	40	0.9
3	25	0.8
2	14	0.7
1	3	0.6
0	0	0.5

(The Probability and Verifiability are taken at the maximum range of 10 and 5 respectively. You can vary the numbers based on the FACTS.)

82. The PEG$^{\circ}$ is an excellent standard to gauge the value of any enterprise based on its existing P/E ratio, its Projected Growth (G) and the Degree of its EVDs, "S" curve and probability/ verifiability of the Facts including Industry Ratios, Growth Rates and other Environmental factors. The table in KEY 85 is used to multiply the PEG (P/E ÷ G). (The PEG INDEX will be between 3 – 0.5). The lower the PEG$^{\circ}$ is from 1 the higher the value of the entity and its ability to lead transformation.

83. RROI/RROE = [LG – F (100% - L)] divided by TP. The rapid return on equity/ energy/ investment is a function of the product of the Likelihood of Success (L), as a percentage, and the expected Gain (G) minus the Product of the Expected Loss multiplied by the balance percentage value of L. This is then divided by the product of the Period of the Return (T) and the current value of Assets (P). The Rapid Rate of Return is expressed a percentage (%). The RROI/RROE has to

281

substantially higher than the Internal Rate of Return or the Hurdle Rate to qualify for evo-devo status.

84. SUCCESS is the Sigma of the Individual Potential (Range: 1-infinity) and its derivative based on the back-flux or resistance to development of the potential. The SUCCESS will be a function of the F (x) minus F (1) based on the value of x or the Individuals within the community. The Sigma effect is applicable when the community attains its maximum potential.

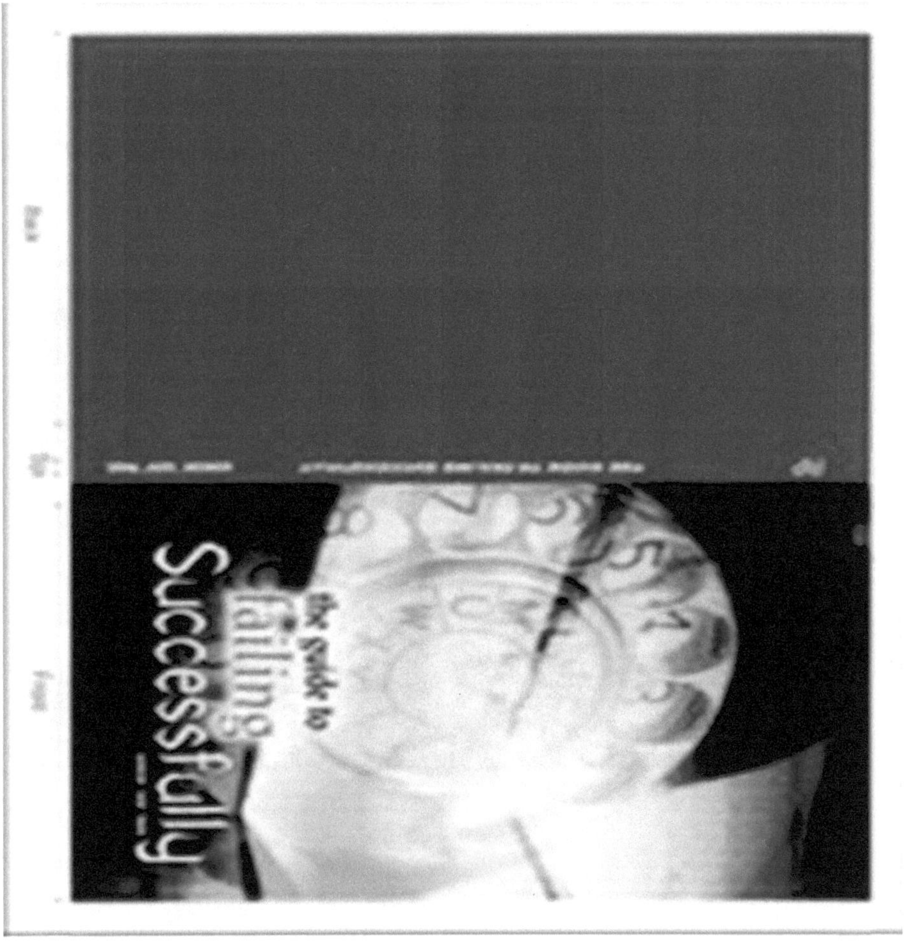

THE ▲ GUIDE TO FAILING SUCCESSFULLY

(A PRE-VIEW of THE FICTION OF YESU- THE LEADER
WHO ATTAINED THE EVO-DEVO "STAR")

By ASHISH "ASH" PAUL

ACKNOWLEDGEMENTS

The website www.legendevodevo.com lists a comprehensive arsenal of reading, learning and practice material that will assist you in the completion of your quest for real SUCCESS. These aids can be acquired, from this one source which will continue to be upgraded as new material that meets the evo- devo benchmarks comes out. The scanning of The QR code at the back cover of the book or on the KEY page will assist us in this matter.

At this point I would like to acknowledge the sources of my epiphany in the quest for the-evo-devo of Leadership:

a) My family and my peers who have stood by me in times of adversity and chaos. My wife who has guided me to earth whenever I am flying to fast. My children who have stood by me across all obstacles mostly self-created.

b) The Teachers, The Boards and the Leaders who have taught me to learn from my errors as well enjoy the fruits of our success, One great example is Dr. Bal from Ohio who is a brilliant Medical Practitioner and a good Human Being at the same time.

c) Stephen Coveys "The 8th Habit".

d)"Relativity- The Special and General theory." - Albert Einstein

e) "The Prince"- Niccolo Machiavelli (Second edition)

f) "The Break-Out Principle "- Herbert Benson M.D. and William Proctor.

g) STEVEN PINKER and ! "How the Mind Works."

h) SEED MAGAZINE/SCIENTIFIC AMERICAN/ USA TODAY / WALL STREET JOURNAL (Var.)

i) John Berry and Wiley Publishing - "OFFSHORING STRATEGIES".

j) Kushwant Singh "History of the Sikhs."

K) OMG Legacy Modernization STAN SEWALL, Jack and the Author created Business Object Libraries and Tools for the extraction of Business logic and migration and modernization in a Joint venture called Aftermath. The Technical Civilization and Digital iQ paradigm is being implemented by the Author using INDO. www.indo-solutions.in

INDEX